BRITISH FIGHTING METHODS IN THE GREAT WAR

BRITISH FIGHTING METHODS IN THE GREAT WAR

Edited by
PADDY GRIFFITH

FRANK CASS
LONDON • PORTLAND, OR.

First Published in 1996 in Great Britain by
FRANK CASS PUBLISHERS
Newbury House, 900 Eastern Avenue,
London IG2 7HH

and in the United States of America by
FRANK CASS PUBLISHERS
c/o ISBS 5804 N.E. Hassalo Street
Portland, Oregon 97213-3644

Website: http://www.frankcass.com

Copyright © 1996 Frank Cass & Co. Ltd.
Reprinted 1998

British Library Cataloguing in Publication Data

British Fighting Methods in the Great War
I. Griffith, Paddy
940.40941
ISBN 0-7146-3495-6 (cloth)
ISBN 0-7146-4468-4 (paper)

Library of Congress Cataloging-in-Publication Data

British fighting methods in the Great War / edited by Paddy Griffith.
    p.   cm.
  Includes bibliographical references and index.
  Contents: Reform in the British Army / Paddy Griffith – British
artillery in the Great War / Jonathan Bailey – Co-stars or
supporting cast? : British divisions in the Hundred Days, 1918 /
Peter Simkins – The operational role of British military police on
the Western Front, 1914–18 / G.D. Sheffield – The treatment of
casualties in the Great War / Geoffrey Noon – the rise of armour /
J.P. Harris – Cavalry and the development of breakthrough doctrine
/ Stephen Badsey – The SHLM project : assessing the battle
performance of British divisions / John Lee.
  ISBN 0-7146-3495-6 (cloth). ISBN 0-7146-4468-4 (pbk).
  1. Great Britain. Army. British Expeditionary Force–History–
World War, 1914–1918. 2. Strategy. 3. World War, 1914–1918–Great
  Britain. I. Griffith, Paddy.
D546.B76 1996
940.4'1241–dc20   95-47978
                                                      CIP

Typeset by Regent Typesetting, London
Printed and bound by Antony Rowe Ltd, Eastbourne
Transferred to digital printing 2005

Contents

Figures and Tables

Notes on Contributors

Dr Stephen Badsey MA, wrote his Cambridge doctoral thesis on the British debate on cavalry, 1871–1921. He became a research assistant at the Imperial War Museum, where he catalogued the museum holding of Great War propaganda films, and then spent five years as an historical consultant and researcher for British television programmes, including 'Timewatch' and the award-winning 'Soldiers'. He is currently a Senior Lecturer in War Studies at the Royal Military Academy, Sandhurst, and a Senior Research Fellow of De Montfort University's Institute for the Study of War and Society. He has written or edited several military history books including *The Crimean War* (with Andrew Lambert), and *The Gulf War Assessed* (with John Pimlott).

Colonel J.B.A Bailey, MBE, RA, is currently Colonel Defence Studies, based at the Army Staff College, Camberley. Before that he commanded a field artillery regiment with the British Army of the Rhine. His book *Field Artillery and Firepower*, covering developments during the whole of the twentieth century, appeared in 1989 while he was a member of the directing staff at the Staff College.

Paddy Griffith is a freelance military author and publisher who worked for 16 years as a Senior Lecturer in War Studies at the Royal Military Academy, Sandhurst. His Oxford doctorate was awarded for a study of the French Army between the two Napoleons, and he has also contributed widely to the wargame hobby; but he is perhaps best known for his books of tactical analysis such as *Forward Into Battle: Battle Tactics of the Civil War* (American), and *Battle Tactics of the Western Front, 1916–18*.

Dr J. P. Harris is a former director of studies at a private college in London and is currently a Senior Lecturer in War Studies at the Royal Military Academy, Sandhurst, and a Senior Research Fellow with the Institute for the Study of War and Society at De Montfort University. He has a doctorate from King's College, London and has published extensively, especially on British military planning between the world wars. He has recently completed a major study on the development of British military thought on armoured warfare up to 1939.

John Lee is Treasurer of the British Commission for Military History and one of the organisers of the SHLM Battle Assessment Study 1914–1918. He has MA degrees in Social and Economic History from Birkbeck College, London, and in War Studies from King's College, London. He is the author of articles and a chapter on aspects of the career of Sir Ian Hamilton, and is currently completing books on Hamilton's life and on the battle of the Menin Road Ridge, 20 September 1917. He works in publishing.

Dr Geoffrey Noon qualified in medicine at Birmingham University in 1954, after which he served on a naval air station for two years and then as a general practitioner in Willenhall and especially the Tamworth area for over three decades, including part-time work as a casualty officer and anaesthetist with a particular interest in trauma and resuscitation. He has now largely retired from practice and is able to follow an interest in the Western Front which originated in the fact that his father and three uncles saw active service there. He is currently chairman of the Wolverhampton branch of the Western Front Association.

Dr G. D. Sheffield is a Senior Lecturer at the Royal Military Academy, Sandhurst, and author of a number of works including *From Vimy Ridge to the Rhine, the Great War Letters of Christopher Stone DSO, MC* (as co-editor); *Warfare in the Twentieth Century*; and the authorised *The Redcaps: A History of the Royal Military Police and its Antecedents from the Middle Ages to the Gulf War*. His doctoral thesis for King's College, London was a study of officer–man relations, morale and discipline in the British Army, 1902–22, and he is currently Secretary-General of the British Commission of Military History.

Peter Simkins, Historian at the Imperial War Museum, is author of the definitive study of *Kitchener's Army: The Raising of the New Armies, 1914–16*, which was published in 1988. He is currently working with Dr G. D. Sheffield and John Lee on a book entitled *Haig's Army*, a study of the organisation, composition and performance of the BEF in France and Belgium from 1916 to 1918. Peter Simkins is an eloquent lecturer on Great War history, and one of the leading authorities in modern military studies.

Introduction

Paddy Griffith

The public has a deep-seated belief that many of the British attacks made between 1914 and 1918 led to needlessly heavy casualties for negligible military gain. This impression arose from the shocking novelty of indus- trialised trench warfare during the first two years of war, when the military machine was largely unable to cope with the massive unplanned expansion of men and *materiél* that was thrust upon it. Then, when the New Armies were finally assembled and thrown forward in what had been heralded as their 'decisive push' on the Somme, on 1 July 1916, they met a notoriously bloody ruin.

For many people the first day of the Somme stands as an almost indelible image of futility, which could have been expunged only by a completely successful and rapid end to both the Somme campaign and to the Great War as a whole. Yet, unfortunately for the reputation of the British Expeditionary Force (BEF), there was to be no such happy outcome. This allowed critics to reinforce their preconceived stereotypes by taking a vindictively selective note of whatever operations could be counted as failures during the second half of hostilities. Thus, the first day of the Somme has been taken as typical of every other day of the battle; the mud and misery of the blighted Ypres salient have generally been taken as the 'norm' during the whole of 1917, while the collapses of the following spring have been seen as encapsulating 1918.

It cannot be denied that by the end of 1917 the BEF had indeed lost both its freshness and much of its political support in Westminster. It was being asked to do too much with too few men, with too little time to rest, and it was particularly weak and inexperienced in defensive operations. Nevertheless, it would do outrageous violence to the historical record[1] if matters were allowed to rest at that, since not all of the Somme battle was disastrous, and it led to a dramatic German retreat in the spring of 1917. That year also saw some spectacularly successful offensive operations – from Vimy Ridge to Cambrai and from Messines to some of the (unexpectedly well-planned) 'bite and hold' attacks at Ypres itself. Then, towards the end of 1918, the BEF succeeded in changing up into a dramatically higher gear, imposing a greater sustainable pace and speed upon operations than had been seen on the Western Front since September 1914.

In its relatively little-known operations of 'the Hundred Days', in the autumn of 1918, the BEF all but restored mobile operations to their traditional status as the military 'norm', even though this was not widely recognised by its critics, either at the time or later. It achieved the sort of pace and momentum that would only occasionally be bettered even in the supposedly more mobile Second World War. The Hundred Days was a brilliant military attainment which deserves far more recognition than it has normally been accorded; neither can it be explained away merely by reference to German war weariness or supply shortages.[2] If not quite Marlboroughs or Wellingtons, the leading British commanders of the Hundred Days may reasonably be portrayed as at least the equivalents of Montgomery or Slim. Indeed, not even Gough's Fifth Army in March 1918 had undergone as great a retreat as either Slim in Burma in 1942 or the Allied forces in the Ardennes at Christmas 1944. The difference was only that Gough had finally run out of credibility, following his failure to effect a breakthrough in either 1916 or 1917, whereas his Second World War counterparts could still be given the benefit of the doubt at the time at which their own retreats took place.

In quite recent times, a number of scholars have indeed underlined the high command's repeated efforts to analyse their past mistakes and improve their tactical efficiency on the Western Front. It has been pointed out that tactics were already being reformed in quite significant ways at least as early as 'the second day of the Somme', 2 July 1916, and that in many of the supporting arms and services a veritable revolution in technique took place during the 12 months after that. Not only did the British lead the way in such key innovations as the squad automatic rifle, the machine gun barrage, the tank and the predicted artillery concentration, but they eventually geared up their whole organisation – including logistics, signals and staff work – to cope with the rigorous demands of mobile warfare. Generals were gradually weaned away from the idea that attacks should be improvised heroically and instantly, even in bleakly unpromising circumstances, or that they should be doggedly continued long after their initial bite had started to fade. The attempt to run every detail from the centre was also gradually abandoned, as it came to be accepted that commanders at lower levels did in fact under-stand the professional realities of their task. Little of this had been true in the first half of the war; but by the second half it amounted to a radical improve-ment in British fighting technique.

This book is intended to collect a few of the modern scholarly perspectives on these changes, and to point the reader towards others. In my own initial essay, I try to take an overview of the subject and set the general scene, after which Colonel Bailey highlights the essential contribution to the BEF's effectiveness that was made by its ever-extending artillery. Not only were the guns, shells and fuses greatly improved during 1916–17, but the concept of pinpoint accuracy advanced from the realm of optimistic theory into that of everyday reality. In 1916, the infantry attack began to be supercharged by creeping barrages designed to make serious infantry fighting unnecessary. Then, in 1917, the enemy's main answer to it – in the shape of defensive artillery fire – was increasingly being neutralised by counter-battery programmes which really worked. 'The deep battle' is perhaps a phrase coined only during the NATO debates of the 1980s, but its reality was already very evident before the start of 1918.

Peter Simkins focuses upon the popular misconception that only the Dominion divisions constituted any sort of sharp assault spearhead in the BEF of 1918. Basing his analysis upon a meticulous statistical study of each division's tactical achievement, he points out just how well some of the British formations managed to perform in the Hundred Days. Perhaps not all British divisions could claim the same sort of 'élite' status that was accorded to their Canadian, Australian and New Zealand colleagues, but quite a large number of them did manage to equal or even exceed that level. A great deal of nonsense has at times been talked about the superiority of colonial over home-grown British troops, and Simkins here sets the record straight in a very welcome manner.

In his essay on the military police, G. D. Sheffield explains some of their essential battlefield roles that are often overlooked by those who prefer to see the red cap only as a symbol of unthinking coercion and authoritarianism. Just as young infantry subalterns learned to collaborate constructively with their subordinates rather than to bully, misunderstand or ignore them, so the same can be said of the battle police. Stragglers would normally be cared for and given 'tea and sympathy', rather than punished, just as road traffic would be helped on its way, in accordance with a comprehensive tactical plan, rather than arbitrarily blocked or jammed. Nor would the military police be personally shy of venturing into the zones beaten by enemy fire. On the contrary, they would be tireless expeditors of victory in all parts of the battlefield.

In a particularly telling essay about the treatment of battle's victims, Dr Noon gives a timely reminder that the British in the Great War made dramatic advances over the medical practices of any previous war and, indeed, over those of some other nationalities in the Great War itself. In very many areas of treatment, the wounded BEF soldier of 1918 enjoyed a much higher standard of care than he had in 1914, but he would not see any particularly radical improvement in those standards even between 1939 and 1945. At least before the arrival of the casevac helicopter in the 1950s, most of the key advances in modern military medicine seem to have occurred mainly during the great trench war on the Western Front, although that fact has not yet been understood as widely as it deserves to be.

In Paul Harris's essay on the rise of armour, there is a detailed analysis of the debates which led to the original creation of the tank, supported by a realistic technical understanding of its limitations and failures on the battle-fields of the Western Front. The tank was by no means the wonder-weapon or secret key to breakthrough that some of its advocates have sometimes liked to claim, at least not during the Great War. It did often give the infantry a helpful short-term shove towards victory, and in later decades it would doubtless rise to a position of much greater prominence. But in terms of the BEF's tactics in 1916–18, it was actually one of the relatively lesser British innovations, rather than the massively important one that far too many historians have so often liked to assert.

Making the converse side of much the same case, Stephen Badsey's discussion of the horsed cavalry represents yet another seminal and overdue re-evaluation. Far from being anachronistic or irrelevant to the Great War battlefield, the cavalry still remained the only conceivable instrument of breakthrough, even as late as 1918. The tanks had far too short a range and the infantry had too little speed for this role, whereas the artillery was lamentably immobile in fluid operations. For all its deficiencies, therefore, the cavalry, or rather 'mounted infantry', as it should all be termed in the conditions of 1916–18, should have been given a far more prominent place in tactical thinking than it actually was. Unfortunately, it suffered from a combination of adverse circumstances, among which enemy barbed wire and machine guns should be ranked as rather less important than 'friendly' politicians and generals who had ceased to believe in any sort of break-through, or signalling technologies which made timely battlefield communi-cations very difficult indeed.

Finally, John Lee adopts a rather different approach from the other contributors. Eschewing the direct reinterpretation of popular stereotypes, he give us a view of how British Western Front studies may be expected to evolve during the next few years. He describes the innovative 'SHLM' project – as already adumbrated in Peter Simkins's essay – and shows how it may give future scholars a far more systematically detailed 'map' of the people and formations that were engaged. By the end of this decade, in fact, the student may well expect to have access to a set of data bases that will decisively trump Edmonds's official histories that have held the field now for over half a century.

All in all, historians can no longer ignore the fact that the BEF was tactically innovative during the second half of the Great War, and must learn to set this perception alongside their cherished traditional stereotype of a 'futile and blundering BEF during the first half of the war'. Equal weight must somehow be given to each of these two perceptions, in order to provide a more balanced general understanding.

NOTES

1. Some recent books on the Western Front are listed in the general bibliography at the end of this volume, although additional details may often be found in the footnotes to individual chapters.

2. A few revisionists, such as John Terraine, have made worthy recent efforts to draw attention to the Hundred Days, while Prior and Wilson's *Command on the Western Front* takes the technical analysis an important step further still. Vols 4 & 5 of Edmonds' official history, *Military Operations, France and Belgium, 1918*, actually provide more of the raw material than is often acknowledged by historians, who rightly distrust Edmonds' habit of making unfair summaries of individual personalities.

CHAPTER ONE

The Extent of Tactical Reform in the British Army[1]

Paddy Griffith

British generalship on the Western Front has often, and rightly, been criticised for major defects of both style and content. The remotely aloof style of command has been discussed too often to require any further elaboration here,[2] apart perhaps from a plea to remember that battlefield communications were often very poor indeed, and 'A General without a telephone was to all practical purposes impotent – a lay figure dressed in uniform, deprived of eyes, arms and ears'.[3] As for content, it is clear that many of the big operational decisions were ill-advised, such as Haig's selection of the Ypres salient as the decisive battlefield for late 1917, or his unbounded faith in Fifth Army's defensive resilience in early March 1918. At lower levels of command, there was a very wasteful tendency to demand that attacks should be launched before they had been properly prepared, or to insist that failed attacks should immediately be repeated.[4] It was only in 1918 that the lesson was fully learned that an attacker should bank his winnings after the first two or three days, and not continue gambling recklessly against a rapidly stiffening enemy defence. Even in the field of minor tactics, there were many mistakes that may be attributed directly to generals, and not to colonels or their subordinates. The blunders between infantry and tanks at the first battle of Bullecourt on 9–11 April 1917, for example, may fairly be laid at the door of the army commander, General Gough, rather than that of any of his subordinates.[5]

MINOR TACTICS

It is nevertheless fair to point out that minor tactics were not really the domain of generals, and that very considerable progress could be, and often was, made in this field by 'colonels or their subordinates', even if the higher generalship was shockingly bad – which was far from always being the case. The true picture seems to be that both General Headquarters (GHQ) and individual army, corps, or divisional commanders often did support the new technologies and the new ideas that were being pushed forward by innovative 'Young Turks' from lower strata of command. It helped a general's reputation if, by picking the brains of his subordinates, he could show his peers that he was energetically abreast of modenity and not merely sitting on his hands. Thus Sir John French himself had won credit for introducing the first motor car into Aldershot command before the war; then he placed the first specification for trench mortars as early as October 1914, and eventually staked at least half of the success of the Loos battle upon a completely untried new weapon – gas. Equally, Gough on the Somme was basing his tactical prescriptions not only upon detailed local analyses submitted by articulate battalion commanders, but also upon hazardous personal observations from aircraft and even from studying cinema films of attacks.[6]

As for the 'Young Turks' themselves, they were almost always keen to find patrons in more elevated ranks, or even in Parliament,[7] and were often successful. Thus symbioses were often established between senior commanders and junior innovators, and centres of tactical excellence gradually accumulated. This was true not only of the more obviously technical specialities such as the Royal Flying Corps or the tanks, but also of certain infantry division or corps headquarters which happened to take a particular interest in tactics. Currie's Canadian Corps, Maxse's XVIII Corps, Tudor's 9th or de Lisle's 29th divisions immediately spring to mind, although there were many more. Once such formations had won a reputation for tactical expertise and dependability, they would be sought out by GHQ – whether consciously or subliminally is not entirely clear – for any obviously difficult job that loomed over the horizon. It is striking to see how often the same 'élite' formations found themselves fighting alongside each other, with their higher staffs in direct contact and exchanging ideas with each other. This type of grouping usually occurred during epic attacks which had failed at first but were subsequently better prepared, such as the final capture of Thiepval, Beaumont Hamel or Passchendaele village itself. The conclusion must be that the association of particular headquarters was by no means a product of chance, but a recognition by the high command that certain command groups were working efficiently in the field of tactics whereas others were still sitting on their hands.

Admittedly, the emergence of such élites was not a uniform development throughout the BEF or in any one particular level of command. Nevertheless, it seems to have been effective. If the tactics of 1916 were generally better than those of 1915, then those of 1917 were very much better than those of 1916. Alas, there was then an exhausted relapse which led to several serious set-backs during the winter and following spring; but by the time of the final 1918 autumn offensive, it seems that British tactics had effectively reached a pitch that would scarcely be surpassed for at least 30 years thereafter.[8]

The axiom that 'practice makes perfect' tends to hold true in every field of human endeavour, unless the immediate consequences of the practice itself are so terminally dire that the practitioners are physically prevented from repeating their experiments. On the Western Front, this prohibiting condition was indeed very much more than merely a distant theoretical possibility: but, in the event, it was usually reached only in personal or somewhat localised cases, rather than for entire units or higher headquarters. Even if a battalion was 'wiped out' in the course of making an attack, it would often still leave a core of experienced survivors which numbered perhaps 20 or even 50 per cent of its starting strength,[9] let alone the official 'nucleus' of perhaps ten per cent that was deliberately left out of action in order to serve as a core for subsequent regrouping. For much of the time, moreover, most battalions were engaged on trench warfare duties which, although certainly uncomfortable and miserable, were not anything like as deadly as a big 'show'.[10] Besides, the casualty rate among a battalion's more senior officers was markedly lower than that among subalterns, and it was the senior officers who were most influential in deciding tactics.

It was up to the survivors of each attack to refine and improve technique in time for the next attack. In doing this, they would be hindered both by the need to absorb large numbers of fresh drafts and by the exhausting routine demands of life at the front. They might find themselves stymied by blithely nonsensical imperatives, showered upon them from the safety of some remote higher headquarters, or they might be thrown into an improvised second attack before there was time to digest the lessons of the first. To a great extent, they would be 'running in order to stand still'. Nevertheless, the incentive for study was enormous, since each attack was such a traumatic event that it greatly concentrated the minds of everyone connected with it. Brigadier Jack summed this up as follows: 'I detest attacks; they mean seeing friends lying about dead and mangled. In addition to this the personal attention to countless details before and during operations imposes a very severe mental and physical strain on one.'[11]

In the case of Lieutenant-Colonel W. D. Croft of 11th Royal Scots (11 RS), the traumatic experience of his successful attack on Logueval on 14 July 1916 spurred him into a careful revision of his training regime, in the spirit of the tactical reflections contained in the influential 1903 pamphlet *The Defence of Duffer's Drift*.[12] Croft's battalion had lost around three-quarters of its strength in casualties, and he was determined that it would do better in its subsequent operations. Energetic and 'thrusting' officers like him would certainly agonise long and hard about every detail and every conceivable source of friction in their future attacks, even though they probably knew in their hearts that too much of what happened would still remain beyond their control when the fatal moment actually arrived.

Before the end of 1915, the preparation for a deliberate attack had been reduced to a routine that was designed to leave as little as possible to chance. The terrain would be reconnoitred both visually and from maps and air photos. A small scale model of it would be constructed for briefing, and then a life-size replica would be taped out as a training area behind the lines. Everyone would be fully drilled in their roles during each of the phases – assembly, assault, mopping up and consolidation. Watches would be synchronised and equipment minutely checked. The assault troops would be rested and fed just before the supreme effort was demanded of them. Security precautions and camouflage would be imposed, supported by diversionary 'Chinese attacks' on neighbouring sectors of the front. Flanking formations would be fully briefed according to the complex rules of professional etiquette and 'staff writing'.

Behind these comprehensive immediate preparations there was also a more general endeavour to set up a network of training schools and short courses designed to cater for every level of command and for every technical or tactical speciality. Not only would these courses give officers precious time out of the line, when they could think and discuss tactical questions, but they would also help to keep all formations briefed about the latest developments and perceptions. Beyond these again, there was a large-scale effort to write and disseminate manuals for the benefit of junior officers, in the hope of stiffening their natural British initiative and sporting instincts with a reassuring framework of doctrine.[13] It should certainly not be imagined that this apparently 'German General Staff' approach was in any way neglected by the BEF. On the contrary, it was an endeavour which gathered momentum remorselessly alongside the steady expansion of the army and its share in the war. By the summer of 1918, there were even complaints that too much doctrine had been originated and too many manuals had been issued.[14] An Inspectorate of Training (IT) was set up under General Maxse in order to co-ordinate the indoctrinators, although one suspects that this merely added one more storey to what he dubbed the doctrinal 'Tower of Babel',[15] rather than bringing the competing diversity of claimants into a more unified tactical authority.

There is a sense in which the central problem of interpretation for the whole of BEF tactics is encapsulated in the way we choose to view Maxse's Inspectorate of Training. On one hand we might regard his attempt to codify practice as a belated but effective wound dressing, staunching an anarchy of half-baked but entrenched opinions which had failed to provide very much positive progress during the preceding four years of war. This was apparently the way in which Maxse himself tended to regard it, and he was often dismissive of his predecessors and rivals in the tactical field. Yet when viewed from another perspective, we may see the IT as the crowning achievement in a long process of evolution and constructive development. Maxse was certainly only one among many forceful tactical analysts and his contribution, although welcome, may to some extent be seen as an attempt to 'fix' a machine that had never really been broken.

No firm final conclusion can probably be reached between these two competing interpretations, except to say that strong elements of truth are contained in both. Many more positive achievements had indeed been made by Maxse's predecessors than he would himself allow, and British infantry attacks had been able to make almost unopposed bounds forward of more than a kilometre on a surprisingly large number of occasions. This phenomenon was even seen in some divisions' sectors at Loos in September 1915, which has generally been written off as an exceptionally dismal example of the BEF's art of attack. It happened again on the Somme right flank on 1 July 1916, which was otherwise a day of still more searing humiliation. By 1917, the process had become almost routine, and the formal 'first days' of Arras, Messines, Third Ypres and Cambrai were all very successful, whatever else may have followed in each case. So brilliant was Plumer's attack at Broodseinde on 4 October that it was acknowledged by the Germans as their 'black day' almost a year before the more famous Amiens attack in August 1918.[16] If the British did particularly well during the Hundred Days following Amiens, therefore, we should see it more as a vindication of the laborious groundwork of the preceding four years than as the instantaneous effect of Maxse's arrival at GHQ.[17]

Yet against these many undoubted successes we must note that Maxse's alleged 'Tower of Babel' did indeed have a certain existence in reality. The problem was not perhaps a matter of doctrine in the strict sense of the term, since there is plenty of evidence to show that all arms were fully consulted and co-ordinated before any important new manual was finally issued, just as the training schools were peppered with fruitful intellectual cross-fertilisation between officers from different branches. To this extent, the higher staffs functioned smoothly and effectively in their work of analysing performance and updating doctrine accordingly across the whole BEF. At a more atavistic or visceral level, however, there was undoubtedly a widespread failure of inter-arm friendship and co-operation which tended to delay and distort the integration of new technologies into the fighting line.

THE PROBLEM OF CAP-BADGES

The popular stereotype of British tactics in the Great War depicts a line of infantry floundering across an impossibly muddy No Man's Land under a hail of bullets, obstructed by barbed wire and hindered rather than helped by supporting artillery fire. This is not an 'all arms' attack, and not even a sensible act of tactics at all, but rather an unequal sacrifice of exposed foot soldiers against a highly efficient all-arms defence. Nor was such a stereotype always far removed from reality, especially during the first half of the war, before artillery had become properly effective. Even after that there were many occasions when, for various reasons, such as the mud in the last month at Passchendaele or the strategic overstretch in March 1918, too few guns could be deployed to support the front line. In these circumstances, the infantry was left to fight its battles almost unaided, and it has not been an accident that by far the most moving and celebrated literature from the war has come from that particular arm. The *servitude et grandeur* of the Western Front has been appropriated almost exclusively by the infantry, and every other arm has tended to be regarded as very secondary.

This effect was heightened within the British Army by a heavy weight of regimental tradition and battalion pride. Despite persistent bureaucratic attempts to draft reinforcements into regiments which were not their own,[18] the cap-badge continued to exercise a powerful magnetism and tribalism throughout the war. Many regiments grew to a strength of more battalions than an entire infantry division,[19] and, through loyalty to their battalion, most soldiers surely felt more loyalty to their regiment than they did to their division. The division was an artificial creation of the war itself, often with a shifting population of battalions,[20] whereas the regiment might be able to trace its battle honours back through the centuries to such epically tribal moments as Sedgemoor, Culloden or the Boyne. For most officers, the regiment was also incarnated not merely in the base depot at which they had probably started their military lives, but very directly and specifically in the tightly knit 'social club' that was their battalion headquarters' mess. This might contain a maximum of 16 members during a time of heavy fighting[21] and was therefore a far less impersonal entity than the all-arms division, which might contain little short of 1,000 officers.

Cap-badge loyalty was a vital and highly constructive force which enhanced the cohesion and fighting will-power of even a mediocre battalion; yet at the same time it was also a seriously damaging obstacle to all-arms co-operation. It tended to encourage soldiers to regard the battalion, and not the brigade or the division, as the true centre of authority and therefore of tactical planning. When elements of the other arms were attached to the battalion, they were often regarded as outsiders and sometimes almost as civilians. This impulse was deeply reinforced by the peculiarly rapid development of unlikely-looking new technologies during the war, which tended to attract somewhat intellectual or other-worldly officers to those branches. Both Lawrence Bragg and H. H. Hemming, for example, selected themselves for the rarefied science of battery location because they disliked horses and therefore did not fit into the hippophile subaltern society of their colleagues in the Royal Field Artillery.[22] They were, in fact, as much out of place as a chess team which happens to find itself accompanying a rugby club tour.[23] Then again, just before the battle of Loos Robert Graves' company commander in 2nd Royal Welch Fusiliers (2 RWF), Captain G. O. Thomas, said of the gas officers that 'their very look makes me tremble. Chemistry-dons from London University, a few lads straight from school, one or two N.C.O.s of the old-soldier type, trained together for a few weeks, then given a job as responsible as this. Of course they'll bungle it. How could they do anything else?'[24] By the same token, the thrusting Lieutenant-Colonel Croft was not the only infantryman to regard his trench mortar officer as 'a wild-eyed enthusiast'; and it is certain that absolutely everyone knew that 'The æsthete does not make a good fighter'.[25]

Not only did the scientific specialities of trench mortars or gas attract graduates rather than the more usual public school men,[26] but both were notoriously difficult to integrate into the smooth running of an infantry battalion. Trench mortars won a bad name whenever they turned up in a battalion's area to fire some bombs, but then hastily retired before the inevitable enemy retaliation descended upon the powerless infantry.[27] It was only in the last year of the war that mortars would habitually be attached to infantry battalions for offensive operations, since more normally they would be held at Brigade Headquarters and regarded as a scarce asset that should be husbanded. In the case of gas, it was an unpopular weapon, not only because leaking cylinders and variations in the wind occasionally caused accidental friendly casualties, but more importantly because the infantry would habitually be called upon to provide large carrying parties, for many nights running before the planned attack, in order to place the gas cylinders in position. By 1918, this particular problem had been solved by releasing the gas from trucks pushed up on tramways running behind the infantry line, which would be evacuated at the time of release: but this, in turn, increased both the physical and psychological distance between the infantry and the Royal Engineer (RE) gas troops.[28] Nor did it solve the underlying problem of co-operation between the engineers and the infantry, since the gas troops were not the only engineer units to be continually demanding large labour gangs.

By 1916, the RE signals service had come to the conclusion that a tele-phone cable was secure from shelling only if it was buried to a depth of six feet, and it was only the infantry which could dig those trenches. When it came to digging field fortifications, the engineers' demands were still more extreme, to the extent that the large number of unkept rendezvous between engineer officers and their infantry working parties became a major source of friction between the two arms of the service.[29] Labour for simple tasks such as digging, carrying or wiring was always at a premium in the BEF, and the drafting in of special pioneer units and Chinese labour gangs appears only partially to have solved the problem. Throughout the war, the infantry was called upon to do more labouring tasks than it had a right to expect, especially in the dangerous zone towards the front line.

The case of the RE Signals was of especial importance in the smooth running of an all-arms battle; yet in 1914 they had only the sketchiest type of existence. They lost most of their equipment in the retreat from Mons, and discovered that they had no chain of command worthy of the name.[30] It took over two years for them to impress the other arms with their importance and to promote appropriate officers to key positions. Even then, some terrific battles still had to be fought in order to impose voice discipline and a due respect for telephone exchange operators. If anything, security seemed to be an ever-growing problem and 'Probably more was given away [to enemy eavesdropping] in 1916 than in 1915'.[31] Thereafter, there was a sharp move to ban all telephones from within at least a mile of the German lines; but this in turn required a considerable effort of re-equipment and retraining with strange new systems, including some that could operate without wires. Runners, pigeons, heliographs and lamps were the most obvious and soonest adopted, but power buzzers and Fullerphones were more effective, and even the quirky radio finally came into its own during the Hundred Days. In the process, however, the signallers were transformed from being an integral part of every battalion, drawn from its own men, into a somewhat alien group of specialists who observed their own chain of command and their own black arts. As one young infantry officer observed, 'The signallers were always with the company, but never of it'.[32]

The introduction of new signalling technology was nevertheless eventually a great success, albeit a somewhat belated one, which undoubtedly helped British tactics to make many important advances. Rather more ambiguous, however, was the chequered history of the Vickers machine gun, from the moment during the winter of 1915–16 when it was taken out of infantry battalions and reorganised as the basis of the new Machine Gun Corps.[33] This measure was designed to ensure a co-ordinated interlocking machine gun defence along the whole front, supervised by brigade machine gun officers, rather than to allow infantry battalions to site their guns according to their own local whims. To placate the infantry for this loss, the Vickers guns were replaced by Lewis guns as company and later platoon weapons, although this was not a popular measure. Only the Vickers was recognised as a 'real' machine gun, and the infantry felt that they had effectively been robbed of it. They failed to accept that its best effect could be achieved only as part of a brigade web of fire, and they distrusted the jumped-up machine gun enthusiasts, with their brand new cap-badges, almost as much as they distrusted trench mortar officers.

The souring of relations between the infantry and the Machine Gun Corps was deepened by two further developments. The first was the failure of GHQ to allow the formation of full machine gun battalions as divisional troops – as opposed to companies of machine guns under brigade command – until the winter of 1917–18. By then, too little time remained for them to shake down properly before the German March offensive, when the infantry was only too ready to blame their supporting machine gunners for the collapse. In theory a properly interlocked web of Vickers guns should have made infantry almost superfluous to a defensive, as Lieutenant-Colonel G. S. Hutchinson would demonstrate triumphantly at Meteren in April.[34] However, in practice, this seldom seemed to happen. The machine gunners felt too remote from the infantry and too inexperienced to fight with flexibility. They either retreated prematurely or were snuffed out too quickly when they attempted to make isolated stands.

A second wedge driven between the infantry and the machine guns was the idea of predicted indirect barrage fire, in which perhaps 30 Vickers guns might fire something like a million rounds over the heads of friendly infantry within a few hours, in order to interdict the enemy's rear areas. As the bullets descended at long range, they would plunge downwards like howitzer shells, scouring all trenches or craters in which the Germans might be hiding, thereby adding a dangerous additional dimension to the artillery barrage. There were many reports of the efficacy of this practice, not least from friendly infantry who drew moral reassurance from the crackling of the bullets overhead as they tried to work their way forward.[35] The Machine Gun Corps was certainly delighted with the effect and made it a touchstone of their specialised expertise, since it marked them out as an arm with a unique status exactly half way between infantry and artillery. However there were doubters among the infantry who were not only wary of 'dropshorts'[36] but outraged that barrage fire represented a distancing of the guns from the front line. The barrage was seen as an over-theoretical concept of dubious efficacy, whereas the use of machine guns for direct fire in or near the front line could achieve very tangible results with a fraction of the ammunition. The March 1918 retreats brought this issue to a head and created a strong backlash against the machine gun barrage and its enthusiasts.[37] Barrages nevertheless continued to be used throughout the Hundred Days, sometimes with as many as 100 Vickers guns firing together against deep targets.

BOMBARDMENT

A major difficulty in attacks was that direct fire with Vickers or Lewis guns could only be guaranteed to suppress concealed enemy machine guns at relatively close range. Yet the latter could reach the attackers at long range or from distant flanking positions. A more comprehensive method for suppressing the defence was essential if attacks were to succeed: it soon became clear that this could be provided only by artillery. During the first two years of the war, an attempt was duly made to hit and destroy every known German position by means of a long preliminary bombardment. Unfortunately, these bombardments could never hope to destroy absolutely every machine gun, and in any event they were often applied on too small a scale.[38] In the case of shrapnel, the shell was of an inappropriate type for reaching into the exceptionally deep bunkers which the Germans liked to provide for their troops. The longer the bombardment continued, moreover, the more the enemy would be forewarned of the coming attack. He could then strike back with disruptive counter-bombardments of his own, while manoeuvring reserves into blocking positions behind his front line.

Especially after its failure on 1 July 1916, the bombardment for 'destruction' was generally discredited for all but very specific tasks, such as wire-cutting or counter-battery fire. Instead, it was being realised increasingly that the much less ambitious aim of 'neutralisation' would suffice in the support of infantry attacks, since the infantry itself could be left to commit the final act of destruction, if only the enemy machine guns could be prevented from firing during the infantry's advance to decisive range. What was needed was a wall of exploding shells advancing ahead of the infantry, and covering its flanks, so that the defenders would be blinded, numbed and unable to intervene before the attackers were already close enough to overwhelm them. This was, in short, the neutralising technique that would be known as the 'creeping barrage'.

It may seem strange that the creeping barrage had been unheard of before the war, or that two years of fighting would pass before it could be perfected and popularised in the BEF.[39] Its widespread adoption came only during the battle of the Somme, which may thus be seen as something of a tactical watershed. The delay may perhaps be attributed to a certain failure of all-arms co-operation since, exactly as with the Machine Gun Corps, the infantry was always wary of dropshorts and resentful of the comfortable remoteness with which the gunners could fight their war. Forward observation officers were often noted more for their absence or intermittent activity than for their scrupulous liaison work, even when they had good signalling links, and it had become a platitude that 'The artillery duels of which one reads too often mean that the infantry are being blown to bits'.[40]

The delay in adopting the creeping barrage was also caused, at least in part, by the improbable or paradoxical nature of the creeper itself. It was designed to be an exceptionally intense form of fire while it lasted, yet it was not intended to destroy the enemy. Still more difficult for the infantry was the fact that they had to advance as closely behind it as humanly possible: 50 yards was often officially cited, but most tacticians knew that 20 was much better. It took a considerable act of faith to trust oneself to this dubious method of fighting, particularly since there were still many technical imperfections in British gunnery techniques which would not be ironed out until the end of 1917. Throughout 1916, British artillery ammunition was unreliable and much of the sciences of survey and accurate gun laying were yet to be fully understood by the gunners. These things would be much improved during 1917, leading to a second tactical watershed at Cambrai on 20 November 1917, when the British artillery was finally able to dispense with preliminary registration and predict its barrage entirely off the map. In the meantime, however, the barrage was recognised as a rather quirky instrument, albeit an absolutely essential one for any attack.

There was much discussion of how fast a barrage should advance and of what munitions it should comprise. It was found, for example, that on ordinary ground the infantry could keep up with it if it advanced at a rate of 100 yards every three or four minutes; but in very muddy conditions they might well lose it even if it advanced only 100 yards every eight minutes. The trick was to pre-set the speed of the barrage to suit the precise tactical conditions expected in the assault; but this was often extremely difficult to achieve in practice. The main limiting factor was that there were usually very poor communications between the guns and the troops actually making the attack, especially after the latter had advanced beyond visual range of the cable-head that had been pre-positioned in the front-line trenches. Therefore one could not routinely phone back corrections to regulate the speed of the barrage or to call down additional concentrations, and so almost everything had to be double-guessed in advance. This made for a major limitation in the flexibility of tactics, although it did not prevent some major offensive successes which have often tended to be overlooked in the literature.

Throughout 1916 and 1917, the main thrust of tactical thinking was to orchestrate an ever bigger and better artillery fireplan which would provide a counter-measure to every conceivable aspect of the enemy's defences. During the preliminary phase, which might continue for several weeks, the bombardment would cut the enemy wire, destroy his artillery and cut off his front-line troops from food and munitions. By a series of false zero hours (or 'Chinese' barrages) he would be left uncertain of the attack's timing and then, when the real zero arrived, he would be neutralised to a depth of 2,000 yards by five or six successive lines of creeping barrage, thickened up in their early stages with trench mortar fire and a machine gun barrage. At the battle of Messines, in June 1917, the effect was further enhanced by the simultaneous blowing of 19 gigantic mines. By this time, also, the artillery planning had achieved sufficient sophistication for an appropriate weight of shell to be calculated for each specific task, thereby avoiding the habitual under-provisioning of earlier years. Some robust multipliers were established for how many shells had to be fired per minute per yard of the attack front in order to make a 'creeper' effective, how many were needed to cut what frontage of wire, and how many to destroy each enemy battery.[41]

In the matter of munitions, it took a considerable time for shrapnel to be superseded by other natures. In part this was the result of a century of tradition, in which the British shrapnel round had been seen as something of a national secret, almost equivalent to the Greek fire of the Byzantine empire. Perhaps more pertinently, the shell shortage of 1915 had led to an over-production of the relatively simple shrapnel shell at the expense of the more sensitive High Explosive (HE), and it was well into 1917 before this imbalance had been corrected. In the event it was the 9th (Scottish) Division which claimed to be the leader in the use of HE for creeping barrages, start-ing with their attack on Longueval on 14 July 1916.[42] They felt that although shrapnel might be effective against defenders who were manning their parapet, the whole point of a creeper was to prevent the enemy from getting that far, and to keep him cowering in his dugouts. For this, only the repeated shock and concussion of HE shells was adequate to convey the full portent of the threat. This theory made good tactical sense, and it gradually spread throughout the BEF during the closing months of 1916. It would make still more sense when the No. 106 Fuse was introduced during the course of 1917. This fuse detonated immediately on contact with the ground and not, as with earlier patterns, after the shell had buried itself deep enough to make a crater. With a creeper composed of HE with 106 Fuses, the infantry would no longer find that the ground ahead of it had been made impassable by the very bombardment that was intended to help it forward. The 106 Fuse also improved wire cutting and reduced the 'back splash' of the creeper, thereby allowing the infantry to hug it ever more closely.

The 9th Division also pioneered the use of smoke shell in their creeper for the first day at Arras (9 April 1917).[43] This type of shell was a novelty in the BEF at the time, pushed through the factories on the initiative of General Furse, a former commander of 9th Division who had risen to become Master General of Ordnance. So scarce was it in April 1917, indeed, that 9th Division used up the entire allocation for Third Army in the course of its attack. Nevertheless, the experiment was deemed to be a great success, since it thickened up the obscuration caused by exploding HE and generally con-tributed to the cocoon of obscurity that it was the artillery's job to weave around attacking infantry, not least on its flanks. By 1918 smoke shell had become an important adjunct to most British attacks.

One final type of munition which should be mentioned is the gas shell. This arrived in the BEF's armoury considerably later than in the Germans', being available to the British in large numbers only in 1918. On the other hand, the British had already perfected two much more concentrated systems of gas distribution which the Germans had not: first, clouds released from cylinders emplaced in the front trenches, and, second, a heavy concentration of gas bombs fired from a massed battery of projectors or heavy mortars. A battery of several hundred projectors, each firing an oil drum full of gas up to a range of 1,000 yards, could lay down far more poison upon a specific target in a short time than was normally possible with the much smaller artillery shells.[44] Nor did a gas shell really enjoy any longer range than a projector or cloud attack, since the wind could easily waft a gas cloud to a depth of 20 kilometres behind the enemy front line, still causing casualties wherever it went. The gas shell, by contrast, offered some distinct advantages through its precision and relative independence of the wind. Its particular strength, like that of the machine gun barrage, was that it could be fired over the heads of attacking infantry to suppress the enemy's depth positions without interfering with the attack itself. Neither a cloud nor a projector attack could offer this degree of discrimination, and it was very noticeable after Loos just how rarely either of them was directly combined with the BEF's major infantry operations. Although the machine gun barrage was eventually accepted with some reluctance as a normal adjunct to infantry attacks, the high-volume gas attack always tended to be relegated to fronts on which the infantry was not attempting to attack at all. Thus, in common with the cavalry during much of the American Civil War, it was regarded as a hit and run, or raiding, weapon rather than an integral part of normal all-arms planning. Only the artillery shell, for all its short-comings could hope to raise chemical warfare to that last lofty status.[45]

No account of artillery support for the infantry would remain complete without an emphasis on the great strides made in counter-battery fire during 1917. This was of crucial importance if the infantry was to avoid a lethal shower of German shells as it formed up, attacked across No Man's Land and then consolidated in captured trenches. The destruction of a defender's artillery was therefore a vital consideration in all tactics, and in 1916 far too little success had been won in this field. The necessary expertise in locating the enemy guns would be built up only laboriously throughout 1917, led by men such as Hemming, Bragg and, especially, the under-recognised Colonel H. St J. L. Winterbotham R. E., who was really their animating patron and responsible for setting up some of the most fruitful programmes.

Between them, these men, and their colleagues in related branches, put in place the very complex but essential apparatus of accurate maps, weather forecasts, gun calibration centres and flash or sound location systems which allowed German batteries to be identified with sufficient accuracy to be engaged at an economical cost in both shells and air observation assets.[46] By the middle of 1917, this effort was bearing fruit to the point that in relatively good conditions, such as the middle part of the Third Ypres battle, the Royal Artillery could subdue the German artillery very considerably. In ideal con-ditions, such as those at Cambrai on 20 November, it could almost entirely destroy its opponent within a single co-ordinated shoot. 'Artillery duels' could no longer be dismissed as merely a blind mutual battering of the infantry, but had become genuine long-range duels between highly skilled teams of gunners and scientists. It should be stressed that although the British artillery certainly suffered some important disadvantages at key moments in this process – notably in the overlooked salient at Ypres or in the misty and overstretched Fifth Army area in March 1918 – they generally held the whip hand over the German guns in both numbers of tubes and quality of science.[47]

Much the same could also be said of the Royal Flying Corps (RFC), which had been seen as a handmaiden of the artillery since at least the battle of Neuve Chapelle in March 1915. It had quickly established both effective air-to-ground radio and the 'zone call' system for calling down fire upon specific targets and, apart from two relatively brief periods at the start of 1916 and in the spring of 1917, had thrown the German air forces onto the defensive.[48] By the time of Messines, it was developing the skills of fighter-ground-attack with considerable success, although liaison with front line infantry, as was the case with so many other new technologies, always remained difficult. From the earliest battles, it had been seen as important that aircraft should be able to identify the foremost lines of friendly troops, not merely to prevent accidental strafing but, more importantly, to inform the generals of what was going on. A whole series of contraptions such as marker panels, flares or smoke signals had been tried out, but in the event they achieved only patchy results. Air observation of a fluid battle remained a very uncertain science. At Passchendaele, there was even a complaint that the all-consuming mud made the Germans look as though they were wearing khaki uniforms.[49] The conclusion that Hemming drew at around this time was that only photographs could provide valuable aerial information on the situation on the ground, since immediate verbal impressions by aircrew could be very ambiguous and unreliable.[50]

THE SAD CASES OF THE TANKS AND THE CAVALRY

One final example of the difficulties of infantry liaison was the sad case of the tanks.[51] Seen as potential war-winners by so many different interest groups, both during and after hostilities, especially following the German armoured victories of 1939–41, they received a far greater propaganda puff than they actually merited. It was surely no coincidence, for example, that Ludendorff and his General Staff started to draw attention to the supposedly unstoppable power of British tanks only during the Hundred Days, and specifically around 30th September 1918; or in other words at the precise moment when the Hindenburg Line was being breached by an overwhelming infantry and artillery assault (in fact supported by relatively few tanks). It was the moment when the inevitability of an early Armistice could no longer be dodged, and so the temptation for the German Army to see the tank as a convenient scapegoat, or *machine ex deo*, must surely have been every bit as overpowering as the temptation to blame civilian politicians for a 'stab in the back'. In reality, the tanks of the Great War were slow, almost blind and scarcely habitable by their crews. The fumes, noise, 'sea sickness' and generally hard labour of life in a tank meant that their combat endurance could seldom be extended much beyond eight hours. This, in turn, made their appearances in the front line seem both rare and fleeting to the long-suffering infantry. Furthermore, since they usually had to arrive in a battle immediately after an approach march of several miles from a concealed laager, tanks quite often failed to meet their rendezvous timings. Even if they did, it was far from inevitable that they would be working alongside infantry who had received adequate training either in what they could expect from the tanks or in how they could themselves help the tanks forward. Inter-arm co-operation remained notoriously difficult in this branch, as in so many others, and the focus upon it in official manuals could never quite catch up with the problem. Nor did GHQ help matters when it ordained, against Tank Corps advice, that tanks should be 'penny packeted' in relatively small numbers in almost every operation in which they took part. Only Cambrai on 20 November 1917 and Amiens on 8 August 1918 could be presented as exceptions to the rule. Even then, the Tank Corps would still complain that too few machines had been used.

After an initial burst of excessive enthusiasm, a mood of disillusionment with tanks swept through the BEF's infantry during the spring of 1917, growing in proportion as they gained personal experience of the tanks' limitations. In vain would the tank experts insist that they had been trying to explain precisely those limitations to their hosts from the very first, in order to promote a finer all-arms understanding. It was too late: the psychological damage had already been done, and it would be only gradually that the infantry would come to understand just what use could and could not be made of the wonderful new land battleships. In essence, the main benefit they had to offer was in cutting or crushing barbed wire. Whereas shrapnel bombardments had taken days, and HE with the No.106 Fuse had taken hours, the tank could plough its way through even the deepest entanglements in only minutes.[52] Once through, it could then act as a rallying point to give the infantry a psychological boost to continue pressing forward, in rather the same way as a creeping barrage might do. When it came to neutralising specific enemy strongpoints, however, it was probably no better than a good squad of machine gunners, bombers or trench mortars. It was also itself very vulnerable to quite a wide variety of anti-tank measures. Hence, in most battles it would itself often be calling upon the foot soldiers to help dispose of troublesome German field guns or anti-tank rifles. It was far from a complete answer to the infantryman's prayer, especially since it was doubly vulnerable when fighting in villages or woods. At Passchendaele–St Julien the tanks were so hampered by the mud that they could not even operate off the roads without bogging. Nevertheless, the tank could still undoubtedly add a certain extra impetus to an attack and, by the time of the Hundred Days, it was generally acknowledged to be a moderately useful auxiliary to the infantry.

If the tank's experience on the Western Front was unfortunate and rather disappointing, that of the horsed cavalry was sadder still. They actually enjoyed little less battlefield success than tanks, but found themselves heaped with unjustified vilification in proportion as the latter were accorded unjustified accolades. This was doubly irksome since the pre-war cavalry had actually been tactically more aware and more advanced than the infantry, and had taken a clear lead in exploiting new technologies such as automatic rifles, aircraft and radios.[53] By virtue of its mobility and dispersed operations, the cavalry had been forced to give special attention to the remoteness of modern command, and because of its specialised tactical history, it had been compelled to look at fire and movement more closely than the infantry. It certainly saw itself as mounted infantry rather than as sabre-charging cavalry; and in practice it often performed quite well during sequences of fluid operations, namely the first few weeks of the war, the early spring advances of 1917, the spring retreats of 1918 and finally the Hundred Days. On one occasion in the last phase, cavalry even made a ten-mile advance in a single bound.[54] However, it has generally been damned for its obvious failures whenever it was called forward to supercharge infantry attacks during phases of predominantly trench warfare. At High Wood on the Somme or at Monchy-le-Preux at Arras, there were openings that might have been exploited successfully if only the cavalry had been available in sufficient force at the right place and the right time. But such was the numbing difficulty of trench warfare, of course, that it was almost impossible to vector the appropriate forces quickly enough to the key point. Cavalry required far more logistic and administrative back-up than infantry, and were accordingly very scarce. More than five cavalry divisions in the BEF were allowed to dwindle to just three and, by reason of their inactivity and starvation of the highest quality manpower, even those lost some of their fine cutting edge. They did at least continue to modernise their tactical concepts, moving by 1916 towards an all-arms mobile force which should include motor machine guns, armoured cars and cyclists as well as mounted infantry.

Overall, the infantry did gradually accumulate an impressive array of supporting arms based on new or relatively new technologies. By the Hundred Days, in the autumn of 1918, it had effectively integrated most of them into a single coherent battle. For too long before that, however, success had been only patchy. Whereas the need for close artillery support was seen early and brought to full fruition during 1917, the perceived importance of the tank first waxed strongly, then waned in 1917, despite its brief moment of glory at Cambrai, and only settled out as a more realistic and workable compromise a year later. With machine guns, the story was that the infantry had always fully appreciated their potential, but increasingly resented their successive administrative withdrawal into ever higher and apparently more esoteric strata of command. Neither trench mortars nor signals experienced a smooth passage to their eventually successful integration during the Hundred Days, and gas was always something to be kept very much 'at arms length'.

THE ALL-ARMS BATTLE

Cap-badge loyalties certainly played an important part in delaying the full integration of all arms into the infantry battalion's battle; but so did the many other institutional and technical problems that were surely inevitable when a whole clutch of new technologies was being invented almost overnight and then instantly promoted to the highest priorities. We must remember that although there had been modern artillery before 1914, there had been no HE round for the British 18-pounder gun, no smoke or gas shell, no creeping barrage, no survey or battery location apparatus and, to all intents and purposes, no air observation. There had been no British trench mortar or Livens projector, no tactical signals, no machine gun barrage, no gas and no tank. All of these things had to elbow their way at short notice into the very core of a sophisticated organisation which had for centuries seen itself as an exclusive club of horse, foot and-dashingly mounted, intrepidly direct firing-field gun. Not even the engineers found themselves especially welcome in the great trench war, any more than Wellington had been able to get enough of them in his great Peninsular sieges. The fact that the Royal Engineers had actually developed gas, mines, signals, survey – and to some extent both aviation and the tank – was apparently set aside rather easily in the BEF of 1916–18.

We may lament the resistance and tribal pride with which the infantry delayed the arrival of new technology which was intended, after all, to be its own salvation. Yet we should also note that this did have one very productive side effect. Far from stultifying the infantry in an outdated pattern of hopelessly unsupported mass attacks, its distrust of technological innovations coming from outside the battalion seems to have persuaded it to make better use of the resources which lay to hand within the battalion itself. It realised that ultimately it would have to find ways of fighting forward on its own, irrespective of the help that might or might not be forthcoming from other agencies.

The battle of the Somme brought these matters to a head, since the creeping barrage could not yet be trusted fully, and the reminder of the innovations still looked extremely unreliable or even simply stupid.[55] The infantry knew that it might be left to fend for itself at almost any stage of a battle, so it put additional emphasis on the principles of fire and movement which had been taught before the war but to some extent forgotten during the first two years of static trench fighting. Lewis guns were by now beginning to be available to each platoon, while both hand- and rifle-grenades had been made sufficiently reliable to be entrusted to non-specialist handlers. Thus there were three new weapons available to every infantry unit, apart from the traditional rifle and bayonet. By the end of the Somme battle, this allowed a set of tactics to be propagated for self-sufficient platoons, in manual SS 143,[56] by which a Lewis and a rifle-grenade section would pin down the enemy by concentrated fire, while a rifle section rushed in from a flank and a hand-grenade section mopped up the dugouts. In essence this brought together a miniature version of all the functions of infantry, artillery and the Machine Gun Corps. Furthermore, since smoke and thermit grenades would also be carried, it even included an element of chemical warfare. It was a formula that would continue to be taught in the British Army, with only relatively minor modifications, for over half a century thereafter.

It was General Maxse who proved to be most voluble in advocating platoon and even section tactics, although he did not approve of every detail in the official manual. His fundamental message was that every battalion should be strictly organised into exactly 16 equal platoons, each always commanded and trained by the same leader. Working against him, he found many local variations in practice, much turbulence of personnel in and out of the battalion, and many distractions from training.[57] His recommendations were never fully implemented even in his own XVIII Corps, which made him sceptical of the fighting value of junior leaders and small units. To a considerable extent, this scepticism seemed to be confirmed by his own large-scale defeat at St Quentin in March 1918 and his subsequent demotion from corps command to direction of the Inspectorate of Training. Nevertheless, the inner concept of fire and movement had in fact became very widely understood in the BEF during 1917, and there are plentiful accounts in the memoirs of junior officers of attempts to put it into practice.[58] Troublesome machine guns were knocked out with platoon weapons on far more occasions than just the famous moments when VCs were won, although it remained true that the infantry would always prefer a good barrage to do the work for it, if that could be arranged.

By a mixture of formal attacks with plentiful all-arms support, and improvised dog-fighting when the infantry was left on its own, British assaults could often make progress even in the unpromising conditions of the Western Front, and even despite the many imperfections in all-arms co-operation. The proof may perhaps be found in the final achievement during the Hundred Days, when the five armies of the BEF advanced an average of 84 miles, with a monthly average advance of 28 miles.[59] This was not as good as the monthly average of 50 miles for the fully mechanised Allied armies in north-west Europe between June 1944 and February 1945; but it was actually better than the 25 miles per month maintained in Italy between

September 1943 and May 1945.[60] Thus Haig's semi-mechanised army performed creditably even by comparison with the norms of the more mobile Second World War. It was no longer simply a mass of unsupported and tactically naïve infantry, but had grown into a complex mixture of many technologies and a high degree of tactical awareness.

NOTES

1. This chapter is based on my *Battle Tactics of the Western Front, The British Army's Art of Attack, 1916–18* (Yale University Press, 1994).
2. Tim Travers, *The Killing Ground: The British Army, the Western Front and the Emergence of Modern Warfare 1900–1918* (London: Allen & Unwin, 1987), the best modern analysis of 'top down' command habits in the BEF.
3. Wyn Griffith, *Up To Mametz* (first published 1931; new edn, London: Severn House, 1981), p. 185.
4. The point is well made in Robin Prior and Trevor Wilson, *Command on the Western Front* (Oxford: Blackwell, 1992), and their 'Summing Up The Somme' in *History Today* (Nov. 1991), pp.37–43.
5. W. H. Watson, *A Company of Tanks* (Edinburgh and London: Blackwood, 1920), pp.41–68.
6. I am grateful to Russell Jones of the Aldershot Military Museum for explaining the detail of the first (1902) military motor car. For Gough on the Somme, see the exceptionally interesting collection of Reserve (or Fifth) Army tactical analyses in Public Record Office (hereafter PRO) document WO158 344.
7. Three particularly 'political' tactical innovators were J. F. C. Fuller: the senior staff officer of the tank staff, C. H. Foulkes of the RE gas brigade and G. M. Lindsay of the Machine Gun Corps, who all conducted extensive correspondence with MPs. A surprising number of MPs themselves fought in the trenches, as opposed to merely visiting them on conducted tours.
8. Bill Rawling, *Surviving Trench Warfare* (University of Toronto Press, 1992), *passim*, and especially pp.216–23.
9. Note that the Welsh Guards in the Falklands were militarily wiped out as a fighting force after losing rather less than 50 per cent of their strength.
10. The *locus classicus* for the comparative safety of routine trench warfare is Tony Ashworth, *Trench Warfare 1914–1918: The Live and Let Live System* (London: Macmillan, 1980), and his 'The Sociology of French Warfare' in *British Journal of Sociology* (1968), pp. 406–21. For a complete explosion of the myth that subalterns' life expectancy at the front was only three weeks, see Martin Middlebrook, *The Kaiser's Battle* (London: Allen Lane, 1978), Appendix 9, pp.405–7.
11. John Terraine (ed.), *General Jack's Diary, 1914–18* (London: Eyre & Spottiswode, 1964), p.209. Compare Siegfried Sassoon's description of planning a trench raid, in his *Memoirs of an Infantry Officer* (first published 1930; new edn, London: Faber, 1965), p.157ff.
12. W. D. Croft, *Three Years With the Ninth (Scottish) Division* (London: Murray, 1919), p.67. *The Defence of Duffer's Drift* was written by Ernest Swinton under the pseudonym of 'Backsight-Forethought'. It was first published in the *United Service Magazine* (1903), but subsequently reprinted several times, most recently by the US Government Printing Office (1985).
13. The first major updating of pre-war manuals came in May 1916 with the *Training of Divisions for Offensive Action* (SS 109, 8 May 1916), supported by Fourth Army's *Tactical Notes* ('The Red Book') of the same month: reproduced in J. E. Edmonds (gen. ed.), *History of the Great War, Based on Official Documents: Military Operations, France and Belgium* (The British Official History (*OH*) in 14 vols. plus maps and appendices, London: Macmillan, 1922–49. Some volumes were recently reprinted by IWM), 1916, Appendices

Nos 17–18. The second major updating occurred during and immediately after the battle of the Somme.

14. A total of 300 pamphlets a year was alleged, and deplored as excessive, in 'The Song' of the Inspectorate of Training, written in the summer of 1918. This figure was annotated by General Maxse as 'A fact': Maxse papers, Imperial War Museum Department of Documents (hereafter IWM), Box 69–53–11, File 53. For a recent listing of the first 600 pamphlets, see Peter T. Scott, 'The CDS/SS Series of Manuals and Instructions, a Numerical Checklist', 11 parts, in *The Great War*, Vol. 1, No. 2 (Feb. 1989) p.50, through to Vol. 3, No. 4 (Sept. 1991), p.136.

15. So described in 'The Song', ibid.

16. OH 1917, Vol. 2, pp.xi, 303.

17. Maxse's organisation had scarcely found its feet by August 1918, and its most important publications tended to appear around November or thereafter. A collection of all the IT publications may be found in the IWM Maxse papers, Box 69–53–12, File 59.

18. See, for example, Dr J. C. Dunn's protests (from 2 RWF) against the 'hairy-eared theorist' who mixed up the regiments, July 1916, in his *The War the Infantry Knew* (first published 1938, new edn with introduction by K. R. Simpson, London: Jane's, 1987), p.245.

19. Apart from artillery and other divisional troops, a division included 12 battalions, later reduced to nine of infantry and one of machine guns. Some regiments, by contrast, numbered as many as 25 battalions in theory, and might indeed have 12 of them scattered around the world in a usable form.

20. These may be traced through A. F. Becke, *Order of Battle of Divisions* (British Official History, 6 vols, London: HMSO, 1937–45, reprinted by Sherwood and Westlake, 1986–89).

21. On the Somme, a total of 20 officers was reckoned to be all a battalion in action really required, and by Passchendaele this had fallen to 16: see J. Ewing, *The History of the 9th (Scottish) Division* (London: Murray, 1921), p.93, and OH 1917, Vol. 2, p.185, respectively. See also John Terraine, *The Smoke and the Fire* (London: Sidgwick & Jackson, 1980), p.125 n2, for the Germans' far smaller officer ratio of eight or nine per battalion.

22. For Bragg, see Appendix L, 'Sound Ranging in France', in M., Farndale, *History of the Royal Regiment of Artillery: Western Front 1914–18.* (Woolwich: RA Institution, 1986), pp.374–9. For Hemming, see IWM microfilm PP MCR 155: Lt, Col. H. H. Hemming, *My Story* (c. 1976).

23. This most uncomfortable situation was once experienced by the present author.

24. Robert Graves, *Goodbye to All That* (first published by J. Cape, 1929; London: Penguin edn, 1982), p.123.

25. Croft, op.cit., p.7; and D. Hanley, *A Student in Arms* (twelfth edn, London: Melrose, 1917), p.245.

26. The recruiting and training of graduates for gas duties is recounted in, among others, C. H. Foulkes, *Gas, the Story of the Special Brigade RE* Edinburgh and London: Blackwood, 1934), pp.47, 57–8, 62.

27. Ashworth, op.cit., p.65.

28. Foulkes, op.cit., pp.242, 293.

29. I. Maxse (ed.), *Hints on Training, Issued by XVIII Corps* ('The Brown Book'; HMSO, Aug. 1918, compiled by IT in May 1918 from a variety of fragments much-used by Maxse during the preceding 12 months).

30. For all discussion of signals, see R. E. Priestley, *The Signal Service in the European War of 1914 to 1918 (France)* (Official RE History, Chatham: Mackay, 1921).

31. Ibid., p.102.

32. Wyn Griffith, op.cit., p.158.

33. See my article 'The Lewis Gun Made Easy', in *The Great War*, Vol. 3, No. 4 (Sept. 1991), pp.108–15.

34. G. S. Hutchinson, *Machine Guns – Their History and Tactical Employment* (London: Macmillan, 1938), pp.234–59.

35. G. M. Lindsay Machine Gun papers, held at the Tank Museum, Bovington, Dorset, File E 15 b, p.3. Further details of late-war machine gun usage are in '*Machine Guns, Tactical and Technical Lessons Learnt*' (IX Corps, Messines), PRO WO158/418; and Col. N. K. Charteris 'Narrative of Machine Gun Operations, Fourth Army April–November 1918,'

WO158/332.

36. For example, Croft, op.cit., pp.124, 167.
37. Lindsay papers, especially the files of series D.
38. Prior and Wilson, *Command on the Western Front*, op.cit., *passim*. For artillery developments I have generally followed J. B. A. Bailey, *Field Artillery and Firepower* (Oxford: Military Press, 1989), and his essay elsewhere in the present volume.
39. See Lt-Col. Bailey's account of the trial and error development of different types of 'lifting' barrages.
40. Lord Moyne, *Staff Officer, the Diaries of Lord Moyne 1914–1918*, (edited by Brian Bond and Simon Robbins London: Leo Cooper, 1987), p.14.
41. Details in planning papers and orders for the battle of Messines in PRO WO158/215 for Second Army and WO158/413, Part 2, for IX Corps' Artillery.
42. Ewing, op.cit., pp.106–7.
43. Ibid., p.187.
44. Foulkes, op.cit., pp.191, 249, 329 ff.
45. Note, however, that the Germans' most potent gas shell, containing mustard gas, could not be used for at least six days before friendly troops were expected to inhabit the target area, due to its persistence. Hence this weapon, in common with British cloud or projector attacks, tended to be relegated to inactive fronts: Foulkes, op.cit., pp.267–71.
46. These aspects are well covered in Shelford Bidwell and Dominick Graham, *Firepower, British Army Weapons and Theories of War, 1904–45* (London: Allen & Unwin, 1982). For survey, see also Peter Chasseaud, *Topography of Armageddon* (London: Mapbooks, 1991).
47. Bailey, and Farndale, op.cit., including Bragg's own evidence, are unanimous in the belief that German gunnery was considerably less scientific than the BEF's.
48. Anon, *A Short History of the Royal Air Force*, (London: Air Historical Branch, 1929).
49. Fifth Army conference, 12 October 1917, in PRO WO158/250, item no.470.
50. Hemming, op.cit., pp.86–7.
51. Apart from Dr Harris's paper later in this collection, my main sources for tanks have been Watson, op.cit., F. Mitchell, *Tank Warfare, the Story of the Tanks in the Great War*. (London: Nelson, n.d. No. 15 in 'The Nelsonian Library', reprinted London: Donovan, 1987); D. J. Fletcher, 'The Origins of Armour' in J. P. Harris and F. H. Toase, (eds), *Armoured Warfare* (London: Batsford, 1990), pp.5–26; and PRO WO158 series, Files No. 834 (second half of 1916), 814 (battle of Arras), 858 (battle of Messines), 803 (includes *Infantry and Tank Co-operation and Training*, issued January 1918), 835 (defensive use, early 1918), 832 (1918, including manual SS 214, *Tanks and their Employment in Co-operation with Other Arms*), 855 and 865 (immediately post-war).
52. Infantry could pass through wire crushed by tanks, but horses often could not, which posed considerable problems not merely for cavalry but also for essential second echelon apparatus – such as machine guns – and re-supply which relied on pack transport: Hutchinson, op.cit., p.219.
53. This section is based on Stephen D. Badsey, *Fire and the Sword* (unpublished doctoral thesis, Cambridge, 1981), and his essay later in the present volume.
54. OH 1918, Vol. 5, pp.219, 527–30, for discussion of vanguards and cavalry operations.
55. For example, the Pipe Pusher (or 'Barratt Hydraulic Forcing Jack') bored a small-diameter hole horizontally through the ground, which could be filled with explosives, telephone cables or gas. Its inglorious uses with explosives are in OH 1916, Vol. 2, pp.128, 187, 195, 224, 255, 269; its help for the signallers, in Priestley, op.cit., pp.127–8; and a gas attack at Arras on 18 March 1917 is reported in Foulkes op.cit., p.196.
56. SS 143, *Instructions for the Training of Platoons for Offensive Action, 1917* (issued by GHQ, 14 Feb. 1917).
57. *Hints on Training, Issued by XVIII Corps*, op.cit., and Imperial War Museum Maxse papers, *passim*.
58. For example, Charles E. Carrington, *Soldier From The Wars Returning* (London: Hutchinson 1965), pp.177–8, and F. C. Hitchcock, *Stand To, A Diary of the Trenches, 1915–1918* (first published 1937, new edn edited by Anthony Spagnoly, (Norwich: Gliddon, 1988), pp.278–80, and especially pp.290–1. See also SS 197. *The Tactical Employment of Lewis Guns* (issued by GHQ, Jan. 1918).

59. The approximate advances, in miles per army, based on OH 1918 Vols 4 and 5, break down as follows:

	1st Army	*2nd Army*	*3rd Army*	*4th Army*	*5th Army*
Average per month	30	22	33	34	21
Total	89	67	98	102	62

60. Not even Gough's Fifth Army in March 1918 retreated as far as either Slim in Burma in 1942 or the Allied forces in the Ardennes at Christmas 1944. For an interesting discussion of the psychic similarities between these campaigns and the Western Front of 1914–18, see John Ellis, *The Sharp End of War* Newton Abbot: (David and Charles, 1980).

CHAPTER TWO

British Artillery in the Great War

Jonathan Bailey

This chapter will explain how the experience of combat between 1914 and 1918 brought about fundamental changes in artillery practice and relationships between the arms. It will show how preoccupation with fire and manoeuvre of infantry gave way to concern for artillery firepower, machine guns, tanks and aircraft and how the art of Command and Control (C2) was seen to lie in the way a commander applied firepower, rather than in the way he deployed foot soldiers.

This transformation was common in varying degrees to all the belligerents and it went through four phases: the realisation in 1914 that existing artillery practice was inadequate, the consequent testing of new methods and build-up of materiel in 1915, the tactics of 'mass destruction' by artillery fire from 1916–17 and, finally, the adoption of 'neutralisation' from 1917–18. The lessons learned from these experiences shaped the foundations of modern artillery operations, and many are still recognisable today.

BEFORE 1914

In 1914, infantry was still required to provide its own covering fire, when artillery was not available. Artillery support, when provided, was almost always by observed fire; Counter-Battery (CB) fire was advocated but generally impractical; harassing fire, let alone continuous fire, was seldom used; and artillery played little part in battlefield deception.

As the First World War approached, British artillery was ill prepared for the future. The principle of massing guns and concentrating fire at the point of decision was known but not followed. British artillery tasks were described as follows: 'Till the enemy discloses his dispositions, artillery must usually limit its action to preparing to support the other arms as soon as occasion demands it', and 'The duty of artillery is to assist infantry to establish superiority of fire over the enemy',[1] in other words winning the fire fight before an attack. The requirement for close support was thus clearly stated, but fire planning was unknown and field artillery could offer only direct fire support.

The British had learned some unfortunate lessons from the Boer War. One was the paramount importance of mobility and the other was the perceived impracticality of indirect fire when tested on the veldt. The Royal Field Artillery (RFA) consequently relied on equipment mobility and did not exploit the advances in fire mobility, made possible through indirect fire techniques and increased ranges. Shortly before the war, gun designers had actually sacrificed range when producing a new gun carriage.

The RFA was renowned for its unscientific approach to gunnery, admiring intuition and subjective judgement, not calculation, when opening fire. The RFA did not practise temperature corrections, map shooting was unknown, and communications were by visual signal, sometimes by short telephone line, but more usually by megaphone. By comparison, the Royal Garrison Artillery (RGA) approach was relatively scientific. By 1914, it was firing from cover and laying guns on line with instruments on calculated data. It shot from maps and corrected for weather before firing. In May 1914, in a lecture at the Royal Artillery Institution, Captain Hill of the RGA was met with hoots of laughter by a largely RFA audience when he said that the RFA would be making meteorological corrections within two months of the start of a war.[2]

Regulations were interpreted to mean close support by the gun not the shell, with masses of pieces grouped well forward with other arms in the style of the 1870s. Artillery regulations in 1914 called for artillery to move forward to positions during battle to get 'a clearer view of the infantry fight', despite the example of the Russo-Japanese War, when this practice was seen to result in the rapid loss of equipment, and so of firepower, for the remainder of hostilities.

Defence received little attention. It was intended that artillery would be evenly distributed behind a strong line and allotted to infantry deployed to the front. Defence in depth was not considered.

The BEF went to war with no artillery above divisional level, and artillery advisers at corps and army level lacked staffs and the ability to command. C2 was decentralised except when equipments happened to be co-located. Telephones were used, but line was in limited supply. In a scenario which judged mobile warfare inevitable, decentralisation of C2 seemed the only answer. Combined with poor communications, this meant that dispersed batteries could not be used to concentrate fire, and this was one reason why increasing range was judged of marginal importance.

Close support might have been better provided by the heavier guns of the RGA; but these were few in number. In 1914, the British Army could find 72 field batteries but only six heavy batteries. By November 1918, there were 568 field batteries and 440 siege or heavy batteries, and only two-thirds of all pieces were lighter than 60-pounders.

The importance of heavier weapons was seriously underrated. Shortly before war broke out, the number of 60-pounders was reduced, as these were considered unsuitable for use with an expeditionary force. The 6-inch howitzer did not even form a part of the Field Army, unlike its equivalent in the German Army.

Firepower could not be generated through mobility if the ammunition was not available. Experience in the Russo-Japanese War had taught that ammunition expenditure could be unexpectedly high. At Lamuntun, during the battle of Sha-ho, Russian guns had fired 166 rounds per gun (rpg) in 40 minutes; but like other European armies, the British learned the wrong lessons, emphasising the need for fire economy rather than increasing the supply of ammunition.[3] Regulations noted that 'Rapid fire cannot be maintained for more than brief periods without exhausting ammunition'.[4] The War Establishments Part I, 1913, noted that every 18-pounder field gun should have 1,000 rounds, with 300 in the United Kingdom and a further 500 to be provided by factories within six months.[5] Of all these, only 176 were held at battery level, and they could sustain firing for just 44 minutes at Rate 4 (four rounds per minute). Six such periods would consume the ammunition with the force, leaving 75 minutes' worth in the UK and another 60 minutes' worth to arrive within six months. With hindsight, the inadequacy was clear.

All ammunition issued to the RFA was shrapnel, which was to prove the most effective munition of 1914. High explosive (HE) was regarded in many quarters as unsporting, because it gave off yellow fumes which were rumoured to be poisonous. The BEF was to find itself outnumbered, outranged and short of many technical skills; but it possessed one outstanding advantage in its ability to burst shrapnel at an effective height, unlike the German artillery, which burst its shrapnel too high at 30 feet.

The shortage of ammunition meant that British artillery could offer only light fire in the initial phase of an attack, building up to a high rate of fire at the decisive moment. Its aim was therefore limited to demoralising the enemy and affecting 'their fire so as to afford the infantry the opportunity to assault'.[6] British artillery expected to neutralise, not destroy, the enemy.

In 1914, European armies and their artillery had little idea what shape the coming war would take. They all regarded artillery as an accessory rather than an essential arm, supporting infantry in mobile operations under what in practice was a decentralised command. There was no question of truly combined arms planning, and while CB fire was deemed necessary, it could not be carried out effectively in the mobile war scenario.

The German artillery was best organised and equipped to deal with the novelties of the First World War, but in 1914 none had settled the outstanding issues: ammunition resupply, the use of heavy artillery, the concealment and protection of guns, the organisation of C2 at high levels and the need to improve communications. When war came, the resolution of these problems would tip the balance away from mobility to satisfy the imperative – firepower.

1914: THE SHOCK OF THE NEW

Four issues of concern to the close battle became apparent soon after the outbreak of war: the relative merits and performance of opposing equipment; the novel primacy of firepower over mobility; the need to fight at night; and the construction of obstacles. The British and French soon appreciated but could not match the power of the medium 5.9-inch howitzer used by the Germans as a field piece. In the case of the BEF, it outranged all but the 60-pounder, which, with a flat trajectory, had difficulty in hitting back.[7]

The value of the howitzer and the need to increase the calibre and range of field equipment was soon realised, but with different results among armies. In 1914, the British 18-pounder frequently held the line after its supported infantry had been overwhelmed; and the advancing phalanxes of German infantry offered ideal targets for shrapnel. It continued in successful service throughout the war. The relatively disappointing performance of their '77' encouraged the Germans to reinforce the success of their '5.9'. While the howitzer had many advantages, it was to prove less accurate than a gun when in barrage fire later in the war. Although the Germans stressed the need to keep close behind a barrage, their infantry were to find it harder to do so in practice than the British. The French '75' was outranged by heavier German guns and, contrary to French expectation, could not compensate for lack of range by mobility or high rate of fire. French medium and heavy artillery was generally at the rear of the column and unable to intervene, rather like Prussian guns in the 1860s. As a result, French infantry was often deprived of the support it might otherwise have had, even though trained to assault without artillery preparation if necessary.

The battles of 1914 demonstrated that mobility was a secondary consideration to firepower and its accomplishment through sound tactical C2. This was evident at the First Battle of Ypres, where the mobility of the German forces, making for the Channel ports, was nullified by combined artillery and infantry fire and their advance brought to a halt. Armies realised that artillery preparation had become a prerequisite for a successful assault.

At the same time, artillery in close support was revealed as more vulnerable than had been feared. The lessons of the Russo-Japanese war had to be learned at first hand before they would be taken seriously.[8] The need for artillery to deploy in depth was clear, but this made liaison between artillery and infantry even harder.[9] The RFA was compelled to revise its method of operation and issued large quantities of telephone line in an attempt to link the two.

New techniques were developed to quicken the response to infantry requests for fire, particularly at night. The British instituted the 'SOS' mission, which is today generally called Defensive Fire (DF), or Final Protective Fire (FPF).[10]

Trench warfare was the product in the first place of superior firepower over mobility, a phenomenon which ran counter to the doctrine of all sides before 1914. Infantry mobility was halted by the power of opposing infantry weapons, and neither side possessed the artillery firepower to silence the latter and restore mobility. The deadlock in the trenches in 1914 reflected the imbalance between infantry and artillery firepower that had existed for 50 years.

Obstacles, and wire in particular, ended the immediate possibility of strategic surprise by stabilising the battlefield. It was accepted that obstacles covered by fire should not be assaulted by infantry without first being cut by artillery. Liaison and joint planning thus became necessities, and artillery ceased to be merely an accessory on the battlefield. The novel demands made on artillery stimulated the generation of enormous resources and imaginative methods of applying them. The irony was that, in unleashing this unprecedented firepower, artillery might sometimes succeed in breaching an obstacle, yet it almost always created another in the form of a devastated terrain. Attempts to restore mobility often proved counter-productive as a result. It was not until late in 1917 that techniques for applying artillery firepower were sufficiently refined to help break the deadlock established in 1914 by its deficiency.

1915: FRESH RESOURCES AND NEW TECHNIQUES

Artillery could only deliver the required firepower by concentrating its slender resources on narrow fronts, expanding as industry delivered fresh equipment and ammunition. The limited battles of 1915 were experiments in the application of concentrated firepower and the lessons learned from them were to shape artillery tactics on all sides until the end of 1917.

The primary lessons were two-fold: artillery required unprecedented supplies of ammunition if it was to win the firefight; and the resulting firepower could best be exploited if it were part of a sound tactical plan under a more centralised command, provided that the gunners could overcome the technical problems of accurate delivery.

By the end of 1915, it had been determined that the committal of infantry to the attack without a certain number of rounds per metre of front would result in failure, and tactical appreciations became dependent on mathematical formulae. This lesson was learned bitterly during the year, and led to the conviction that there could never be enough artillery support. From this conviction stemmed the gigantic consumption of munitions in 1916 and 1917.

In 1914, the usual allocation of ammunition for a British offensive was up to 100 rpg. By 1915 it had trebled,[11] but this was small compared to that of subsequent years.[12] The British and, indeed, the French problem was not in deciding how many rounds to fire but how to find the rounds. Ammunition establishments were already inadequate in theory, and by 1 June 1915 there were often less than half of these available in practice.[13] Both Britain and France initiated major reorganisations of their munitions industries in order to meet the demand, but quality was often sacrificed to quantity. Hastily manufactured '75' ammunition proved defective. In the first nine months of war the French lost 1,440 pieces, often through accidents.[14] All tactical plans were dependent upon ammunition supplies. The British experience in the battles of 1915 shows how this realisation dawned and illustrates the new techniques of gunnery that emerged from it.

The British learned from French and German experience at, for example, Perthes and Soissons in January 1915, and Artois in May, that a preliminary bombardment was essential for an infantry assault. The first British attack of penetration was at Neuve Chapelle from 10–12 March 1915. The attack was by three brigades on a narrow sector with an army in reserve on a ten-mile front. There were 354 pieces deployed against 60 German on a sector of just 1,200 yards, a concentration not matched until 1917 on a much broader sector at Ypres; but at Neuve Chapelle British guns could fire only 200–400 rpg, a fraction of what became available two years later. The choice of a narrow sector was in part determined by the shortage of ammunition and indicated an appreciation of the need for concentrated firepower to break through obstacles.

Such an operation required a degree of joint planning not previously achieved. The plan of attack was secret. For the first time, detailed maps were specially produced from aerial photography. Unlike the French offensive earlier in the year, the preliminary bombardment lasted only 35 minutes, in order to reduce the time for the Germans to react, and registration was concealed over a period of three weeks. Field guns were brought up to cut the wire with direct fire, and howitzers engaged the trenches. The wire was cut successfully, but the howitzers firing off maps were wildly inaccurate and the trenches were barely damaged.

The preliminary bombardment paralysed the defence and initial objectives were secured, but the advance soon ground to a halt. The problem was that the planners had focused on obstacles as the key to successful defence, rather than on the fire from the trenches, which the obstacles enhanced. If enemy firepower had been tackled effectively, the obstacles would have been of less importance. Where success was achieved, it was through the 'neutralisation' of the defence with a short, intense bombardment, not through the 'destruction' of obstacles alone. By 1917 this was appreciated, and short 'hurricane' bombardments became the norm, but in 1915 the lesson was misread.

The failure of the attack was put down to obstacles remaining intact, rather than to the failure of howitzers to hit enemy infantry in their trenches. This experience led to a belief in the need for the total destruction of everything that stood in the path of attacking infantry, irrespective of damage to the terrain and loss of surprise. The only arm which could deliver this firepower was artillery, and its massive expansion continued until within a year it had assumed the dominant role on the battlefield.[15]

The British plan for the battle of Loos on 15 September 1915 was significantly different from that of Neuve Chapelle. The front was eight times longer, but with little increase in artillery. Consequently there was only one piece per 23 yards, or one-fifth of what there had been in March. To achieve what was judged to be adequate 'destruction' on a longer front with fewer weapons, it was necessary to reduce the density of fire but to fire over a longer period, sacrificing surprise. The four-day preliminary bombardment lost not just tactical but also strategic surprise. This failure was in part because of GHQ's estimate that the planned gas attack would double the effectiveness of the guns: an expectation that was badly disappointed when the wind failed to co-operate with the gas.

The co-ordination of artillery fire was of unprecedented complexity and led to novel arrangements for C2. The preliminary bombardment and initial phases of the assault came under centralised control, but this was decentralised for subsequent phases to accommodate the flow of battle. The British I and IV Corps each created artillery headquarters to co-ordinate divisional plans; but the heavy artillery still remained separate from the field branch, which caused difficulties when these weapons were used in close support.

The most significant development in tactics was the use of the 'lifting barrage'. Rather than fire advancing at arbitrary intervals – the 'straight barrage' – the 'lifting barrage' moved in parallel lines but from trench to trench, concentrating fire on the lines of greatest resistance. The idea was an improvement on previous practice, but although observers accompanied the infantry, the expertise to make best use of the barrage was lacking. With imperfect indirect fire techniques, map shooting was extremely inaccurate and difficult for infantry to follow.[16] By 1916 the 'piled-up barrage' had been developed, and later, as enemy positions became harder to locate, the 'creeping' or 'rolling barrage' was adopted (see Figures 2.1, 2.2 and 2.3).

The British reviewed their performance for the year and blamed their disappointment on a failure to win the firefight before committing the infantry to the assault. Artillery was directed to produce larger and heavier 'destructive' bombardments, and a better barrage to shield the infantry. Attempts to improve the barrage had foundered on technical inadequacy.

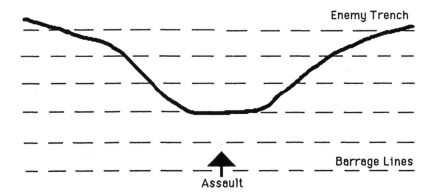

FIGURE 2.1: THE STRAIGHT BARRAGE, 1915

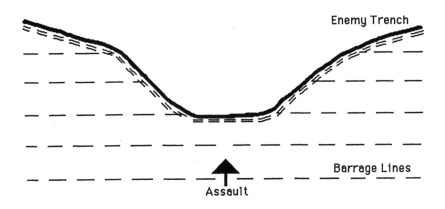

FIGURE 2.2: THE PILED-UP BARRAGE, 1916

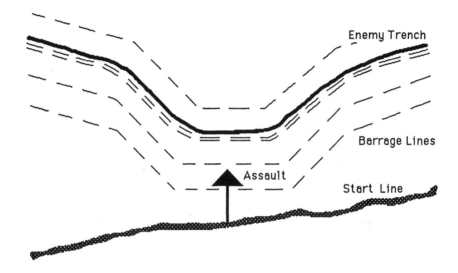

FIGURE 2.3: THE CREEPING BARRAGE, 1917

Communications to control fire were rudimentary, but experiments were being conducted by observers in aircraft and balloons using a clock code for ranging.[17] Maps made from air photographs suffered from the inaccuracies of camera distortion. As a result, artillery still insisted on registration, with a consequent loss of surprise. Although cartography soon improved, an understanding of the need for deception did not. Surprise, traditionally achieved through infantry mobility, might have been won by the fire mobility which was replacing it. Instead, this was used merely to concentrate fire for mass destruction and surprise was abandoned. To create greater destruction, heavier weapons were introduced, in particular 6 inch and 9.2 inch howitzers, and naval guns on railway mountings. While medium and heavy guns were used for close support, they were also required for CB fire, which had become recognised as a separate but interdependent part of combined operations. By 1918 that deep battle had surpassed close support as artillery's prime activity.

1916: 'DESTRUCTION'

By 1916, British leaders were inclined to think that the effect of a massive bombardment would be to 'crush all resistance, and that it would be necessary for the infantry only to march forward and take possession'.[18] Artillery was tasked to restore infantry mobility by winning the firefight at the cost of surprise. The quantity of artillery available determined the scope of operations, and all-arms planning was based on the tasking of artillery. Those tasks were to be conducted methodically on an unprecedented scale, and were best illustrated by the preparation for, and initial experience of, the battle of the Somme in the summer of 1916.

That battle typified the tactics of mass 'destruction' which required the adoption of novel gunnery techniques and tactics as well as a keener appreciation of logistic problems. The scale of artillery planning and the danger of excessive complexity made simplicity essential. This ruled out the use of mass enfilade fire, and encouraged gunners to develop techniques to improve the firepower of whatever pieces were allotted to a particular sector. Aircraft were increasingly used to inspect the effects of artillery fire; but in 1916 observers were still relatively inexperienced.[19] When intelligence was produced by aerial observation, artillery needed to react quickly and new, faster and more accurate methods of calculation were devised.

C2 became more centralised in an attempt to make best use of resources.[20] The creation of an artillery commander at corps ensured that improved all-arms liaison would be matched by improvements in co-ordination of the close and deep battles, which had been weak in 1915. Although greater attention was paid to C2 for operations in 1916, it was recognised that it was not possible to guarantee the destruction of all or even most enemy guns, and so the close battle retained prominence. This was divided into three phases: the preliminary bombardment, the barrage, and the exploitation and consolidation phase.

The preliminary bombardment on the Somme lasted for seven days. Its primary aim was the destruction of machine guns, which were the main source of infantry firepower, the obstacles which they covered, and the communications that were needed to control the battle and summon artillery fire. In addition, new varieties of barrage were tested, concealed in the bombardment, and at the same time a number of feints were made in the hope that tactical deception might compensate for the loss of strategic surprise.

High explosive shells still had no effective fuse for cutting wire, a task consequently given to trench mortars and 18-pounders firing shrapnel.[21] Batteries were allotted sectors of territory and times at which to fire at the wire. The task of destroying trenches and machine guns was given to the heavy artillery under corps command. Infantry units were asked to state the degree of destruction they desired on their objective. This care for good liaison was admirable, but such decentralisation incurred penalties. Leading infantry units usually requested as much destruction as possible – which was understandable, given their limited objectives; but the devastation to terrain militated against the success of subsequent waves of units whose opinions had not been sought. The supported arm did not always know what was best for it.

The week of preliminary bombardment ended with 30 minutes of intense fire, which in effect signalled the start of the assault, and sacrificed the tactical surprise that some had still hoped to preserve.[22]

The idea of assaulting with small groups of infantry, rather than in waves, was discussed by army commanders at a conference on 15 June 1916. All three commanders opposed the idea. They were advocates of the linear artillery barrage and reluctant to adopt a plan that would require local concentrations of artillery support which might miss pockets of resistance. They wanted guaranteed and uniform destruction.[23] The barrage of 1 July was relatively simple, but its weakness was lack of speed, which could not be modified as the battle demanded.[24] The barrage was not uniform. Different formations used a variety of shapes, often with very different results.[25] There were different views on how close infantry should keep to a barrage,[26] but bitter experience soon taught that troops should keep as close to the barrage as possible. When it became clear that the preliminary bombardment had been insufficiently 'destructive' and that surprise had been lost, GHQ urged the infantry to stay close to the barrage, even at the risk of taking casualties from it.[27]

Fresh issues arose as the battle of the Somme developed. The British were committed to a battle of attrition in a series of offensives with limited objectives – the product of Anglo-French experience in 1915. The Germans countered by deploying in greater depth. On 12 October, machine guns were reported to be firing from beyond the limit of the barrage,[28] setting a trend which caused Lord Cavan (commanding XIV Corps) to advocate a deeper barrage and a smoke-screen. It also became standard practice to 'superimpose' some guns on a fire-plan for use against contingency targets, a measure still practised today. The area of immediate importance to the supported arm had stretched further away from the front line, and it became clearer to the infantry that artillery operations in greater depth were not a separate matter but of direct benefit, through their suppression of weapons in deep defence and the breaking up of German counter-attacks.

The 'protective barrage' designed to prevent counter-attacks in the summer of 1916 was far from ideal. It usually consisted of a wall of fire around the objective, but lacked the flexibility to accommodate changes in timing and objective.[29] By the autumn, British bombardments were being fired deep into German defences. This required yet more heavy artillery, which by the battle of Beaumont Hamel was often being operated as if it were part of the field branch. The guns of a division could cover only 1,200 yards, less than a normal divisional front. It was hoped that the tank, which was still undergoing assessment, might eventually make up for this deficiency in firepower, not so much through its own firepower as by its

armoured mobility, making artillery firepower less important. In the meantime, more and heavier guns were required, and to fire at a higher rate. It was
also generally accepted that the artillery must not only lead the infantry on to
its objective, but also provide fire at least 2,000 yards beyond them in order
to deal with the machine guns in depth. It was also necessary for artillery to
move forward to provide support for subsequent, and perhaps unplanned,
operations. There was no longer any question of infantry trying to exploit
beyond the range of friendly guns.

The tactics of 'destruction' called for vast logistic support, particularly in
the supply of artillery ammunition. The enormous weights required and the
conditions under which ammunition travelled were largely responsible for
the cumbersome character of operations. No attack could be planned until a
commander was confident that he had sufficient ammunition, and this often
determined the scale of an operation. When planning an attack, Foch was
more interested in the number of guns than in the number of divisions available. It was useless to have more guns or order a higher rate of fire if ammunition was not available. If supplies were limited, it was sometimes
necessary to narrow the sector of attack to generate the required density of
fire.[30]

Balck had observed before the war that 'The line on which artillery is to
fight the decisive action forms the framework of every defensive position'.[31]
It was a characteristic of German planning that a defensive line should
optimise the value of artillery support by providing observation, good fields
of fire and communications. This was evident from the first year of the war at
Ypres, and in its most dramatic form in the construction of the Hindenburg
Line in 1917, which was sited with artillery requirements as the foremost consideration. The deliberate siting of defensive lines, often on fresh undamaged
terrain, also gave the defender logistic advantages because roads and railways
were relatively unscathed. The existence and positioning of field workshops
also became tactical matters for consideration in a commander's plan. The
number of serviceable guns and the rate at which battle 'casualties' could be
repaired were important elements in its formulation.

In 1914, infantry had determined the face of battle. By 1916 only the
logistician carried more influence than the gunner; and the infantryman was
reduced to carrying out such operations as these two deemed feasible. The
war became what the Germans called a *Materialschlacht*, in which, by fighting on two fronts, they were at a severe disadvantage. They, above all,
had an interest in developing more effective tactics to minimise this disadvantage. They had been encouraged by the effectiveness of their machine
guns against infantry, but their artillery could not match the support given to
British infantry. They therefore sought to nullify the effect of that support by
luring British infantry into areas where German infantry could fight on equal
terms, or into attacks on elaborately prepared defences.

The British and French, for their part, believed that in their tactics of 'destruction', admittedly expensive, they had established a formula for success. They were confident that with sufficient artillery they could take any limited objective. Greater success by penetration would depend upon extending the range of artillery, and upon improving CB fire. Without the latter, an infantry attack could be halted in its tracks by forewarned enemy guns.

1917: DESTRUCTION REACHES ITS ZENITH

The tactics of destruction reached their climax in 1917, which was also a year of change. The German Army withdrew to the Hindenburg Line, and the British Army advanced across devastated terrain in preparation for an assault. The offensives which accompanied the German withdrawal illustrated the refinement that had taken place in 'destructive' planning.

The Canadian assault at Vimy Ridge in April 1917 was a success and its limited objectives were achieved;[32] but the consequences of 'destruction' were a devastated terrain and a wrecked road system which hampered exploitation. The destruction of tactical obstacles had created administrative ones and, in the process, had alerted enemy reserves, which moved to block penetration. It was suggested by officers of Third Army that this form of attack be replaced by a shorter 'hurricane' bombardment of greater intensity, but the idea was rejected. 'Destructive' firepower had become like an addictive drug. Armies preferred the near certainty of limited, if costly, success to the political and military risks of operations which reduced 'destruction', even though their might have achieved greater penetration and mobility.[33]

Despite flaws in its application, the strength of Allied artillery ensured that, in a duel, it would defeat German artillery.[34] British tactics seemed to offer sufficient return for their high cost, and were consequently repeated at Third Ypres, but geography multiplied that cost. British positions suffered the inherent logistic and tactical disadvantages of a salient. In addition, the terrain was dependent on a fragile drainage system to remove surface water. There could have been few less promising choices for an offensive marking the zenith of the tactics of 'destruction'. It soon became apparent that conditions for an offensive were thoroughly unfavourable; but the British persisted with an attack which could have been switched to another area by moving medium and heavy artillery, as in operations earlier that year; and the opportunities for movement were not exploited.

However given that an attack was to be made at Ypres, 'destruction' was probably the best option. German positions were protected by such heavy wire that a short preliminary bombardment would have been inadequate, and breaching the wire was still a prerequisite for a successful infantry attack.

The effect of the bombardment was so severe that in the last week of July, German troops withdrew from a large area, opposite XIV British Corps, without orders.[35] Artillery fire swept the whole sector of operations, while aircraft sought out dead ground. But a major advance was not achieved, largely because of effective German counter-attacks on 31 July and 15 August.[36]

The 'clockwork' German counter-attack could be anticipated, and elaborate precautions were taken by artillery to protect British infantry once they had reached their objectives, so long as these were little more than 1,000 yards from the start lines. Another two or three equally limited successive phases were planned once artillery had moved forward. These tactics were tested on 20 and 26 September with great success, but by 2 October the Germans had again developed counter-measures. Reserves for the counter-attack were moved even further back, and, with less fire falling on their forward positions, held these in strength supported by massed machine gun fire from the rear. The British responded by reverting to the tactics of the Somme in 1916, with massive bombardments causing the Germans to change once more to an even stronger chequerboard of concrete strong points.

By 17 October, the Germans had taken drastic but effective measures to avoid British artillery fire. They withdrew from their forward line shortly before the anticipated British zero hour, and 15 minutes after that brought down a heavy bombardment on British forward positions, through which attacking waves would have to pass. German troops retired by another bound and brought down another defensive bombardment close in front of their own positions by light signal.[37]

The last months of 1917 marked the end of the tactics of 'destruction'. By then it was possible, using a mathematical formula of guns and ammunition set against length of front and infantry bayonets, to guarantee a local success of 2–3,000 yards in depth but at the expense of surprise. This enabled an enemy to prepare his defences and to minimise his casualties without fear of strategic defeat. The demands of 'destructive' firepower had created a vast munitions industry whose products it consumed voraciously.[38] Even if the tactics of applying fire were soon to change, the demand for shells continued to rise until the Armistice.

In 1916, the tactics of 'destruction' had been met by deepening lines of defence, the deep deployment of reserves for the counter-attack, and the deeper siting of artillery. Throughout 1917 offensive tactics were modified to tackle this deeper dimension to the battlefield, and the process of tactical action and reaction continued without breaking the strategic stalemate.

1917–18: NEUTRALISATION – NEW IDEAS
FOR THE OFFENCE

By the winter of 1917, circumstances were ripe for a major change in artillery and all-arms tactics. The nature of these changes was determined by the tactical experience gained earlier in the year, advances in technology and the realisation that strategic success could not be achieved without them. Both sides adopted new but different approaches in the hope of achieving the same end.

The British learned during their advance to the Hindenburg Line that medium and heavy artillery could be almost as mobile as field artillery, given the opportunity. But years of static warfare had discouraged belief in mobility.[39] The advent of tanks revolutionised artillery close support. They had been used in experimental attacks where artillery firepower was lacking, had met with initial success, but had then been stopped by artillery. The idea that the firepower of a tank could equal that of artillery was a mistake – one that has frequently been repeated since.

The battle of Cambrai, which opened on 20 November 1917, tested the new ideas and equipment in a full-scale operation, intended to gain both strategic and tactical surprise. The fire plan was in its way as remarkable as the employment of tanks, featuring for the first time massive and accurate predicted fire to neutralise the enemy. This allowed for a shorter overall plan. It was significant that tanks were used to break through the obstacle belt, dispensing with a preliminary bombardment by artillery. Despite its limited firepower, the 'shock' of their armoured mobility was judged sufficient to overcome the infantry in their path, who in the event proved little threat to the tank, which could be stopped only by direct artillery fire or mechanical failure.

The relationship of artillery to other arms was thus redefined. Artillery was not required to aid mobility for the infantry by destroying obstacles and machine guns. Instead, it aided mobility by destroying or 'neutralising' enemy artillery and whatever infantry firepower might escape the tank. Surprise could not be achieved without forbidding registration. In earlier battles the techniques of predicted fire were too crude to guarantee accuracy, but by November 1917 major progress had been made. Target location for CB fire, which did not exist in 1914, had been transformed from an art into a science. Indirect fire, which had proved dangerously inaccurate in 1915, was a routine and reliable method and gas and smoke shells had become available in quantities that made 'neutralisation' with these munitions a feasible alternative to 'destruction' with HE. Accurate maps were available and compensation was routinely made for meteorological conditions, variations in ammunition and the muzzle velocities of individual guns.

Artillery's efforts were not reduced but redirected. The same mass of guns and equipment was still required, and, as observation by the enemy might have compromised operations, all unit moves were made in darkness and at the last possible moment, with great attention paid on arrival to camouflage. Artillery was unlikely to neutralise all opposing pieces with HE, so extensive use was made of gas and smoke.[40]

The Battle of Cambrai showed how the strategic stalemate might be broken if a variety of innovations were developed further. Infantry was no longer dependent solely on the artillery, but looked to the tank for support as well. Yet the role of artillery in the design for battle was undiminished, since the tank needed artillery support as much as the infantry, and the possibility of a decisive breakthrough was opened up by the decision to allow artillery to turn its attention to the deeper battle.

In 1917, the German Army in the west was still on the defensive, but experiments had been made on the Eastern Front which were to form the basis for future offensives in the west. Their aim was to break the strategic stalemate, but without the help of the tank.[41]

By the end of 1917, the Germans had moved away from the thinking of *Materialschlacht*, of limited gain through attrition, to a more flexible concept: 'To fire merely in reply or reprisal while the enemy is firing is misconceived. Surprise, co-ordination of fire according to space and time, and regulation of fire according to the right moment are often decisive for effectiveness.'[42] The pioneer of the new thinking was Colonel Georg Bruchmüller. He did not advocate the complete destruction of enemy trenches and obstacles, rather the shattering of the morale of their defenders and their defeat by unexpected assault – in other words, 'neutralisation'. The weight of a bombardment was not enough; it was necessary to apply it in a manner that would demoralise an enemy.

By March 1918, the Germans had begun trying to devise new ways of controlling barrages from the front line, although the British experience was that this was not possible in a large centralised plan, since information rapidly became out of date.[43] Great attention was paid to co-ordinating the close and deep battles. The neutralisation of enemy forward positions would have offered little advantage had enemy guns been left intact and its C2 system unparalysed.

German tactics evolved quickly in 1917, in imaginative ways requiring great skill. Ironically they failed, not because they were unsound, but because Germany had already lost the *Materialschlacht* in 1916 and 1917. This became clear only in 1918, after both sides had abandoned the tactics of attrition which had proved decisive in the long term. The new tactics of neutralisation were in part an expedient to derive greater tactical efficiency from expensive (and, in Germany's case, dwindling) logistic resources. The significance of the new thinking of 1917–18 lay not so much in how it determined the outcome of the First World War, but in how it formed the

seed-bed for the new techniques of fire and manoeuvre developed in the
1920s and 1930s and practised in the Second World War.

1917–18: NEUTRALISATION – NEW IDEAS
FOR THE DEFENCE

In 1917, both sides had studied new offensive techniques. However, in the
winter of 1917–18, it became clear to the British that their defences would
soon be put to the test by the switching of German strategic efforts to the
west. British defences had remained virtually untested for three years, having
dealt only with small raids and with warding off counter-attacks. The army
had grown used to feeding on vast quantities of ammunition provided by an
elaborate logistic machine; and the concentrations of guns at vital sectors
assured mutual support. The standard defensive tactic was to bring down
heavy fire at a density of one field gun per 20 metres. Nevertheless on many
quiet sectors of the front the British had just one field gun per 300 yards and
could not achieve adequate defensive densities if the Germans should mount
a surprise major offensive.

To ease this problem, artillery was reorganised to concentrate on vital
areas, leaving the intervals to be covered by the machine guns and mortars of
the infantry. The power of concentrated artillery in the offence had raised the
stakes in the firefight to a level where artillery in defence could not provide
a comprehensive response. It had to be supplemented by infantry firepower,
which itself had first provoked the growth of artillery offensive power.

Defensive fire was most effective when used against troops preparing for
attack, and was termed 'counter-preparation' fire. It was extremely difficult
to time such fire correctly, especially if the enemy were taking precautions to
disguise the end of their preliminary bombardment. It was also hard to judge
when to switch fire away from counter-preparation, to the defensive barrage,
brought down close to defending positions at the decisive moment. By 1917,
SOS fire, which had been practised since 1915, was seen to be a handicap.
The right to call for SOS fire had been devolved to units in the front
line who, understandably, often called for it at the slightest indication of
increased enemy activity, even if that merely turned out to be reconnaissance. Numerous false alarms drew artillery assets away from counter-
preparation fire, and consumed large quantities of ammunition at the expense
of the main defensive barrage when it was required. Given the power of
infantry weapons in defence, it is arguable that British artillery should have
left the leading assault waves to be dealt with by the infantry, and put its
main weight into attacking the succeeding echelons, which constituted the
greater threat.

In earlier British offensives, the depth of attack had been limited by the need to remain within range of the protecting artillery, whose targets could be predicted readily, given foreknowledge of the objective.[44] In the defence of linear positions, however, where the attacker held the initiative, it was harder to predict suitable deep targets, since intelligence and techniques of target acquisition were inadequate.[45] From 1917, the Germans practised a more open form of warfare in defence as well as offence. The vulnerability of shallow linear defence using deep dug-outs and the terrible effects of 'destructive' bombardments had caused them to reduce the manning of forward areas and to increase the strength of concealed infantry and artillery reserves for the counter-attack.[46]

1918: NEUTRALISATION – THE FRUITION OF NEW IDEAS

The new ideas tested in 1917 came to fruition in the great German offensive in the spring of 1918 and the later Allied sweep to victory which followed the Second Battle of Amiens in August. Despite an awareness of the force massing against them, and fresh thinking on how to meet it, the British were ill-prepared when Ludendorff's massive onslaught was launched on 21 March and were surprised by the offensive tactics used. Artillery densities were generally low in the sectors attacked, and such obstacles as existed were insufficient to stop infantry attacking after a hurricane bombardment. British defences were not sufficiently strong to force the Germans to neutralise them with a lengthy bombardment – a measure that would have sacrificed surprise. The depth and size of British reserves eventually halted the offensive, but not until spectacular German successes had vindicated their offensive tactics.

The lessons of spring 1918 were that artillery in defence must produce sudden and annihilating concentrations of fire on demand; that it must be sited in depth; and that artillery commanders should use their initiative to influence the close battle. To do this, they needed good observation and communications. Their primary task was to delay attacking infantry and put it out of synchrony with its supporting barrage, thus making it vulnerable to infantry firepower. It was also appreciated that as offensive mobility returned to the battlefield, artillery in defence would have to respond with greater flexibility and a capacity to react to the unforeseen.

The return of mobility through German shock tactics brought fresh perils for artillery. British pieces had to be positioned within 2,000 yards of their infantry if they were to engage enemy infantry assembling to attack, yet this proximity made them vulnerable to enemy trench mortars and to capture. How to balance the deployment of field artillery became a fine decision.

There were several ways of employing close support artillery under these circumstances. It could withdraw, or, like the Germans in 1917, remain in position as the backbone of defence after most friendly infantry had withdrawn to the reserve. The British favoured holding forward, it being considered bad for morale to see some troops withdrawing. The best method was judged to be the creation of strong points with heavy artillery support. Unfortunately, in March 1918 the Germans infiltrated these positions and large numbers of encircled troops were captured. Nevertheless, artillery played a key role in the defence in many places.[47]

The experiences of spring 1918 brought about the final demise of SOS fire. By the summer of that year, calls for SOS fire by the infantry were for artillery information only, not executive orders to fire.[48] For the first time the infantry could not count on dedicated close artillery support. Based on higher intelligence, artillery fire was directed instead at targets of a higher priority, albeit in the best interests of the infantry and artillery commanders played a more decisive tactical role in the close battle,[49] where artillery was asserting itself as an autonomous arm.[50] By the end of the war, however, British defensive tactics placed greater emphasis on the artillery's deep battle than on the close battle. Fire was concentrated on 'counter-preparation', which continued deep into enemy lines, striking succeeding echelons with intense bursts, instead of merely shifting a defensive barrage. Artillery fire was no longer so important on targets which the infantry could handle; instead it found targets which the infantry was unable to engage.

The British advances of the summer of 1918 displayed an awareness of lessons learned by artillery of all sides. There were initially no preliminary bombardments, so as to preserve strategic surprise. Batteries deployed at night, ammunition dumps were concealed, comprehensive and accurate survey was completed to ensure the accuracy of predicted fire, and infantry start lines were designed to fit in with convenient artillery barrage lines.[51]

Once strategic surprise had been lost, artillery bombardment returned to a normal pattern, but not to cutting wire. This task was carried out by tanks which also destroyed the machine guns covering it. Artillery's main task was to support this armoured mobility against the threat of enemy artillery.[52] The role of artillery might have changed, but not its importance. The speed of the advance was still governed by artillery and the ability of the logistic organisation to sustain it.

The new role of artillery was seen in its deployment for the battle of Amiens, which opened on 8 August 1918. Despite the large force of tanks, artillery density was only slightly less than it had been in 1917, and because there was no preliminary bombardment the number of guns and the weight of fire generated during the assault was far greater.[53]

In the battles that followed, the infantry sometimes resented the apparent loss of heavy pieces in close support. They failed to appreciate the importance of the deep battle, which occupied the majority of artillery assets – even though deep operations played a direct and important part in the close battle by reducing casualties from enemy artillery.[54]

Preparations for the attack were carried out at army level, but corps controlled the deployment of its own artillery. Once the assault had begun, C2 was decentralised to divisions and the two artillery brigades which supported each of them. Poor communications made it impossible for advancing troops to modify the close support fire plan on demand, and consequently one of the two divisional artillery brigades advanced with the assault, one and a half hours after zero hour, to permit closer all-arms liaison. Artillery was once again faced with the problem of how to keep up in a mobile battle, a problem it had not faced for over three years. By September 1918, gun sections were being deployed with the infantry but suffered heavy casualties without adequate protection. The need for mobility and protection was identified, but this problem was not to be addressed successfully for many years.

After the early success in August 1918, artillery staff turned their attention to deeper targets for subsequent phases, in particular the Hindenburg Line, which was assaulted on 26 September. By that stage, strategic surprise had become unimportant and there was every advantage in reverting to a massive 'destructive' bombardment. This lasted for 56 hours and was fired by over 1,000 guns on a 21,000-yard front, concentrating on lanes through the defence and on demoralising the enemy as much as possible. This allowed the Staffordshire infantry of 46th Division to make famous progress at zero hour early on 29 September, and cross the St Quentin canal in fine style.

By November massive destructive artillery fire was seen as a means of reducing unnecessary infantry casualties, and artillery densities relative to infantry numbers reached their highest levels. For example, at Valenciennes on 1 November 1918, 1,500 men of the Canadian Corps were supported by one gun to every six men on a front of just 2,500 yards. Artillery not only reduced infantry casualties, but also made up for infantry losses which might otherwise have slowed the offensive.

Clausewitz asked, 'How much artillery can one have without inconvenience? An excess of artillery is bound to cause operations to partake more and more of a defensive and passive character. A shortage of artillery will on the contrary enable us to let the offensive, mobility and manoeuvring predominate.' [55] The experience of artillery in the First World War challenged this assertion. The need for more guns, shells and logistic support became the dominant theme in military planning. Vast resources and the evolution of accurate predicted fire enabled artillery to concentrate fire as in Napoleonic times – but now through fire mobility, not just the massing of equipment.

New tactics were required to make best use of the firepower thus harnessed. At first these were characterised by the 'destruction' of everything in the path of advancing infantry. Realisation that 'destructive' tactics carried severe penalties led to the adoption of 'neutralisation' in its place. The use of short but heavy bombardments restored the element of surprise and the possibility of achieving deeper penetrations. These tactics generated a greater awareness of the need for depth in attack and defence. As a result, fewer resources were devoted to the close battle, and, eventually, the greater part to the deep battle, allowing artillery to achieve an importance as an offensive arm not seen for 100 years.

NOTES

1. Colonel Commandant L.C.L. Oldfield, 'Artillery and the Lessons we have Learnt with regard to it in the Late War', *RUSI Journal*, Vol. LXVII, No. 468 (Nov. 1922), pp.579–99.
2. Colonel R. M. St G. Kirke, 'Some Aspects of Artillery Development during the First World War on the Western Front', *Royal Artillery Journal* (hereafter *RAJ*), Vol. CI, No. 2 (Sept. 1974), pp.130–40.
3. Lieutenant-Colonel A. F. Brooke, 'The Evolution of Artillery in the Great War: Part 1', *RAJ*, Vol. LI, No. 5 (1924), pp.250–67. Alan Brooke (later to become a Field Marshal and chairman of the British Chiefs of Staff in the Second World War) was a pioneer of artillery tactics at corps and divisional levels in the Great War.
4. Oldfield (1922), op. cit.
5. Lieutenant-Colonel A. F. Brooke, 'The Evolution of Artillery in the Great War: Part II', *RAJ* Vol. LI, No. 6 (Jan. 1925), pp. 359–72.
6. 'Field Artillery Training: 1914', quoted in Brooke (1924), op. cit., p.266.
7. The Germans frequently managed to position observers on high ground and the British were forced to conceal their guns, where possible on reverse slopes, which were less suitable for their flat trajectories. A British pamphlet of 30 October 1914 emphasised the need to occupy reverse slopes in view of the superior range and firepower of the 5.9-inch howitzers which opposed them: quoted in Lieutenant-Colonel C.N.F. Broad, 'The Development of Artillery Tactics 1914–1918', *RAJ*, Vol. XLIX, No. 2 (May 1922), p.67. Thus at Ypres, Messines, Aubers Ridge and in many subsequent battles the Germans won observation over British guns, while their own remained covered from view.
8. At Le Cateau, British artillery of 5th Division deployed in the open within 500 metres of supported infantry and was swept away. If artillery fell back, crests often prevented it from supporting the infantry. To remain forward may have been good for infantry morale, but at a severe price in artillery casualties. The vulnerability of guns deploying in forward areas was demonstrated at Bertrix in August 1914. German guns suffered as they engaged French infantry at 50–1,200 yards and French guns at 400 metres. Lieutenant-Colonel A. H. Burne, 'The French Guns at Bertrix 1914', *RAJ*, Vol. LXIII, No. 3 (Oct. 1936), pp. 345–60.
9. There were many examples of the confusion common to all wars: at Bezu on 9 September 1914 a British battery fired on the Lincolnshire Regiment in error, Brigadier J. E. Edmonds, *Official History* (hereafter) *OH) 1914*, Vol. I (London: Macmillan, 1922), p. 290; and on 10 September an attack on German positions near Priez by battalions of the Sussex and Northamptonshire Regiments was actually forced to fall back under friendly fire, ibid., p.309. At the Aisne, the artillery of II and III Corps was unable to give proper support to its infantry, which was deployed across the river to the north, because of poor communications between observers and guns.
10. Artillery was laid on fixed lines and opened fire automatically if rifle fire was heard to the front. This was expensive in ammunition, but became an important element in defensive plans. SOS fire became increasingly sophisticated, but by 1917 had been largely discredited; nevertheless, in 1914 it helped to break the mould of traditional gunnery practice.
11. Broad (1922), op.cit., p.70.
12. The French were already firing considerably more. In their offensive in Champagne and Artois, starting on 25 September 1915, 1,100 field guns fired 850 rpg. By 1918, the Germans were producing 11 million shells per month. In July and August 1916, they fired 14 million shells, equal to three times the ammunition reserves of 1914. Jurg Meister,

'Arms Production in time of War – Some Sobering Thoughts', *Armada International*, Vol. 9, No. 3 (May 1985), p.2.

13. In the worst case, the British 6-inch howitzer with an establishment of 495 rpg had only 73 rpg: Lieutenant-Colonel A. F. Brooke, 'The Evolution of Artillery in the Great War: Part 5', *RAJ*, Vol. LIII, No. 1 (April 1926), p.87. The French responded to the ammunition crisis in early 1915 by re-equipping 100 batteries with the obsolete *90 de Bange*, which had large reserves of ammunition. This helped to compensate for the inadequacy of French industry which was producing only 3–14 rpg per day. The British had similar problems and rationed artillery to 5–10 rpg per day.

14. In one morning, ten out of 12 guns in a *Groupe* burst, a consequence of the pre-war mis-calculation of ammunition expenditure rates. For a description of accidents in the Second World War, the Korean War, and the Vietnam War see Brigadier C. D. Y. Ostrom, 'Leaders, Lanyards and Losses', *Field Artillery Journal*, Vol. 54, No. 2 (March–April 1986), pp.35–7.

15. The first application of the new tactics of 'destruction' by the British was seen at Festubert in May 1915, when the preliminary bombardment lasted for 48 hours, compared to the 35 minutes of Neuve Chapelle. Despite the cutting of heavy wire obstacles with slow observed fire, the attack was a failure, at a cost of 24,000 casualties. Artillery was held substantially to blame for failing to inflict sufficient 'destruction', although with hindsight it is apparent that better results might have been achieved by an intense, short bombardment and an element of surprise.

   Even though the infantry made three successful assaults at Givenchy in June 1915, they were expelled each time from their objectives. This was blamed on artillery's failure to give support on those objectives, and led to the development of SOS fire as a means of crushing counter-attacks. But the practice of SOS fire became so common that large quantities of ammunition were wasted on unwarranted false alarms, and attention was diverted from more important tasks. This problem of defence was not considered fully, the emphasis being on the offence as the British and French planned their operations for the autumn of 1915.

16. The French also employed the 'lifting barrage' when they attacked in Champagne and Artois ten days later; but their three-day preliminary bombardment had also cost them surprise. The warning gave German reserves time, and hence the mobility, to achieve con-centration to meet the attack in depth. It failed, despite the expenditure of over one million rounds of '75' ammunition. In January 1916, the French Army published fresh instructions for the conduct of artillery in the close battle. These required that combined offensives should take the form of successive attacks, each of limited depth and within range of friendly artillery support. Objectives were to include German artillery positions, which were recognised as the backbone of the defence. This was hard to achieve, as German guns outranged those of the French and were often positioned in depth. It was hoped to penetrate defences by mounting a series of such attacks in rapid succession, maintaining the momentum otherwise lost against a forewarned enemy. A prerequisite for this was that artillery should accompany the infantry advance and have sufficient ammunition to produce concentrated fire. Close liaison with the infantry was also important, and so special liaison detachments and joint command posts were established.

17. Kirke (1974), op.cit., p.135.

18. *OH 1914* (1922), op.cit., p.34.

19. Broad (1922), op.cit., p.72.

20. The artillery adviser at corps headquarters became the commander of all the divisional artillery in that corps. In 1915, after the battle of Loos, all heavy artillery in the divisions had been placed under army command. These pieces were now put under the command of corps and only the 'super-heavies' remained under army. This reflected the need for heavier artillery at corps level to assist in close support, but at the same time the corps artillery commander took command of the deep battle, causing some resentment at divisional level where it was seen that the heavy artillery, now relied on for close support, was being directed at more distant targets.

   Centralised command improved security and efficiency. Corps set the timings for the close support programme and divisions were tasked to carry them out. Corps even allocated Forward Observation Officers (FOOs) to the batteries in the divisions. It was the corps that issued co-ordinating maps and issued a plan based on divisional requirements, including the desired infantry plan, speed and objectives. There were still conflicts between neighbouring divisions on inter-corps boundaries, but these were later overcome by the issue of comprehensive barrage maps from army headquarters. While artillery might be the dominant arm, it still tried to provide a service, and from this stemmed genuine combined-arms planning. The development of C2 is described in Annex C to General Sir Martin Farndale's *History of the Royal Regiment of Artillery: Western Front 1914–1918* (London: RA Institution, 1986).

21. For a description of wire-cutting techniques in the First World War, see Brigadier R. J. Lewendon, 'The Cutting of Barbed Wire Entanglements by Artillery Fire in World War I', *RAJ*, Vol. CXII, No. 2 (Sept. 1985), pp.115–17.

22. On 14 July 1916, the artillery-commanders of 3rd and 9th Divisions protested that this had merely warned the enemy to put down a protective barrage. On 1 July, for instance, 2nd Battalion The West Yorkshire Regiment lost 250 men to enemy artillery before the assault in which they were to lose only 179 men to machine guns: *OH 1916*, Vol. 2, p.79. This lesson was learned and when 3rd and 9th Divisions next attacked, the preliminary bombardment was reduced to just five minutes. As a result, much of the enemy return fire fell behind the attacking troops, a tactic equally successful at Thiepval on 26 September.

The Germans had used a ten-hour bombardment at Verdun in 1916, but it proved too long to 'neutralise' the French defence, which recovered from the initial shock, yet too short to achieve the level of 'destruction' required for immediate success. In subsequent German attacks, the bombardment was denser and shortened still further.

23. A few well-placed machine guns could have held up the offensive on 1 July 1916, and to be sure of hitting every enemy weapon it was calculated that one 18-pounder shell would have to fall in every 25 metres of trench, in each successive line of trenches. Accordingly, one 18-pounder was allotted to every 25 metres and one 'heavy' or howitzer to every 60 metres. The barrage moved at prearranged times from trench to trench in an attempt to keep the enemy from manning his weapons before the attackers could bring their own small arms to bear. At times the lifts were so short, relative to the zone of the pieces, that the whole ground was swept and a 'creeping barrage' created. The development of the barrage in 1916 is described in Captain W. R. Young, 'The Barrage Comes Back', *RAJ*, Vol. LXX, No. 2 (April 1943), pp.117–23.

24. Many heavily protected German machine guns survived the preliminary bombardment and held up or stopped advancing infantry; but the barrage continued to advance. The further it went, the more enemy were able to emerge from cover, and the more exposed the attackers became. Because of this problem, the speed of the barrage, which had been 100 yards in three minutes on 1 July, was reduced to 100 yards in five minutes by the end of August. In contrast, there were problems if the barrage advanced too slowly, for this consumed larger quantities of ammunition, replacement of which could delay subsequent phases of battle, perhaps causing a fatal loss of momentum.

25. The 7th, 18th and 34th Divisions used 'creeping barrages', but the 34th had less success than the other two. The 30th and 36th Divisions used 'lifting barrages', but only the 36th made a deep penetration. In 21st Division, 64th Brigade used a successful 'creeping barrage' that swept the entire ground, whereas the 50th Brigade of the same Division used lifts of 500 and 250 metres and was repulsed with heavy loss.

By August 1916, it had become a standard German practice to position machine guns in shell-holes in No Man's Land and between trench lines, making it necessary to clear the whole area in the path of an attack. The 18-pounders, firing at Rate Four, had insufficient range to knock out weapons sited in depth, and 4.5-inch howitzers were brought forward to deal with them.

The infantry wanted a barrage to take the shape of the trench line it was attacking, and so hit the whole length simultaneously to avoid being taken by enfilade fire. But most trench lines were of irregular shape and to deal with this the gunners developed the 'Piled-Up Barrage' (see Figure 2.2), which called for artillery to linger when it reached a trench until all other parts of the barrage had reached that line, at which time the infantry would be expected to assault. Unfortunately, gunnery calculations could not match this level of tactical sophistication, and serious mistakes were made in its execution.

26. Brigadier-General Jardine, commander of 97th Brigade of 32nd Division, ordered his men to within 30–40 metres of the enemy trenches before zero hour. As the bombardment lifted, his Highland Light Infantry overran the Leipzig Salient in a successful tactic that owed something to its author's experience as an observer of the Russo-Japanese War: *OH 1916*, Vol. II, p.400.

27. On one occasion, 5th Division ordered its infantry to keep just 25 yards behind the barrage in a tactic that the French had advocated before 1914. The French later held that if 10–15 per cent of their casualties were not suffered from the friendly barrage, then the troops were not close enough: Brigadier H. W. Wynter, 'The Revival of the Barrage', *RAJ*, Vol. LXX, No. 4 (Oct. 1943), p.274. One French general said that there was 'Nothing less than the out-right massacre of friendly infantry by its own artillery', quoted in Lieutenant-Colonel C. R. Shrader, 'Artillery Amicicide', in *Amicicide the Problem of Friendly Fire in Modern War* (Combat Studies Institute Research Survey No. 1, US Army Command and General Staff College, Fort Leavenworth, Dec. 1982), p.2. General Percin estimated that 75,000 French casualties were caused by 'friendly' artillery, largely through lack of co-ordination and the excessive use of heavy artillery. This, however, represented only about 1.5 per cent of French casualties and was a problem common to all combatants.

28. *OH 1916*, Vol. I, p.442.

29. As early as 4 September, the 'protective barrage' was seen as a hindrance to exploitation. 95th Brigade of 5th Division had reached Leuze Wood, but 'here the British barrage prevented further progress': ibid., p.258. The next day 15th Brigade was little bothered by desultory German fire; 'it was the British "protective barrage" which discouraged further advance'. Poor communications between forward troops and the guns were hard to overcome. Visual signals were easily obscured, and line and runners were repeatedly blown away. The problem was not resolved and became worse as German procedures improved. By 1917 German defences mounted counter-attacks by a timetable starting automatically at the British zero hour.

30. Appreciation of these problems often caused the Germans to attack on a salient, where the defender would find himself with a narrow line of supply through atrocious terrain. For example, at Verdun, most 75s received just 250 rpg per day, or half to one-third of their firing capacity – poor logistic communications reduced their firepower by half. By contrast, the attacker had more numerous options for re-supply, the advantage of space in which to disperse his assets, and a greater opportunity to concentrate enfilade fire from them.

31. Colonel W. Balck (trans., Lt W. Krueger), *Tactics* (London: Hugh Rees, 1914), Vol. III, p.442.

32. The offensive on Vimy Ridge in April 1917, which was a part of the battle of Arras, was subsequently used as a model for its highly centralised C2. Four divisions attacked from positions previously held by just two. The artillery staffs of the latter were tasked to prepare for the arrival of others, after which artillery command was centralised at corps headquarters. Artillery assets were distributed to divisions according to their attacking frontage and depth of objective, but every battery position was selected by corps. In the south, where objectives were too deep for normal artillery support, 90 18-pounder guns were sited in silent positions just 1,000 yards from the front line: Lieutenant Colonel A. F. Brooke 'The Evolution of Artillery in the Great War: Part 6', *RAJ*, Vol. LIII, No. 2 (July 1926), p.241.

   'Destruction' was still the aim, and the preliminary bombardment lasted for seven days, following a gradual build-up over 20 days. Mortars and 18-pounders were again tasked to cut forward wire, with medium and heavy artillery attacking deeper lines of wire and trenches. Medium and heavy pieces fired 91,000 rounds on 42,000 yards of trench and 8,000 rounds on 8,000 yards of wire. The preliminary bombardment included a more sophisticated deception plan with a number of feint barrages, which rolled forward luring troops to leave shelter, only to roll back onto them again. The logistic effort for this operation was formidable. Dumps were established with 600 rpg for 18-pounders, and the ammunition column to sustain this stretched ten miles every night during the preliminary bombardment.

   The assault was supported by a barrage that took account of the depth of the defence. Two-thirds of all 18-pounders fired at targets immediately in front of the leading infantry, one-third fired on targets 100 metres ahead of that, while the 4.5-inch howitzers and 'heavies' engaged targets not less than 200 yards behind the forward line. Some 18-pounders fired over 1,000 rpg and some 60-pounders 200 rpg: ibid., p.244.

33. The French at this time also adhered to a policy of 'destruction' and, like the British, were attempting deeper penetrations, with artillery reaching further into German positions deployed in greater depth. General Nivelle hoped to achieve a decisive breakthrough on the Aisne in spring 1917, starting with a nine-day preliminary bombardment, fired by 5,500 pieces on a 40-kilometre front, heavily weighted against deep targets. This idea had merit, but forward targets received insufficient attentions and the attack failed.

34. At Messines in June 1917, X British Corps attacked on a five-kilometre front with 800 pieces, the British for the first time making effective use of air observers to control the cutting of enemy wire: Wynter (1943), op.cit., p.273. The Germans saw that British tactics were heavily reliant on artillery and had devised new methods of CB fire. Large-scale artillery duels developed, in which the Germans were out-gunned and their artillery withdrawn; but the length of the bombardment disclosed the sector of attack, and the Germans took the precaution of withdrawing their infantry as well before the attack, which then hit 'thin air'.

35. Broad (1922), op.cit., p.131.

36. British infantry was operating at the extreme limit of artillery support, and after hard fighting to reach objectives could not hold them against fresh German infantry and artillery – which had often been withdrawn deliberately from the sector under attack as the preliminary bombardment started. German trenches were often sparsely manned but reinforced by concrete 'pill-boxes'. These, in effect, did away with the concept of tactical linear defence. Once this was realised, the need for a linear barrage was also questioned. It seemed more appropriate to meet concentrations in defence with concentrations of fire-power.

For this reason, and to regain tactical surprise, the British soon stopped the arbitrary bombardment of trenches, firing only on known targets. Pieces engaged in CB fire were withdrawn to thicken up this fire after zero hour and for as long as the infantry was mobile. These then returned to CB tasks and to the bombardment of reserves up to 9,000 yards behind enemy lines.

37. The extraordinary conditions of the terrain, which turned any manoeuvre into confusion, made it hard to assess this ploy, but it was used with great success in 1918 by the French General Gouraud, south of Reims, when French infantry withdrew before an attack by German infantry, which was then annihilated by French artillery.

38. At Malmaison, for example, the French fired 360 train-loads of ammunition between 13 and 27 August 1917: Brooke (1926), op.cit., p.248.

39. In many cases, artillery positions were quite literally dug into the trench system, and took orders only from a centralised command system. Few junior commanders had training or experience of the mobile operations which had been the norm before autumn 1914. Special schools were set up in France to re-educate officers in the mobile warfare which might bring the war to an end.

40. At Cambrai, 70 60-pounders fired 16,000 rounds of tear-gas to force enemy gunners into respirators, to reduce their efficiency, and a smoke-screen was planned to cover the advance. 18-pounders spaced every 25 yards fired smoke 300 yards ahead of the tanks, lifting from trench to trench along a 10,500-yard front, firing 93,000 rounds. At the same time, the 6-inch howitzers fired 500 yards ahead of the tanks and the 'heavies' fired 15-minute concentrations on selected targets.

41. Artillery was still a relatively neglected arm in the German Army, although it was recognised that artillery was no longer a mere accessory but an offensive arm, able to engage targets on its own initiative. This called for a greater rather than a lesser appreciation of the tactical scene, and closer liaison with the supported arm; but the supported arm remained supreme. German Battle Regulations, *Gefechtsvorschrift für die Artillerie*, still cast artillery in a secondary role, which caused resentment during the *Materialschlacht* of 1917, when clearly its operations were of primary importance. *Deutsche Militaergeschichte: Band 6 Militaergeschichtliches Forschungsamt* (Munich: Bernard und Graefe Verlag, 1983), pp 513–14.

42. A report by Army Group Crown Prince Rupprecht on 14 December 1917 stated that for a powerful breakthrough surprise was most important and that, in consequence, preliminary bombardment should be heavy but short. Quoted in ibid., p 514. Bruchmüller's techniques have been analysed in detail in *Steelwind* by David Zabecki (Westport, CT: Praeger, 1995). See also Bruce I. Gudmundsson, *On Artillery* (Westport, CT: Praeger, 1993).

43. Where FOOs had succeeded in modifying a fire plan, there were often adverse effects on neighbouring units. The Germans tried to organise a system of control on a precise, narrow, but decisive sector. Each battery had one or more observers in the front line, often advancing with the infantry. Communications were by line via an 'anchor OP' or through signalling detachments, which were collocated at every battalion headquarters with an artillery liaison officer. But these communications proved inadequate, and the Germans had limited success, although they did indicate artillery's desire to establish a closer relationship with the infantry after a period when it had often seemed to operate as an autonomous arm.

44. The Germans noted that their counter-attacking forces barely reached their own front line without heavy losses in a situation where the British were content with limited territorial gain: Broad (1922), op. cit., p.134.

45. A situation analogous to that 60 years later.

46. This policy had been successful in the summer of 1917, when the British advance inflicted relatively few casualties. As the British tried to strike deeper against these reserves, the latter were pulled even further back. The Germans calculated that they would have two hours from the outset of a British attack to bring up these reserves, positioned up to 9 kilometres to the rear. As the British limited their advances and covered them with massive fire plans, reserves sited so far back became ineffective. For example, on 23 September 1917, a superior force of German infantry advancing to counter-attack on Poelcapelle was annihilated by artillery fire: Oldfield (1922), op. cit. For a time during the battle of Passchendaele, the Germans had returned to their old tactics of holding forward in strength, but had been smashed by 'destructive' fire. By October 1917, the Germans had settled for the withdrawal of forward troops as the British attacked and the summoning of defensive barrages by light signal.

47. For example, at a crossing over the La Bassée canal near Hinges on 12 April 1918, two observers of the RFA held their position for six hours after their supported infantry had virtually collapsed, ibid., p.470.

48. It could only be fired on the order of the artillery commander, and special authority was required before fire could be switched away from counter-preparation.

49. For example, in April 1918, three German companies moved to attack opposite positions of the British 61st Division defending a bridge near Pacaut. The divisional artillery commander put down a bombardment in an area of 1,000 yards square inside enemy lines and destroyed two companies. The third advanced and surrendered *en bloc*, ibid., p.469.

50. This trend has a parallel in the British Army of the 1980s, where the ties between infantry battalions and the fire of affiliated batteries have been weakened to ensure that fire is concentrated on targets of highest priority on the direction of the artillery C2 organisation.

51. An example of what could happen if surprise were compromised was seen on 15 July 1918, when the French Fourth Army received advanced warning of a German attack and withdrew its infantry, putting down a massive counter-preparation and CB fire programme just before the German 'hurricane' bombardment. The attack failed on a 90-kilometre front.

52. The success of the lone German gunner who held up the tanks of 51st Division at Flesquières on 20 November 1917 had not been forgotten. Some 60 per cent of artillery was engaged on CB fire missions, and others on smoke missions to mask the advance of the tanks. Other tasks included the disruption of C2 and harassing fire to lower enemy morale. It should however be noted that after the first day of an attack few tanks remained in action, because of mechanical failure and crew exhaustion.

53. At Passchendaele, 75 per cent of 18-pounders, 65 per cent of 6-inch howitzers, and 35 per cent of 60-pounders had been used. At Amiens, 98.5 per cent of all artillery was used on the day of the assault: Lieutenant-Colonel A. F. Brooke, 'The Evolution of Artillery in the Great War: Part 7', *RAJ*, Vol. LIII, No. 3 (Oct. 1926), p.323. Like the Germans, the British favoured shorter and more intense bombardments; but the weight of munitions was still

formidable: Fourth Army fired 3,700 wagon-loads of 18-pounder ammunition on 8 August alone.

54. The British Fourth Army reported few cases of shrapnel wounds and 70 per cent from small arms. In contrast, the Germans reported an exceptionally high incidence of shrapnel wounds.

55. Quoted in Balck (1914), op.cit., p.241.

CHAPTER THREE

Co-Stars or Supporting Cast?
British Divisions in the 'Hundred Days', 1918[1]

Peter Simkins

Despite the renewed surge of interest in the Great War over the last 20 years or so, the overall tactical performance of the BEF on the Western Front has, until very recently, received low or negative ratings from the majority of writers and historians. Martin Samuels, in his book *Doctrine and Dogma*, comparing German and British infantry tactics between 1914 and 1918, states: 'The British Army in the First World War was characterised by its unsubtle and inflexible approach to battle. Having once adopted this approach, it proved virtually impossible to alter it'.[2] Similarly, Bruce Gudmundsson, in *Stormtroop Tactics*, claims that most British officers worked hard to maintain an air of 'detached amateurism'. According to Gudmundsson, the few regular officers who took their profession seriously found themselves concentrated on staffs, 'leaving small unit leadership to enthusiastic but tactically incompetent schoolboys'. In his view, whereas the French were provided with the answers to tactical questions before they were asked, the British, at least at the regimental level, 'rarely even bothered to ask what the questions were'.[3] Denis Winter observes that whenever Haig planned a breakthrough or faced a particularly obdurate German position, 'British units were pushed aside and Dominion troops put in charge'. Judging it to be poorly trained and ill-equipped, supported by low-quality staff work and commanded by generals inadequate to the task, Haig's BEF, he asserts, 'was, indeed, the bluntest of swords'.[4]

With such views still largely occupying centre-stage, it is hardly surprising that British *popular* perceptions of the First World War remain almost wholly dominated by images of futile frontal assaults in Flanders and of brave but naive troops being slaughtered at the whim of uncaring and bungling nincompoops. As I have written elsewhere, one should never seek to underplay the horrors and tragedies of the front-line soldier's experience during the war.[5] On the other hand, those successes – such as the three and a half-mile advance of XVII Corps on 9 April 1917, Plumer's operations in the latter half of September, or Third Army's assault at Cambrai on 20 November that year – which do indicate a distinct improvement in the BEF's collective tactical ability – are all too often undervalued or simply ignored. These remarks apply in equal, if not greater, measure to the victories of the 'Hundred Days' offensive of August to November 1918. The carnage of the first day of the 1916 Somme offensive and the mud of Passchendaele are firmly rooted in the British folk memory, but the BEF's achievements at Amiens or Albert or in the battles of the Canal du Nord and the St Quentin Canal in the late summer and autumn of 1918 are unknown to the average British citizen. It is not just the ordinary man or woman on the proverbial Clapham omnibus who is at fault here. Sadly, the hundreds, if not thousands, of after-action reports and narratives contained in the army, corps, divisional, brigade and battalion war diaries – which clearly demonstrate that a great deal of post-battle analysis and evaluation was, in fact, carried out by the officers of the BEF – remain unfamiliar territory for all too many writers on the conflict.

There are, of course, exceptions to this rule. It is significant that those scholars who have been prepared to undertake the necessary historical foot-slogging through such sources have, in the main, produced the most balanced and thorough assessments of the BEF's performance. Their conclusions, in addition, are frequently at variance with the more widely accepted conventional judgements on the conduct of British operations on the Western Front. Bill Rawling, for example, suggests that there was a well-defined and more or less continuous tactical learning curve between the Somme and the Armistice, not merely in the Canadian Corps – with which he is primarily concerned – but in the BEF as a whole. One aspect of this was the way in which the infantry platoon was reorganised and given greater firepower in the form of Lewis guns and rifle grenades. In the end, Rawling contends, tactics based on artillery support and small unit manoeuvre played a key part in the defeat of the Imperial German Army.[6]

Here Rawling echoes the sentiments of Robin Prior and Trevor Wilson, who believe that the battles fought by the BEF from July to November 1918 were a demonstration of superior employment of weaponry and manpower at a time when the right relationship between the two was vital to success. On the Somme, two years earlier, they remark, German garrisons in any one of a series of woods and villages might have represented a serious obstacle, but, in the summer and autumn of 1918, 'the British forces had weapons and tactics sufficient for their suppression'.[7] Prior and Wilson also point to the greater degree of tactical decentralisation in the BEF by 1918, commenting that 'as the British army at every level became a more complex, sophisticated, and above all specialist organisation, any detailed intervention by the commander-in-chief became increasingly inappropriate'. Hence, they contend, Haig's job, like that of Rawlinson and other individual army commanders, was

> diminishing not expanding as the forces under his direction grew in expertise and complexity. And Haig, again like Rawlinson, proved far more effective as a commander once the sphere of his activities began to diminish to an extent that brought them within the limits of his capabilities.[8]

These claims have recently been powerfully reinforced by Dr Paddy Griffith in his book *Battle Tactics of the Western Front: The British Army's Art of Attack, 1916–18*. Dr Griffith argues convincingly that, on the eve of the Somme offensive of 1916, the BEF's doctrine already bore a marked resemblance to the much-praised German 'stormtroop' tactics in its emphasis on 'an aggressive front line to push forward wherever possible, and rearward lines to mop up and consolidate', while the British, during that year, also revealed that they had grasped the principles of 'mission orders' and 'directive command' – a system again usually ascribed to the Germans.[9] Trench raids, too, provided a valuable means of familiarising front-line units with assault tactics which included infiltration, close fire support and decentralised initiative. Despite their unpopularity with the troops themselves, such operations – which the British tended to mount more frequently than the Germans – thereby made a substantial contribution to the BEF's tactical education.[10] The Somme, in Dr Griffith's view, underlined the value of trench mortars, Lewis guns and rifle grenades as close support weapons which enabled infantrymen to fight their own way forward and prompted 'the decisive "third generation" of tactical reappraisal in the BEF' in the winter of 1916–17. The results of that reappraisal were crystallised in the key manuals *Instructions for the Training of Divisions for Offensive Action* (SS 135), published in December 1916, and *Instructions for the Training of Platoons for Offensive Action* (SS 143), issued in February 1917.[11] Dr Griffith maintains that SS 143, in particular, is essentially a 'stormtrooper's handbook', incorporating 'instructions for a miniature all-arms battle in which every section plays a distinct part.'[12] It can therefore be seen as a 'milestone in tactics' leading to the era of 'flexible small groups built around a variety of high-firepower weapons'. The accompanying improvement in artillery techniques – especially in the widespread adoption of the creeping barrage and the development of effective counter-battery fire and the concept of the 'deep battle' – combined with the advances in infantry tactics to produce notable successes for the BEF on 9 April 1917, the first day of the battle of Arras. From this point on, apart from obvious refinements, such as predicted fire, British tactics in the First World War were less a matter of revolution than of evolution.[13]

Like Prior and Wilson, Paddy Griffith acknowledges the degree of tactical decentralisation that took place in the BEF during the last two years of the war, paying particular attention to 'grand tactics', the fighting methods employed within the corps, division or brigade. These, he writes, might embrace such things as the timing of a creeping barrage or the co-ordination of low-flying ground-attack aircraft squadrons. Battalions, brigades and divisions, he adds, often 'invented their own characteristic tactics and operating procedures. ... The whims of commanders, in fact, were always a very major determinant of how every battle would be fought.'[14] Shared recognition of these points has stimulated a number of other British historians to embark upon a much more systematic examination of divisional organisation, composition, command and performance in the BEF.[15] Much of this work, both individually and collectively, is in its early stages, so this chapter represents a preliminary bulletin from base-camp rather than a report from the summit. However, at least British historians are now increasingly attempting the difficult ascent.

A great deal of the credit for the success of the final Allied offensive in 1918 has rightly been attributed to the Australian, Canadian and New Zealand formations on the Western Front. There were 60 active infantry divisions in the BEF during the 'Hundred Days' offensive of 8 August to 11 November 1918 and, of these, ten were Dominion divisions – one New Zealand, four Canadian and five Australian. In preparing this chapter, I analysed a sample of 221 individual attacking operations by Dominion divisions in the 'Hundred Days' (42 by the New Zealand Division, 79 by the Australians and 100 by the four Canadian divisions).[16] The operations examined range from strong offensive patrols and battalion actions to full-scale set-piece assaults by several divisions at a time, such as the attack at Amiens on 8 August 1918. Not surprisingly, my findings confirm that the success rate of the Dominion divisions was indeed remarkably high.

The first interesting statistic to emerge from the survey is that only 9.04 per cent of the attacks by Dominion divisions could be said to have failed totally, in that no real forward progress was made. Looked at another way, this means that some progress was registered in 90.96 per cent of the operations under review. Even if one allows for the fact that a further proportion – 19 per cent – of the attacks resulted in only limited gains, and also that in another 3.16 per cent of the Dominion operations the divisions were facing a retreating enemy who put up little or no opposition, one is still left with an overall Dominion success rate of 68.8 per cent in *opposed* attacks – this latter statistic being arguably the most accurate indicator of all of the fighting performance of the divisions in question. It must be added that the successes of the Dominion divisions in this period encompassed some of the truly outstanding offensive operations of the war, including major advances by the Canadians and Australians on the first day of the battle of Amiens (8 August), the Australian capture of Mont St Quentin and Péronne (31

August–2 September), the Canadian assaults on the Drocourt–Quéant Line (2 September) and the Canal du Nord (27 September), and the seizure by the New Zealand Division of the walled town of Le Quesnoy (4 November).

Many Australian soldiers were critical of the quality of British troops on the Western Front in 1918. Derogatory opinions about the morale or the command and fighting abilities of the 'Tommies' are by no means difficult to uncover in the letters and diaries of Australian officers and other ranks alike. Writing to the Australian official historian, C. E. W. Bean, some 12 years after the war, Brigadier General H. E. 'Pompey' Elliott, who commanded the 15th Australian Brigade (5th Australian Division) in 1917–18, declared that 'Sir Charles Harrington [*sic*], Plumer's Chief of Staff, was the only one of the British Staff officers who ever impressed me that he had a proper conception of his job – to save the infantry casualties by the measures which they took'.[17] The British were the target of particularly biting criticism for their performance in the face of the German offensives of March and April 1918. Lieutenant S. R. Traill, of the 1st Battalion, AIF, noted in his diary, following the German capture of Mount Kemmel: 'The name of the Tommy stinks in a good many quarters now, for it is coming out that they retreated a long way further than they need, and that the staff was a hell of a failure – Damn them.'[18] Earlier that month, Sir John Monash, then a major general commanding the 3rd Australian Division, remarked: 'Some of these Tommy divisions are the absolute limit, and not worth the money it costs to put them into uniform.' Shortly afterwards he reflected: 'If we only had twenty Divisions like the 5 Australian, 4 Canadian and 1 New Zealand there would have been a different tale to tell.'[19] Such views were so commonly expressed in the spring of 1918 that Lieutenant General Sir William Birdwood, who, at that time, was still commanding the Australian Corps, felt it necessary to intervene. In a letter circulated to his senior officers on 30 April he observed:

> You have probably noticed, as I have done, the great tendency there is now-adays for a certain number of officers and men to criticise and make disparaging comparisons between their own units and others that may be serving alongside of them. ... I do hope that you will do everything in your power to see that this practice is stopped. ... More particularly would I urge the restriction of comparison between Dominion and English troops.[20]

Australian successes at Hamel on 4 July and at the start of the 'Hundred Days' offensive in August 1918 merely encouraged Australian soldiers to indulge in a renewed wave of criticism of British troops. On 10 August, Sergeant Lionel Elliott of the 56th Battalion, AIF – who was himself born in England in 1890 – told his mother and sisters: 'Our boys have the *real* bulldog spirit in them, not the milk and water specimen we see occasionally from England.'[21] Captain G. W. Parramore of the Australian Army Medical Corps, serving with the 4th Australian Division, recorded in his diary: 'The British Tommy when led will go anywhere but usually his officers are absolutely incapable and apart from the officers the B[ritish] Tommy has no resource or initiative.'[22] Monash, who had taken over the command of the Australian Corps on 31 May, was also unwilling to retract his earlier statements about British units. In a letter to his family on 11 September 1918, he described British troops as 'brave enough' but 'simply unskilful'. He went on:

> They would be all right if properly led, but their officers, particularly the junior officers [such as platoon and company leaders], are [very] poor [stuff]; young men from the professions and from office stools in the English cities, who have had no experience whatever of independent responsibility or leadership. [The fact remains that] very few English divisions can [today] be classed as first-class fighting troops [who can be] relied upon to carry out the tasks set. On the other hand, the Canadians and Australians have never failed to achieve all their objectives strictly according to plan.[23]

Monash and the other Australians quoted here can perhaps be forgiven for a tendency to boast of their own successes while denigrating the deeds of British troops.[24] Even so, as Eric Andrews suggests in his book *The Anzac Illusion*, deserved recognition for, and pride in, splendid tactical achievements by Australian soldiers has become somewhat distorted, helping to create the myth of the 'colonial superman'.[25] In the process, the contribution of the British soldier to the ultimate victory has been overshadowed. But just how important was the part played by the British regular, New Army and territorial divisions in the 'Hundred Days' – and have their achievements been obscured to an unjustified extent by the often brilliant feats of the Dominion contingents?

Of the 50 British infantry divisions in the BEF during the 'Hundred Days', nine were regular divisions, 16 were territorial or dismounted Yeomanry units and the remaining 25 (if one includes the 63rd (Royal Naval) Division in this category) were New Army formations. All but seven had been heavily engaged during the German *Michael* offensive in March or the *Georgette* attack on the Lys in April, and 17 – or around one-third – had been involved in both; five of these 17, in turn, had then been unfortunate enough to become embroiled in a third German attack, the *Blücher* offensive on the Aisne in May 1918. Another four divisions had taken part in the second battle of the Marne in July. Two divisions, the 52nd (Lowland) and the 74th (Yeomanry), were relatively new to the Western Front, having been transferred from Palestine. Finally, a total of nine divisions – just under one-fifth of the British infantry divisions in the BEF – had been reconstituted in the late spring and summer of 1918. Apart from the two which had come from Palestine, only five divisions – the 11th (Northern), 37th, 38th (Welsh),

46th (North Midland) and 57th (2nd West Lancashire) – had not been seriously involved in major operations on the Western Front between 21 March and 8 August 1918.[26]

Given that the BEF could hardly be portrayed as 'fresh' when the 'Hundred Days' started, the success rate of the British divisions in the offensive was impressive. In the case of the British divisions, I surveyed a total of 966 individual attacking operations between 8 August and 11 November 1918. As with the Dominion divisions, the sample surveyed does not include every single offensive operation undertaken by the British divisions during that period, but it does take account of the vast majority of those mentioned by the British official history and is, I believe, sufficiently thorough and extensive to offer some reasonably accurate conclusions about performance. Applying the same criteria as for the Dominion units, one finds that 168 of these operations (or 17.39 per cent) could be classed as outright failures or, conversely, that some progress was achieved in 82.61 per cent of the attacks. A further 119 attacks (12.31 per cent) secured only limited gains while in 111 operations (or 11.49 per cent), the British divisions concerned encountered negligible or minor resistance from a retreating enemy. Thus, in 58.81 per cent of the British attacks, some or all of the objectives were taken against opposition, the quality of which was sometimes extremely high, including, for instance, the Alpine Corps, the 2nd Guard Division and the 27th (Württemberg) Division.

At first glance, these statistics seem to support the claim that the performance of Dominion divisions in the 'Hundred Days' was significantly superior to that of the British units, the proportion of British failures (17.39 per cent) being almost double the Dominion figure. However, on closer examination, the statistics, in several respects, tell a rather different story. First, the average success rate in *opposed* attacks of the nine British divisions which served in Rawlinson's Fourth Army for most, if not all, of the 'Hundred Days' was 70.7 per cent – identical to the average success rate of the five Australian divisions (70.7 per cent), only slightly lower than the average for the four Canadian divisions (72.5 per cent) and higher than that of the New Zealand Division (64.5 per cent). The corresponding success rate of the 17 British divisions which spent all or most of the 'Hundred Days' in Byng's Third Army was 64.38 per cent – a figure which is admittedly lower than the average for the Dominion divisions, but not by a huge margin. Secondly, five British divisions – the 19th and 66th (with 100 per cent), the 9th (93 per cent), the 25th (85 per cent) and the 16th (80 per cent) – each had a higher success rate against opposition within an overall total of ten or more attacks than any of their Dominion counterparts, the nearest of which were the 2nd Australian Division (with a comparative success rate of 77.75 per cent against opposition in an overall total of 18 attacks) and the 4th Canadian Division (77.5 per cent in 31 attacks). True, one Australian division – the 4th

– had a success rate of 80 per cent but this was in only *five* attacks surveyed and the figure might therefore be misleading if taken as a yardstick. It should also be remembered, in this context, that the Canadian Corps had hardly been engaged at all in the great defensive battles of the spring of 1918 and that its divisions, on 8 August that year, were thus relatively fresh and intact. Thirdly, six Dominion divisions (1st, 2nd and 5th Australian and 1st, 2nd and 4th Canadian) achieved a success rate of between 70 and 80 per cent in opposed attacks while five British divisions (Guards, 18th, 24th, 34th and 38th) also came into this category. In other words, one could infer from these figures that, in general, ten British divisions performed at least as well as – and in a few cases possibly better than – the leading six or seven Dominion divisions. It is also interesting to note in passing that, of the British divisions with the highest success rates, all, apart from the Guards (regular) and 66th (territorial), were New Army formations.

If one then considers the number of attacks carried out by individual British and Dominion divisions, and also the number of 'battle days' on which each division saw meaningful action, the British units again stand up well to the comparison. Judging from the overall sample of 1,187 operations surveyed – all of which were deemed worthy of mention by the British official historian – the 58th (2nd/1st London) Division (46 attacks over 37 'battle days') or the New Zealand Division (42 attacks in 31 'battle days') appear to have been more heavily engaged than most divisions, although a minute examination of every divisional war diary might well throw up some other examples. Nevertheless, the survey suggests that as many as 33 British divisions took part in more attacks than the Australian divisional average (15.8 attacks) and nine in more attacks than the Canadian divisional average (25). Similarly, 34 British divisions fought on more 'battle days' than the Australian divisional average (12.6) and 11 on more than the Canadian divisional average (20.75 'battle days').[27] The statistics, then, seem to indicate that, far from being the 'bluntest of swords' or a mere supporting cast, the British divisions in the 'Hundred Days', in spite of the crises they had experienced earlier in the year, actually made a very weighty contribution to the Allied victory.

The overall figures inevitably conceal a fairly wide degree of variation between the performances of individual divisions. The 9th (Scottish) Division, the third most effective of those surveyed, had a success rate of 93 per cent against opposition in 14 attacks. The 19th (Western) Division's 100 per cent success rate in 12 opposed operations was achieved over a shorter time-span, mainly after 20 October, while all of the 66th (2nd East Lancashire) Division's operations which are covered by this survey, and which attained the same high success rate, were carried out after 7 October. In contrast, seven British divisions had an outright failure rate of 25 per cent or more. This group included the 33rd Division, with a failure rate of 35.25

per cent, the 46th (North Midland) Division (30.75 per cent), 61st (2nd South Midland) Division (30 per cent), 41st Division (29.5 per cent), 63rd (Royal Naval) Division (27.25 per cent) and the 6th and 56th (London) Divisions (both with 25 per cent). Three of these were territorial divisions, three were New Army units and one was a regular division. Only 12 of the British divisions had a partial or total success rate in opposed attacks of less than 50 per cent, the majority falling into the 50 to 70 per cent category.

One might bear in mind that a failure rate of 25 per cent in opposed attacks was by no means discreditable on the Western Front and, in any case, did not necessarily signify that a particular division was always ineffective. The 46th Division, for example, suffered a setback at Pontruet on 24 September but, less than a week later, took part in one of the outstanding operations of the war when it crossed the St Quentin Canal and helped to breach the Hindenburg Line. Similarly, the 63rd (Royal Naval) Division failed on three occasions near Achiet le Petit and Thilloy between 24 and 27 August, the divisional commander, Major-General Lawrie, subsequently being removed. Yet, on 2 September – again barely a week after a reverse – the division, in action in the Quéant–Inchy sector, enjoyed what one of its brigade commanders later described as a 'very happy day which I will never forget'. The troops, he recalled, 'did grand work, and the way in which they manoeuvred in the open and made use of ground was most encouraging'.[28]

It could be argued that the high success rates of both British and Dominion divisions were made possible by the fact that the German defences in the autumn of 1918 were much less solid and integrated than they had been on the Somme or at Passchendaele and thus provided more opportunities for infiltration. This may be so, although it is also important to point out that the Hindenburg Line, the Drocourt–Quéant Position and the Canal du Nord were still formidable obstacles which required major set-piece assaults before they could be overcome. Furthermore, the advantages gained by the soldiers of the BEF when facing less elaborate defences were more than offset by the wide variety of conditions and terrain which they had to negotiate and the many different tactical tasks with which they were confronted in the space of a few weeks – particularly as, after three years of attrition, the divisions were comparatively inexperienced in the art of attacking in conditions of semi-open warfare. Quite apart from dealing with the enemy, British and Dominion troops in the 'Hundred Days' had to cope with the challenges posed by valleys, villages, farms, woods and forests, ridges and spurs, rivers and canals, railway embankments and cuttings, walled and ruined towns, marshes and floods, orchards, pasture land enclosed by thick hedges, industrial suburbs and even old battlefields.

What factors, therefore, may have contributed to the often unrecognised achievements of the British divisions in the period from 8 August to the Armistice? When analysing the performance of the Australian and Canadian contingents, the British official historian ascribes their success partly to the fact that they retained their social and organisational homogeneity. Whereas the British reduced the number of infantry battalions in a division to nine early in 1918, the Canadian divisions kept the 12 battalion organisation throughout, and even those Australian divisions which eventually lost battalions at least stayed relatively intact until late September. The Australian and Canadian Corps also remained together as formations, so enhancing morale and team spirit, improving confidence and cohesion through familiarity and making it easier to disseminate lessons learned on the battlefield. Their wounded, if and when they recovered, would normally be drafted back to their own units.[29] The British divisions, however, lacked these benefits. The coming of conscription in 1916 saw men recruited for general service and posted to units as required, rather than being encouraged to enlist in formations with a strong local connection. From then onwards, the drafting of reinforcements and casualty replacements from a parent regiment to its own units at the front was no longer guaranteed. During the battle of the Somme in 1916 there was a major reorganisation of the reserve and drafting system itself which henceforth made the impact of losses on particular communities less concentrated and dramatic but also diluted the social and geographical cohesion of the units on active service. As a case in point, in the 1/6th Cheshires, a territorial battalion with the 30th Division, only 20 per cent of the men by 1918 were from the unit's original recruiting area around Stockport and barely half were from the county.[30] Regular, New Army and territorial brigades and battalions had been interchanged between divisions at the front almost from the beginning, a process which, coupled with the reconstitution of nine divisions in 1918, resulted in the composition of nearly half the British divisions in the BEF being wholly or partly changed by the time hostilities ceased. The distinctive, highly localised character of the BEF of 1916 had consequently disappeared and an increasingly 'nationalised' force had taken its place.

Having said all that, I am not entirely convinced that, in the end, such changes made an overwhelming amount of difference. Three of the ten British divisions which performed best in the 'Hundred Days' – the 9th, 19th and 24th – had seen at least one-third of their original battalions replaced by others, while four – the 16th, 25th, 34th and 66th – had been wholly, or almost completely, reconstituted in 1918. Indeed, the fact that the 9th (Scottish) had lost its splendid South African Brigade, which, having joined the division in 1916, had been reduced to a Composite Battalion before August 1918 and left altogether at the end of that month, does not seem to have significantly affected the division's success rate during the final weeks of the war.[31] Good infantry could be created by good divisions within a few months, so long as the formation possessed an experienced cadre around which it could rebuild.

A similar verdict might be reached when one considers the question of continuity of command. It is true that British units were shuffled round from corps to corps 'like cards in a pack'.[32] Of the 50 British divisions under review, only 16 remained in the same corps throughout the 'Hundred Days'; 22 served in two different corps; and 12 fought in three different corps, even during this limited period. But, here too, if one re-examines the ten British divisions with a success rate of 70 per cent against opposition within an overall total of ten or more attacks, one finds that five stayed in one corps throughout, four of them each served in two different corps and one served in three different corps. It is also difficult to detect any consistent patterns at the divisional command level. If one widens the sample slightly to include all British divisions with a success rate in opposed attacks of 60 per cent or more, one discovers that the commanders of 14 of them had been in post less than six months, eight had been in command of their divisions since 1917 and the remaining four since 1916. The 18th – Ivor Maxse's old division – had only two commanders in its entire service on the Western Front, yet the 9th (Scottish) Division had experienced nine changes of command and seven different commanders since crossing to France and Major General H. H. Tudor, who led it during the 'Hundred Days', had only been in post since March. Thus good battlefield performance did not always hinge upon a settled existence in the same corps with a long-serving divisional commander. What mattered far more than even the individual personality of the divisional commander, influential as he might be, was the creation and maintenance of a divisional 'command culture' or ethos – a way of doing things within the formation which could be passed on to others over the longer term, regardless of constant changes of personnel.

The morale factor is harder to quantify. However, there is strong evidence from postal censorship reports that, despite the low point of late 1917 and the crises of March–April 1918, British units and soldiers remained committed to winning the war – a vital element in their performance in the latter half of 1918.[33] They had survived, albeit narrowly, the worst the German Army could hurl at them and, from July onwards, at last had tangible proof of success in ground gained and prisoners and guns captured. As Charles Douie, an officer in the 1st Dorsets, wrote: 'The infantry at least had no doubt that they were winning, and their faith was justified when the greatest military Power of modern times finally collapsed in disordered retreat.'[34] While British units at the front certainly still contained a nucleus of combat veterans in the autumn of 1918, they were, by then, mostly composed of young conscripts who had not experienced the wearisome years of trench warfare and were therefore arguably more resilient after temporary setbacks. This would help to explain why, with casualties of 379,074 in the BEF from August to November 1918, including 41,901 British dead – and with 14 British divisions each suffering casualties of over 2,500 in the last six weeks of the war alone – the offensive did not grind to a halt.[35] In addition, Prior and Wilson have emphasised the point that nearly 20,000 had been killed on 1 July 1916, providing a sharp contrast between the price of failure on one day in 1916 and of victory in more than three months in 1918.[36]

Good relations between officers and other ranks were central to the maintenance of morale in front-line units. In this respect, British officer–man relations have frequently been compared unfavourably with those which prevailed in Australian and Canadian formations.[37] But the socio-military gulf between British officers and men has probably been exaggerated. The social base of the British officer corps was unquestionably widened during the war. In February 1916, with the creation of the Officer Cadet Battalions, a new system was adopted for selecting and training junior officers. From then until the end of the war, the majority of the 107,929 officers who passed through the Officer Cadet Battalions and received temporary commissions had previously served in the ranks.[38] Consequently they were more likely to have earned their commission on the battlefield, not simply because they came from a particular social class. Recent research in Britain, notably by Gary Sheffield, shows that, even if British officer–man relations were different to those in Dominion units, this should not be taken to imply that there was inevitably less mutual respect, admiration and affection between the ranks in British formations. The paternalistic ethos of the pre-war regular officer infused the entire wartime officer class and was a crucial factor in maintaining the morale of the British soldier. In turn, perhaps 41 per cent of young Edwardian males may have belonged to a uniformed youth organisation at some stage and were accustomed to military-style discipline and obedience.[39] In Gary Sheffield's view, deference was recognised in the British Army as part of an interdependent, reciprocal relationship which worked so long as the officers were prepared to keep to their paternalistic side of the unspoken bargain, acting in a way that inspired trust and permitting the socially conservative British working man – who was neither abjectly submissive nor revolutionary – to retain his self-respect. In any case, as Dr Sheffield has found, the relationship between officers and other ranks in the wartime British Army tended to assume the more informal style which had existed in pre-1914 auxiliary units rather than that of regular formations.[40]

The real keys to success were, nevertheless, the weapons system which the BEF had assembled by mid-1918 and the manner in which those weapons, especially the artillery component, were now being employed. The generally high level of performance of the gunners, which lay at the heart of the vastly improved co-operation between infantry and artillery in 1917–18, ensured that, in the majority of assaults, even the rawest young conscripts could be shepherded onto their objectives by creeping barrages of great weight and accuracy. I disagree with Tim Travers when he implies that officers who relied principally upon infantry and artillery were necessarily unprogressive in comparison with the mechanical warfare enthusiasts, particularly the advocates of the tank.[41] At the 'sharp end' of operations in 1918, the battle had to be conducted with the weapons that actually worked best, not just those which fuelled the visions of the new technocrats. In my own survey of operations during the 'Hundred Days', tanks – while extremely useful on some occasions – appear to have exerted a significant influence on the outcome of 16.75 per cent of the attacks by Dominion divisions and on only 7.75 per cent of those undertaken by British divisions. A captured German officer told the commander of the 188th Brigade in the 63rd (Royal Naval) Division: 'If you attack with Infantry plus Artillery plus Tanks you will always get your objectives....If you attack with Infantry plus Artillery you will get your objectives 3 times out of 4....If you attack with Infantry plus Tanks only you will get your objectives only once in 4 times.'[42] One concedes that tanks were not omnipresent in the 'Hundred Days' but their general lack of impact after the opening phases of the battle of Amiens often had as much to do with mechanical beakdowns or vulnerability to artillery fire as to the numbers available on a given day.

Historians have, on the whole, also tended to underestimate the improvement in the BEF's small unit infantry tactics and in the standards of junior leadership by the final months of the Great War. The extent of the improvement is well illustrated by the action of the 9th Northumberland Fusiliers, part of the 61st Division, in crossing the Plate Becque and taking Rennet Farm, near Merville, on 18 August 1918:

> Taking cover under a hedge and a ditch, one section rushed a sunken barge in the river. This was an enemy machine-gun post, and the first man to rush was killed by the only shot the enemy was allowed to fire ere being captured. From the barge, the same section rushed a house on the far side of the river, again capturing a machine-gun team, this time without any casualties. The platoon riflemen, about a dozen strong, worked their way along a hedge in the rear of the enemy's left flank, and rushed into the open towards the enemy trench. This move from their rear so surprised the Germans that they immediately surrendered. Rennet Farm, about sixty yards in the rear of the enemy's right flank, held two gun teams and was causing much havoc. Six men of No. 5 platoon rushed to attack it, and timely aid was given by one of our low-flying planes. The enemy surrendered.[43]

Another well-executed small unit attack, described in the British official history, was carried out by the 5th Duke of Wellington's Regiment (186th Brigade, 62nd Division), north of Bapaume, during the battle of the Scarpe, on 29 August. The objective was a 1,300-yard section of the old 1917 British front line which ran at right angles to the position held by the battalion, so that the attack had to be made *along* the German front and support trenches, which converged at the eastern end of the objective. The operation was helped by a smoke-screen on the northern flank and by a creeping barrage. Beginning at 5.30 p.m., the initial assault was made by one company, with a second in close support, and was led by two groups of nine bombers each, who worked along the main trenches. Lewis gun teams, moving over the open on each side of each trench, prevented the Germans from getting out of the trenches and kept their heads down. The remainder of the leading company followed about 150 yards behind, operating in two platoons – one to each trench – and dropping off section posts as flank guards on the way. The support company also furnished four Lewis gun teams to proceed over the open ground 100 yards to the rear of the leading company and 50 yards north and south of each trench. At first, the Germans offered stubborn resistance but their own bombers were disorganised by cross-fire from the British Lewis guns, enabling the attackers to close with the bayonet. The attack was all over and the objective taken within an hour. Having suffered only slight casualties, the battalion had killed 35 Germans and captured 93 more together with 15 machine guns.[44]

The day before (28 August), the 35th and 36th Brigades of the 12th Division had stormed the Hardecourt aux Bois–Maltz Horn Farm ridge, greatly assisted by overhead fire from the 12th Machine Gun Battalion. The action of the 9th Royal Fusiliers (36th Brigade) in clearing Favière Wood, occupying Hardecourt and capturing 16 machine guns, was particularly note-worthy as the battalion contained some 350 recruits, aged between 18½ and 19½, who had been in France barely a week. The 6th Buffs, part of the 37th Brigade in the same division, twice employed infiltration tactics in three days – first at Favière Wood on 27 August and then at Maurepas on 29 August. On the second occasion they penetrated to the rear of a German company without being observed, cutting off and capturing two officers and 60 men. Just under three weeks later, on 18 September – when, fighting alongside the 18th Division, they attacked the Ronssoy–Epéhy position – five battalions of the 12th Division succeeded in ejecting 12 *Jäger* battalions of the famed German Alpine Corps from a stronghold which the latter had been ordered to hold at all costs. Then, on 24 October, the 6th Buffs, having crossed the Scarpe the previous day, moved along the banks of a small tributary – the Traitoire – to reach Cubray and Haute Rive prior to seizing Buridon under covering fire from skilfully-sited Lewis guns. On 25 October, the Buffs launched a swift attack on Bruille, a large village on the banks of the Canal de l'Escaut (Schelde Canal). Dispensing with artillery preparation, the battalion caught the Germans unawares, secured the village with little loss to itself and thus turned the German position between two rivers, causing the enemy units on the left to be withdrawn.[45]

These are certainly not isolated examples. From numerous similar instances one might quote the 37th Division's attack at Achiet le Grand on 23 August, when the 13th Royal Fusiliers overcame opposition from a brick-works by a flanking movement, pushing out small parties, under covering fire from trench mortars and Lewis guns, to bring the defenders under enfilade fire and force 400 of them to surrender;[46] the night advance of elements of the 21st Division over a distance of more than 3,000 yards on 23–24 August to secure most of an important spur south-east of Miraumont – an operation during which Brigadier-General A. J. McCulloch, commander of the 64th Brigade, cleverly modified the original plan at least three times in 12 hours to meet altered or unforeseen circumstances;[47] the 25th Division's attack on Beaurevoir from the flank and rear on the evening of 5 October, and a fine series of small unit attacks by the division's 75th Brigade – despite the fact that its rifle strength was under 700 – over the course of several hours near Pommereuil on 23 October, during the battle of the Selle;[48] or the 35th Division's flank march and subsequent flank attack under a creeping barrage on 20 October, when it helped to take two ridge lines and breach the Courtrai Switch position.[49] Of the 966 British divisional attacks surveyed for this chapter, 201 (or 20.8 per cent), even at a conservative estimate, clearly succeeded because of good, flexible small-unit or all-arms tactics. The average number of outstanding operations of this type per division was four – or just over one-fifth of the average number of attacks of all types carried out by each British division. Significantly, only six out of the 50 British divisions failed to contribute to this total of outstanding attacks. Twenty-eight divisions (that is, over half) took part in four or more such operations and 16 (nearly one-third) exceeded the divisional average. Since 15 out of the 28 divisions which figured most prominently in these impressive operations do not feature among the formations identified by Paddy Griffith as constituting the *British* element of the élite 'assault spearhead' of the BEF from 1916 to 1918, it is difficult to avoid the conclusion that the *general* level of tactical ability in the BEF had indeed improved markedly by the 'Hundred Days'.[50] That the Germans opposing the BEF were weaker than before is undeniable, but then so were the British and Dominion formations. The 1/2nd London Regiment, a battalion in the 56th (London) Division, was, for example, down to only 11 officers and 193 other ranks on 28 August during the battle of the Scarpe, and the 140th Brigade of the 47th (2nd London) Division was reduced to around 700 rifles by 2 September, after several days' fighting east of Albert.[51]

Given the overall improvement in small-unit tactics in the BEF's British divisions, it follows that the standards of junior leadership were also higher than some authorities have cared to acknowledge. One particular case which can be used to illustrate the many is the 18th Division's attack at Bousies, Robersart and Renuart Farm, around the *Hermann Position II* on 23–24 October, during the battle of the Selle. On the first of those two days, the division advanced some 8,000 yards, a splendid accomplishment considering the darkness at zero hour (4 a.m.), the broken ground and the obstacle posed by the Richemont river. The division captured Bousies along with 700 prisoners and 56 guns. On 24 October it took Renuart Farm, where Lieutenant F. W. Hedges of the Bedfordshire Regiment – attached to the 6th Northamptonshires – won the Victoria Cross while leading a sergeant and a Lewis gun section in the capture of six German machine guns. The division also gained a footing in the western outskirts of Robersart, finally clearing the village in the evening. The original creeping barrage and the subsequent artillery support on 24 October were not as effective as usual and the division had become embroiled in hand-to-hand fighting in the orchards between Bousies and Robersart. Such success as its battalions achieved over the two days was mainly due to their platoon and section commanders and their small-unit tactics, not to tanks and artillery.[52]

The BEF's ability in the 'Hundred Days' to overcome such a wide variety of tactical obstacles and challenges – ranging from set-piece operations to street fighting and canal crossings on improvised rafts – would simply not have been possible without good junior leadership. Paddy Griffith is surely correct in laying the blame at the door of the official historian for encouraging the belief that British junior leaders were poor in 1918.[53] In Griffith's opinion, the decentralisation of tactics to the level of the temporary officer and citizen-soldier NCO was a profoundly unsettling innovation to many regulars, since it was, in effect, an erosion of the powers of the old regular army and its senior officers. Edmonds's 'apparently cynical scape-goating condemnation' of 'poor junior leaders' in 1918 can consequently be explained partly in terms of a backlash reaction against this erosion.[54] It did not always suit old regulars like Edmonds to concede that citizen-soldiers who had enlisted merely 'for the duration' could achieve high levels of tactical skill and initiative.

To be fair, Griffith himself recognises the role of GHQ in helping to create a climate or 'culture' in which, by 1918, local initiative could flourish. 'The system', he writes, 'was designed to stimulate local originality through leadership from the centre. Sometimes it succeeded and sometimes it failed; but…it was never a complete free-for-all.'[55] Only now are historians beginning to make a proper assessment of the part played by the training schools, and by the wide distribution of training and instructional manuals, in disseminating tactical ideas throughout the BEF.[56] The general improvement in standards also probably owed much to cross-fertilisation and a steady exchange of views, lessons and information at corps, divisional and brigade level – the same sort of process, in fact, which Bill Rawling detects as having occurred between the Canadian Corps and the rest of the BEF.[57] A lot more research in this area is required, however, before we can reach any firmer conclusions.

In any discussion of the BEF's performance in the last three months of the Great War, one should never forget that the fighting character of the British front-line soldier was arguably as important – and perhaps even more important – than the methods he employed. The 12th Division, for example, had five prolonged spells in the line or in actual battle during the 'Hundred Days': from 6 to 13 August, 22 to 30 August, 4 to 8 September, 18 to 30 September, and 6 to 29 October. As a result, the division was involved in some of the heaviest fighting, such as the battles of Amiens, Albert and the Scarpe in August, the advance to the Hindenburg Position, the battle of Epéhy and the battle of the St Quentin Canal in September, and the advance to, and battle of, the Selle in October. During this period it suffered some 6,940 casualties, including 86 officers and 879 other ranks killed, 241 officers and 4,987 other ranks wounded, and nine officers and 738 other ranks missing. Yet, despite these casualties and the fact that it had been almost continuously in action since 6 August, with only brief periods of rest, the 12th Division achieved a success rate of 69.5 per cent in opposed attacks and, as late as 25 October, was still capable of mounting such operations as the surprise attack by the 6th Buffs at Bruille.[58] In this context, it might be recalled that the German divisions, after spectacular initial progress in March, April and May, had little real bite left after one or two weeks of each of those offensives. The average British division in late 1918, on the other hand, had the capacity to maintain the pressure on the enemy – allowing for limited spells of rest – over much of the three-month period of the 'Hundred Days'. It was this relentless pressure which, coupled with the dash customarily displayed by the Dominion divisions, did as much as anything to bring about the battlefield defeat of the German Army. In short, by the 'Hundred Days', the sum of the BEF truly mattered more than its individual parts.

NOTES

1. This chapter is based on a paper presented at the Australian War Memorial's twelfth annual History Conference, held at the Australian Defence Force Academy, Canberra, in September 1993. The theme of the conference was '1918 and Beyond'. I am grateful to my colleagues and friends at the Australian War Memorial, particularly Dr Peter Stanley of the Historical Research Section, for permitting me to reproduce parts of that paper here.
2. Martin Samuels, *Doctrine and Dogma: German and British Infantry Tactics in the First World War* (Westport, CT: Greenwood Press, 1992), p.180.
3. Bruce I. Gudmundsson, *Stormtroop Tactics: Innovation in the German Army, 1914–1918* (New York: Praeger, 1989), pp.175–6.
4. Denis Winter, *Haig's Command: A Reassessment* (London: Viking, 1991), pp.144, 150.
5. Peter Simkins, 'Everyman at War: Recent Interpretations of the Front Line Experience', in Brian Bond (ed.), *The First World War and British Military History* (Oxford: Clarendon Press, 1991), p.311.

6. Bill Rawling, *Surviving Trench Warfare: Technology and the Canadian Corps, 1914–1918* (University of Toronto Press, 1992), pp.5–6, 89–91, 134, 167–87, 189–215.

7. Robin Prior and Trevor Wilson, 'What Manner of Victory? Reflections on the Termination of the First World War', in *Revue Internationale d'Histoire Militaire*, No.72 (1990), pp.91, 96.

8. Prior and Wilson, *Command on the Western Front: The Military Career of Sir Henry Rawlinson, 1914–18*, (Oxford: Blackwell, 1992), p.305; see also pp.300, 339. Another scholar, Tim Travers, argues that, during the 'Hundred Days', Haig and GHQ became irrelevant from a tactical standpoint. In the transition from positional to mobile warfare, when the BEF had to cope with a mixture of set-piece assaults and periods of movement, the methods used, says Travers, 'had nothing to do with the prewar principles preached by the top brass at GHQ, but resulted from developments at army, corps and divisional level'. See Tim Travers, *How the War was Won: Command and Technology in the British Army on the Western Front, 1917–1918*, (London: Routledge, 1992), pp.109, 145–51.

9. Paddy Griffith, *Battle Tactics of the Western Front: The British Army's Art of Attack, 1916–18* (New Haven and London: Yale University Press, 1994), pp.52–9.

10. Ibid., pp.60–2.

11. Ibid., pp.76–7.

12. Ibid., p.194.

13. Ibid., pp.78, 84–5, 93.

14. Ibid., pp.22–3, 27.

15. They include John Lee, a group led by Dr John Bourne and Dr Bob Bushaway of the University of Birmingham, Dr G. D. Sheffield of the Department of War Studies at Sandhurst, and Chris McCarthy, Bryn Hammond and myself at the Imperial War Museum. Similar work has been undertaken in Ireland, notably by Dr Terence Denman and Nicholas Perry.

16. The principal sources for the survey were the appropriate divisional war diaries, housed at the Public Record Office, Kew, under class WO 95; and the *Official History (OH), 1918*, Vols. IV and V.

17. Elliott papers, letter to C. E. W. Bean, undated (*c*. 1930), Australian War Memorial (AWM) 2DRL/513, Item 42A.

18. Diary of Lieutenant S. R. Traill, entry of 29 April 1918, AWM 2DRL/0711, File No. 12/11/5106.

19. Monash papers, typescript of 'War Letters of General Monash', Vol. II, see under 4 April 1918, AWM 3DRL/2316. Judging by the content of the letter in question, part of it, including the second of these two short quotations, was actually written on or around 9 April, soon after the start of the German Lys offensive.

20. A copy of this letter can be found in the Elliott papers, AWM 2DRL/513, Item 16. There is also a copy in the Monash papers.

21. Letter from Sergeant L. F. S. Elliott to his mother and sisters, 10 August 1918, AWM 2DRL/0213, File No. 12/11/1191.

22. Diary of Captain G. W. Parramore, entry for 27 Aug. 1918, AWM PR 00212, File No. 93/0012.

23. Monash papers, typescript of 'War Letters of General Monash', Vol. II, see under 11 Sept. 1918, AWM 3DRL/2316. The words in square brackets have been crossed out in red ink on the original typescript, presumably to tone the letter down, as most of them do not appear in the version published in F. M. Cutlack (ed.), *War Letters of General Monash* (Sydney: Angus and Robertson, 1935), p.268. The words 'unintelligent' and 'sheep-like', which Monash also uses in this letter to describe British troops, are similarly omitted from the published version.

24. See also Bill Gammage, *The Broken Years: Australian Soldiers in the Great War* (Canberra: Australian National University Press, 1974), especially Chs 7 and 8.

25. Eric Andrews, *The Anzac Illusion: Anglo-Australian Relations during World War I* (Cambridge University Press, 1993), pp.60–3, 86, 101–2, 143–51, 154–9, 178–9.

26. Major A. F. Becke, *History of the Great War: Order of Battle of Divisions, Parts 1 to 4* (HMSO, London, 1939–45), *passim*. The 66th (2nd East Lancashire) Division, which was reconstituted during the summer of 1918, contained battalions drawn from Salonika and

Palestine as well as the South African Brigade, which was subsequently transferred from the 9th (Scottish) Division.

27. From the details given in *OH, 1918*, Vols. IV and V, it would appear that the Canadian and Australian divisions which saw most action in the 'Hundred Days' were respectively, the 4th Canadian Division (31 attacks in 26, 'battle days') and the 3rd Australian Division (29 attacks in 21 'battle days').

28. General Sir John Coleridge to Brigadier-General Sir James Edmonds, 15 April 1938, PRO CAB 45/184.

29. *OH, 1918*, Vol. V, p.179. See also Winter, *Haig's Command*, p.148; and Desmond Morton, 'The Canadian Military Experience in the First World War, 1914–18', in R. J. Q. Adams (ed.), *The Great War, 1914–1918: Essays on the Military, Political and Social History of the First World War* (London: Macmillan, 1990), pp.89–90.

30. David Kelsall, *Stockport Lads Together: The 6th Cheshire Territorials, 1908–1919* (Stockport Metropolitan Borough Council, 1989), p.39.

31. John Ewing, *The History of the 9th (Scottish) Division, 1914–1919* (London: Murray, 1921), pp.82, 332–3; John Buchan, *The History of the South African Forces in France* (London: Nelson, 1920), pp.209, 224–5.

32. Winter, op.cit., p.148.

33. 'The British Armies in France as gathered from censorship', Haig Diary, Appendix to July 1918, PRO WO 256/33.

34. Charles Douie, *The Weary Road: Recollections of a Subaltern of Infantry* (London: Murray, 1929), pp.15–16.

35. *Statistics of the Military Effort of the British Empire during the Great War, 1914–1920* (London: HMSO, 1922), pp.269–71.

36. Prior and Wilson, *Command on the Western Front*, p.391.

37. See, for instance, C. E. W. Bean, *Official History of Australia in the War of 1914–1918* (Sydney: Angus and Robertson), Vol. I (1921), pp.7, 47, 607, and Vol. VI (1942), p.1085; also Pierre Berton, *Vimy* (Penguin edn, Canada, 1987), pp.49–50, 61, 63, 160–1, 236–7, 298.

38. *Statistics of the Military Effort of the British Empire*, p.235; Keith Simpson, 'The Officers', in Ian F. W. Beckett and Keith Simpson (eds), *A Nation in Arms: A Social Study of the British Army in the First World War* (Manchester University Press, 1985), pp.79–83.

39. Peter Simkins, *Kitchener's Army: The Raising of the New Armies, 1914–16* (Manchester University Press, 1988), p.20; John Springhall, *Youth, Empire and Society: British Youth Movements, 1883–1940* (London: Croom Helm, 1970), pp.14–16, 29–30, 37–46, 53–64, 124–6; P. Wilkinson, 'English youth movements, 1908–30', *Journal of Contemporary History*, Vol. 4, No. 2, (1969), pp. 3–24; M. D. Blanch, 'Imperialism, nationalism and organised youth', in J. Clarke, C. Critcher and R. Johnson (eds), *Working Class Culture* (London: Hutchinson, 1979), pp.103–120.

40. G. D. Sheffield, 'Officer–Man Relations, Morale and Discipline in the British Army, 1902–22', unpublished PhD thesis, University of London, 1994. I am greatly indebted to Dr Sheffield for allowing me to read his doctoral thesis while I was preparing this chapter.

41. Tim Travers, *How the War was Won*, pp.7–9, 175–82.

42. General Sir John Coleridge to Edmonds, 15 April 1938, PRO CAB 45/184.

43. Captain C. H. Cooke, *Historical Records of the 9th (Service) Battalion Northumberland Fusiliers* (Newcastle and Gateshead Chamber of Commerce, 1928), p.107; 9th Northumberland Fusiliers, War Diary, June 1918–August 1919, PRO WO 95/3062.

44. *OH, 1918*, Vol.IV, p. 345; 1/5th Duke of Wellington's Regiment, War Diary, Feb. 1918–April 1919, PRO WO 95/3086; 62nd Division, War Diary, Aug. 1918–Aug. 1919, PRO WO 95/3071.

45. *OH, 1918*, Vol.IV, pp.333, 484–8; Major-General Sir Arthur B. Scott and P. Middleton Brumwell (eds), *History of the 12th (Eastern) Division in the Great War, 1914–1918* (London: Nisbet, 1923), pp.198–200, 206–7, 222–3; 9th Royal Fusiliers, War Diary, June 1915–June 1919, PRO WO 95/1857; 6th Buffs, War Diary, June 1915–March 1919, PRO WO 95/1860; 35th Infantry Brigade, War Diary, Jan. 1918–May 1919, PRO WO 95/1849; 36th Infantry Brigade, War Diary, Jan. 1918–June 1919, PRO WO 95/1855; 12th Division, War Diary, Aug. 1918–June 1919, PRO WO 95/1827.

46. *OH, 1918*, Vol. IV, pp.230–2; 37th Division, War Diary, July 1918–March 1919, PRO WO 95/2515.
47. *OH, 1918*, Vol. IV, pp.243–7; 21st Division, War Diary, Jan. 1918–Aug. 1918, PRO WO 95/2133; 64th Infantry Brigade, War Diary, June 1917–March 1919, PRO WO 95/2160.
48. *OH, 1918*, Vol. V, pp.175–8, 357–9; 25th Division, War Diary, May 1918–Feb. 1919, PRO WO 95/2227; 75th Infantry Brigade, War Diary, Sept. 1916–Feb. 1919, PRO WO 95/2249.
49. *OH, 1918*, Vol. V, pp.428–30; 35th Division, War Diary, July 1918–March 1919, PRO WO 95/2470.
50. See Paddy Griffith, *Battle Tactics of the Western Front*, pp.79–83. The élite 'assault spearhead' identified by Dr Griffith included most of the regular formations as well as the 9th, 11th, 14th, 15th, 18th, 19th, 21st, 30th, 33rd, 36th, 46th, 47th, 51st, 55th and 56th Divisions. The other formations which appear to have employed skilful small-unit tactics most frequently during the 'Hundred Days' were the 12th, 17th, 24th, 25th, 32nd, 35th, 37th, 38th, 41st, 42nd, 50th, 52nd, 57th, 58th and 62nd Divisions.
51. *OH, 1918*, Vol. IV, pp.335, 395.
52. Captain G. H. F. Nichols, *The 18th Division in the Great War* (Edinburgh and London: Blackwood, 1922), pp.433–50; *OH, 1918*, Vol. V, pp.355–61, 372–5; 18th Division, War Diary, Jan. 1918–March 1919, PRO WO 95/2017.
53. See, for example, *OH, 1918*, Vol. IV, pp.82, 183, 192, 515.
54. Griffith, op.cit., p.22.
55. Ibid., pp.185–6.
56. See, for instance, Griffith, op.cit., pp.179–91. A detailed checklist of the tactical instruction manuals and pamphlets in the CDS/SS series, which were distributed through the Army Printing and Stationery Services in France, appeared in successive issues of the journal *The Great War, 1914–1918*, edited by Peter T. Scott, between 1989 and 1991.
57. Rawling, *Surviving Trench Warfare*, pp.6, 46, 67–8, 86, 97–8, 136, 187.
58. Scott and Brumwell (eds), *History of the 12th (Eastern) Division*, pp.190–230; 12th Division, War Diary, Aug. 1918–June 1919, PRO WO 95/1827.

CHAPTER FOUR

The Operational Role of British Military Police on the Western Front, 1914–18[1]

G. D. Sheffield

The morale and discipline of the BEF on the Western Front has aroused considerable scholarly and popular interest. However, surprisingly little attention has been paid to a body which had a central role in the enforcement of discipline, namely the Corps of Military Police (CMP, or Redcaps). Furthermore, one of the principal duties of the CMP – traffic control – has been almost entirely ignored. The relationship between an army and its military police is rarely easy, and the Great War perhaps marked the nadir of this relationship as far as the British Army was concerned. Other ranks[2] and officers[3] united in whole-hearted condemnation of the CMP. Two former infantry privates claimed that military police were never to be seen 'in the danger area', and that few civil policemen became Redcaps; the latter's job 'was voluntary and few decent men would undertake it if they realised what it implied'.[4] Historians have mostly been content to accept such judgements at face value,[5] and for Redcap have read, it seems, 'martinet', 'sadist', and 'enemy of the ordinary fighting soldier'.[6] This chapter will seek to demonstrate that such views contain a strange mixture of fact, error, opinion and prejudice.

The military police are certainly worthy of study, if for no other reason than that their numbers grew dramatically during the war years. Englander and Osborne have calculated that the growth rate of the CMP 'greatly exceeded that of the army itself'.[7] They link this growth rate to an increase in disciplinary problems in the British Army; but this chapter will argue that other factors should also be considered. Military police were not used solely in their traditional role of enforcing discipline. They also formed traffic control companies, were responsible for disposal of prisoners of war (POW) and came to have an important role on the battlefield, to mention just three of their duties. The growth of the CMP can be seen as a paradigm of the growth of the BEF as a whole, from a small, relatively unsophisticated organisation into a large and vastly more complex body. The expansion of the numbers of military police should be viewed in the context of the general proliferation of specialist units – such as tank and machine gun units and trench mortar batteries – that became necessary as the BEF adapted and changed to suit the conditions of modern industrialised warfare. In short, the war saw the CMP develop from a small organisation 'concerned solely with the enforcement of discipline at military stations and in the base towns of overseas theatres of war, to a Corps containing thousands of men, which had acquired an essential operational role both in the rear and in the forward areas'.[8] Although tasks such as the enforcement of rear area discipline were important, this chapter will, after a brief survey of organisation and personnel, concentrate on the operational role of the military police in controlling stragglers and traffic, with a particular case study of the 1918 spring retreats.

In 1914, British military policemen fell into three categories: Regimental Police (RP), Garrison Military Police (GMP) and members of the CMP. The first were simply soldiers chosen to perform police duties on a temporary basis in their unit.[9] The GMP were somewhat similar, being seconded from their units to police garrison towns; in 1916 most were incorporated into the CMP.[10] The CMP itself was divided into the Military Mounted Police and Military Foot Police (MMP and MFP).[11] Members of the CMP were volunteers who had served at least four years in the army, were of exemplary character and had transferred to the corps from their parent regiments. They were the only MPs who were entitled to wear the red cap cover.[12]

On 4 August 1914, the strength of the CMP was a mere three officers and 508 NCOs and men. This meagre figure was increased to 776 by the influx of reservists on mobilisation.[13] The demand for military policemen soon outpaced the supply. As early as 2 September 1914 the CMP was opened to direct enlistment for the first time, and (*pace* Brophy and Partridge) a number of civilian policemen did join the corps.[14] In addition, some units were transferred *en bloc* to provost work, without becoming members of the CMP. Paradoxically, considering the strictly limited opportunities for cavalry on the Western Front, the mobility of the mounted military policeman made him an extremely desirable asset for patrolling behind the static front. Three parties from the Bedfordshire Yeomanry, for example, were transferred in the autumn of 1914 to serve as the divisional police of 48th Division.[15] Yeomen were also called upon to serve as dismounted policemen. In January 1917 it was reported that 460 men of the Hampshire Yeomanry, serving in IX Corps, had been trained in traffic control duties – of whom 51 were so employed at any one time. Cyclist units were also much used in this role.[16] While Yeomanry and cyclists had other duties in addition to provost work, some units were transferred permanently to it. From the beginning of 1917, two garrison battalions of infantry regiments served in France under the orders of the Provost-Marshal. In addition, from 1916 onwards, substantial numbers of men who had been serving as GMP were temporarily transferred to the CMP, and the CMP received a small number of con-scripts.[17] Englander and Osborne calculated that in 1914 the ratio of military policemen to soldiers stood at 1:3,306. In 1918 the ratio was 1:292.[18] Impressive as these figures are, they exclude a large number of men who were used on provost work but did not wear the badge of the CMP. The highest estimate of the number employed on provost duties suggests that some 25,000 were involved world-wide. The Provost-Marshal in France claimed to have 12,000 men under his command on the Western Front, and this figure seems plausible.[19]

Although the CMP expanded to a peak of 151 warrant-officers and 13,325 other ranks in 1918, the corps could still boast only three officers.[20] Other officers were drafted in as varying grades of Provost-Marshal to command detachments of military police. In October 1918, there were 175 of these officers serving in France. The most common variety of Assistant Provost-Marshal (APM) were those graded as staff captains. An analysis of the provenance of those 64 officers appointed to this position from August 1914 to May 1915 reveals that about a third were regular officers who had retired or were on the reserve. If one adds in special reserve, territorial and other categories of reserve officer, one arrives at a figure of approximately 75 per cent of APMs drawn from reserve sources.[21]

The Great War saw something of a leap in the social quality of the Provost-Marshal. The highest ranking provost officer in 1914 had been Major R. J. A. Terry who acted as Provost-Marshal and Commandant of the CMP. By the end of the war, there were two brigadier-generals who served as provost-marshals in France and Britain respectively.[22] Numerous Guards-men served as provost officers, including the Honourable Clive Bigham, later Lord Mersey, who was the Provost-Marshal at Gallipoli.[23] The evidence suggests that many provost officers were older men, or men who had been wounded. In short, many officers of the provost branch were not taken from 'teeth-arm' units, but were 'dug-outs' or men who, for one reason or another, were no longer fit for front-line duty. Service as a provost officer allowed them to fulfil a valuable, and increasingly socially acceptable, role.[24]

Did the military police deserve their unsavoury reputation? Some probably did. Much of the fury of the men who mutinied at Étaples Base Camp in September 1917 was directed against military policemen rather than against their own officers,[25] leading one historian to describe the disturbance as 'a case of loyal indiscipline'.[26] As early as May 1916, there seem to have been cases of military policemen abusing their authority at Étaples,[27] and the APM, Captain E. Strachan of the 10th Lancashire Fusiliers, seems to have been an unpopular, although efficient, officer.[28] It was the shooting of an infantryman by a military policeman, Private H. Reeve, which sparked off the mutiny, although, interestingly, Reeve seems to have been a Camp Policeman (a 'species' of GMP) rather than a member of the CMP.[29]

However, before damning the entire provost branch on the evidence of Étaples, one must consider certain factors. By the very nature of things, relations between an army and its military police are seldom harmonious. In the case of the Great War, many soldiers felt that they were in the hands of an arbitrary and impersonal military machine,[30] and that the Redcaps were a visible symbol of authority and liable to be hated as such, even if the individual military policeman was not officious. In addition, one cannot ignore the strong probability that the antipathy of the working class towards civilian police was carried over into the army and transferred to the CMP.[31] There was a sharp division between front-line soldiers and those who served in the rear, and a common misperception existed that the CMP carried out their duties very much in the rear, safe from every danger. As will be demonstrated, this was not the case. Broadly speaking, the MFP (many of whom were not fit for front-line duty)[32] performed duties on the lines of communication, while the MMP served just behind the front lines. Controlling traffic within the battle area was a particularly dangerous activity. C. S. Havers, a former Essex policeman, was wounded by shell fire while on traffic duty near Ypres in 1917 and while he was recuperating in hospital his Chief Constable wrote to say that, to date, 17 other Essex constables, many of whom apparently served in the CMP, had been killed or died of disease.[33] Over 50 members of the CMP received the DCM and over 85 were killed on active service or died of wounds on the Western Front alone, in addition to an unknown number of cyclists, yeomen and the like who became casualties while carrying out provost duties.[34]

What were the attitudes of yeomen, cyclists and other temporary military policemen towards their new employment? Evidence on this point is not easy to find. One historian wrote, somewhat lamely, that 'It has not been recorded that any of these units objected to the transfer',[35] and, in fact, the men of the Bedfordshire Yeomanry, who transferred in autumn 1914, reacted with great enthusiasm to the move, believing that it would mean they would soon see active service – and, indeed, they did cross to France three months before their parent regiment.[36] However, before too rosy a view is taken, it is worth mentioning the evidence of 'Howard', a member of the Royal Wiltshire Yeomanry who was attached to the APM of 4th Division. In a letter of June 1916 he mentioned that, having had several previous posts, he was now serving as a policeman. Two weeks later he wrote that he was now attached to the APM of 7th Division and was not entirely happy in this new role, in part because his peripatetic lifestyle meant that he had difficulty in receiving his mail.[37] Although this is the evidence of just one, possibly unrepresentative, soldier, it acts as a salutary corrective to the traditional 'infantryman's' view that the military police were a collection of danger-shirking martinets who joined this corps in order to give free rein to their sadistic tendencies.

The BEF of 1914 had no clearly defined battlefield role for military police.[38] At the end of the year GHQ found it necessary to issue guidance on provost duties, based on the experience of 5th Division. These instructions amounted to only 14 paragraphs, of which only one referred to duties on the line of march, and none gave any indication that the CMP might be of use on the battlefield.[39] Nevertheless, by early 1915 they had begun to play a minor but significant role on the battlefield: a role which was to become increasingly important as the war went on.

The CMP had first proved useful in rounding up large numbers of men who straggled from their units during the retreat from Mons, and in shepherding them back to their units – a duty which was reflected in the GHQ instructions mentioned above. Although some limited use was made of military police as a 'battle stop' as early as the battle of Le Cateau (26 August 1914), the fighting on the Aisne in September was the first occasion on which the CMP were deployed on a large scale to round up battle stragglers.[40] During the first battle of Ypres, in October–November 1914, the problem began to escalate alarmingly.[41] Haig noted in his diary on 4 December 1914 that 'we have to take special precautions during a battle to post police, to prevent more men than necessary from accompanying a wounded man back from the firing line!'[42] The small numbers of military policemen available – 25 MMP were allocated to each division, and a further six (or possibly seven) were included in the establishment of a corps – proved to be woefully inadequate and their numbers had to be supplemented by untrained personnel.[43] This seems to have been arranged informally during First Ypres, but by the time of Neuve Chapelle, in March 1915, men were detached before the battle from their units for provost work.[44] Neuve Chapelle was the turning point in the history of the CMP: it established beyond a shadow of doubt that the CMP did indeed have a battlefield role.

What was this role? Essentially, the deployment of a line of 'straggler posts' acted as a barrier to men attempting to leave the front line, but it would be wrong to see straggler posts simply as a way of keeping reluctant soldiers in the killing zone. Under the conditions of battle, many men became separated from their units for quite legitimate reasons, and straggler posts served to collect these men, if necessary rearm them, and direct them back to their units. Indeed, a post-war report compiled by the CMP recommended the use of the terms 'battle stop' and 'collecting post' rather than 'straggler post', as the latter term 'is one of often undeserving reproach to a soldier, frequently only anxious to discover his Unit.'[45] A 'battle stop' was defined as the forward straggler post, located just behind the front lines. At Loos, for example, those of one formation of IV Corps, 7th Division, were situated 'at the end of every communication trench'.[46] Those of another corps were situated considerably further back and proved to be far less useful because, in the words of a post-war report, 'the further back stragglers get, the longer is the journey to rejoin their units.'[47] Collecting posts, as the name implies, were the positions where stragglers intercepted by the battle stops were sent, ready for distribution to their units. From First Ypres onwards, the practice was for one CMP NCO to be placed in charge of the battle stop and one or two at each collecting post, with three or four non-CMP personnel under their command.[48] Interestingly, given the CMP's reputation, one of the functions of these posts was to provide food, water and hot tea for stragglers, a policy which foreshadows the modern practice of sympathetic forward treatment of psychiatric casualties.[49] At Neuve Chapelle, in March 1915, for example, a number of men who had lost their way were collected by military police, fed at the collecting posts and escorted back to their units on the following morning.[50] Straggler posts also proved themselves useful in many other ways: in directing traffic, escorting POW to the rear, and guiding reinforcements.[51] On occasion, straggler posts served the function of a last ditch fighting reserve. On 11 November 1914, the APM of 1st Division won the DSO leading a mixed party of military police and stragglers in a counter-attack near the Menin Road.[52]

Notwithstanding these 'positive' aspects of battlefield provost work, it did of course contain a strong element of coercion: of preventing unauthorised personnel from leaving the battle area. The growth in the importance of this work can be seen by comparing the thin red-capped line of 1914 with the vastly more sophisticated provost arrangements of Third and Fifth Armies in March 1918. By that time Fifth Army had three separate lines of straggler posts, organised by division, corps and army respectively, each comprising forward battle stops and rearward collecting stations as shown in Figure 4.1. Patrols of MMP visited the posts at regular intervals. VI Corps of Third Army also had military policemen posted at separate collecting stations for walking wounded, ready to remove them to straggler posts if the medical officer believed they were malingering. Behind these three lines were to be found both traffic control units and patrols of MMP, with orders to round up stragglers. Beyond them again were two lines of 'examination posts', which served the same purpose as a fielder placed on the boundary of a cricket field. Unlike the full range of straggler posts which were deployed immediately before action, examination posts were a permanent fixture.[53]

Apart from serving as a general deterrent for would-be absconders, the importance of straggler posts varied with the circumstances of battle and the morale of the army at any given time. Between 1 April 1917 and 11 November 1918, a total of 67 men were arrested as absentees from their units at the examination posts manned by D Company of 2nd (G) Battalion, King's Own Yorkshire Light Infantry (KOYLI). As one might expect, there was a degree of correlation between numbers of arrests and dates of battles. The two months in which most arrests were made coincide with the dates of the battles of Arras and Amiens in April 1917 and August 1918 respectively, although records for the vital March–April 1918 period are incomplete.[54] The

usefulness of straggler posts also varied from battle to battle. At Loos, in
September 1915, they proved extremely useful in rounding up and reorganising the survivors of the ill-fated attack of 21st and 24th Divisions as they fell
back in disorder through the British positions.[55] On the Somme, on 1 July
1916, however, there were very few stragglers; despite the disaster to British
arms, morale remained relatively high. The APM of 4th Division could
remember coming across only one straggler on that day, while 30th Division
recorded only seven, and none at all during operations conducted on 23
July.[56] Generally speaking, it would appear that there was a greater need for
straggler posts during defensive operations than during offensive ones, and
that successful operations produced fewer stragglers than unsuccessful ones.
At Bullecourt in 1917, 70 men routed and were stopped by the straggler
posts, while during the taking of Messines Ridge several months later, IX
Corps deployed 44 men on straggler post duties, but had to deal with only 19
stragglers in all.[57]

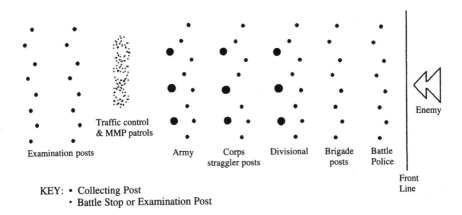

FIGURE 4.1: THE NOMINAL LAYOUT OF MILITARY POLICE
BEHIND FIFTH ARMY'S POSITIONS, MARCH 1918

Before they could even reach the lines of straggler posts, stragglers were
often confronted with 'battle police'. It is often difficult to disentangle fact
from fiction when discussing this subject. According to one historian, before
the Somme offensive in July 1916, many units were informed that men who
hung back in an attack would be summarily executed by military police. This
author goes on to cite an example, based on uncorroborated oral evidence, of
the execution of two soldiers by 'Red Caps' [sic]: in the trenches.[58] There are
a number of difficulties involved in accepting this story, quite apart from the
illegality of the executions. Firstly, it is difficult to see what purpose such
executions would serve, since it was the policy of GHQ to publicise

executions in the belief that they would serve as a deterrent to others.[59] Secondly, MMP were husbanded as a precious resource for use behind the lines and it is unlikely that two Redcaps would have been available to patrol the trenches: the CMP seem to have had responsibility for policing the area behind the trenches but not the trenches themselves.

Although the evidence is not entirely clear, in one corps at least the responsibility for policing the trenches on 1 July rested with the individual brigades, with a troop of yeomanry being provided for patrolling the rear-most communication trenches.[60] Other evidence suggests that 'battle police' were drawn from sources other than the CMP. The 2 West Yorkshires deployed their Provost-Sergeant and the Regimental Police to arrest – but not shoot – men who 'returned improperly' from their attack on Ypres on 3 July 1917. Similarly, in August 1917, 3rd Australian Division was posting its RPs in communication trenches to 'form the first line of Battle Stops', among other tasks.[61] Battle police were undoubtedly useful. This is illustrated by the suggestion of one officer that insufficient numbers of them were deployed by 36th (Ulster) Division on 1 July 1916. After their initial attack, the trenches were crowded with stragglers, many of whom were unwounded but were lacking arms and any form of organisation, and in some cases blocking com-munication trenches.[62] At this point, battle police, if available in sufficient numbers, would have been invaluable in reorganising these stragglers. It would also appear that the deployment or otherwise of battle police depended upon the whim of an individual unit or formation commander. It was not a universal practice, and one historian has concluded that 'most privates were not sure whether [battle police] existed or not'.[63]

Some extravagant claims have been made about the use of battle police in maintaining the discipline of the BEF;[64] but it is clear that, whatever their composition, on rare occasions they were sometimes used to shoot stragglers. However most decisions to begin shooting at one's own men seem to have been taken entirely unofficially, at a local level by harassed officers or NCOs faced with routing troops. Rarely was this officially sanctioned. It is instructive to compare the orders given on 25 June 1916 to the straggler posts of the New Zealand Division to fire on men who refused to halt when ordered to do so,[65] or the behaviour of the notorious Brigadier-General F. P. Crozier, who had considerable enthusiasm for the practice of shooting his own men, with the reaction of the British high command to the situation on the Aisne in May 1918.[66] During that period of crisis the commander of 19th Division asked GHQ for the power to 'confirm and have carried out' death sentences on stragglers. This request was refused.[67] Although British military justice of the period can be criticised, the fact remains that the processes of military law, which demanded that death sentences be confirmed by the commander-in-chief, were adhered to even at a time of crisis. In sum, the evidence suggests that the image of the brutal

Redcap, deployed by a cynical high command to patrol the trenches and force the 'PBI' into action at the point of a revolver, is a misleading caricature of the truth.

The German offensives of March–April 1918 presented the provost branch with its greatest challenge of the war. The experience of XIX Corps may stand as representative of the way in which that challenge was met. This corps, commanded by Sir H. E. Watts, held a frontage of about 12,000 yards on 21 March, and was sandwiched between Congreve's VII Corps to the north and Maxse's XVIII Corps to the south. Two divisions – 66th and 24th – were stationed in the front line.[68] Their divisional straggler posts were established on a line between 3,500 yards and about 6,000 yards from the front line. This was much further back than had been the practice in earlier battles, but is probably a reflection of the fact that defence in depth had been adopted by this stage, and in fact the divisional straggler posts ran down the centre of the Battle Zone, in which the main fighting was expected to take place. Four collecting posts had been established with the furthest, at Montigny Farm, lying about 6,500 yards behind the front line. The straggler posts were manned at about 6.00 a.m., and by 11.00 a.m., the enemy were attacking the Battle Zone, having already cleared the obstacle of the forward zone. This brought chaos to the British line. At about 12.30 Captain Westmacott, APM of 24th Division, arrived at Vermand, where there was both a battle stop and a collecting post. He found a body of wounded and unwounded men from the infantry and artillery, many lacking weapons, streaming back as a mob across the bridge with the military police doing little to prevent them crossing. Westmacott held up the crowd with his revolver, helped by a sergeant in the North Staffords. He then armed 40 men with rifles taken from the wounded, and pressed them into service as temporary military policemen. As soon as his back was turned, these men ran away. Westmacott then took more drastic action, pressing another 20 stragglers into service. Arming his own Redcaps with rifles (normally they only carried revolvers), he ordered them to shoot these men should they attempt to abscond. He and his military policemen then served under the battalion headquarters of 13 Middlesex until he was ordered to retire, having been lightly wounded by shellfire.

This was the pattern for the remainder of the retreat: as the enemy approached, provost personnel fell back to fresh positions and resumed their duties until the approach of the enemy once again forced them to retire. They shared most of the discomforts and many of the experiences of the infantry. On 27 March, the situation was so critical that Westmacott was forced to send most of his police to fight in the front line. On other occasions he was able to distribute much-needed rations to the infantry. From his reports, it is clear that the military police were not always as efficient as they might have been. A report of 1 April was extremely critical of XIX Corps straggler posts for being too lenient, and he used his divisional police to conduct a house-to-house search in rear villages to flush out stragglers, even though this should have been a corps responsibility. Nevertheless, it is clear that the provost staff of XIX Corps on the whole coped well with the enormous responsibilities placed upon them by the retreat.[69]

What were the achievements of military police in the March retreat? A post-war report estimated that at least 25,000 stragglers were collected, fed, and put back into the fighting.[70] This figure is almost certainly an underestimate. A detailed set of figures has survived which reveal that 11,214 stragglers (of whom four were officers) were collected by XIX Corps from 21 March to 5 April.[71] Admittedly this corps was very heavily engaged; but it was only one of four corps in Fifth Army. Third Army also suffered a number of stragglers: for example IX Corps collected 200 in the first two days of the battle.[72] Where possible, stragglers were directed back to their original units, but sometimes they were formed into composite battalions. Occasionally, at particularly desperate moments, military police led them into action.[73] One account of the fighting by a member of Carey's Force (an *ad hoc* force) who clearly was no admirer of the Redcaps, serves to illustrate the importance of military police during the March retreat. This soldier, A. W. Bradbury, saw men fleeing from their trenches, which were being shelled, only to be rounded up and returned to their positions by armed military police. Although Bradbury expressed incredulity at the notion of military policemen appearing in a place of danger, he admitted that the poor standard of the infantry justified such drastic measures.[74]

The effectiveness of the provost arrangements is indicated by the fact that, according to the report of Fifth Army's Deputy Provost-Marshal (DPM), less than 100 men from the fighting arms got back as far as army headquarters and he was able to state categorically that 'At no time during the retreat was the straggler position out of hand, and much larger numbers could have been dealt with.'[75] In effect, the CMP maintained a tight cordon behind the Fifth and Third Armies, a cordon which undoubtedly helped maintain cohesion during the retreat. The problem which would have resulted if the BEF had not developed relatively sophisticated provost arrangements by 1918 is demonstrated by the situation which arose when the Guards Division went into action having neglected to deploy straggler posts. This formation, according to one source, claimed that it simply did not need them. As a provost officer of a neighbouring formation drily commented, 'This sounds very well in theory but in practice it broke the continuity of the Straggler Post lines, and allowed the leakage of a number of troops from various divisions. Had these stragglers been directed to their units by posts well up behind the front lines, they would have never have wandered as far back as they . . . did.'[76] In fact, relatively few Guardsmen were separated from their units, but those who did wandered a considerable distance before reaching a straggler post that could direct them back; a further reminder that not all 'stragglers' were deliberately running towards safety. Thus not only did the absence of straggler posts from behind the Guards Division allow stragglers from neighbouring formations to get much further back than would otherwise have been possible, but valuable time was wasted in getting troops, fit and ready to fight, back into the firing line.

There is much to be learned about the morale and discipline of the army as a whole from a study of straggler control. The impression created in 1918 by Lloyd George and others was that Fifth Army collapsed in rout, a line which has been followed by some historians.[77] It is thus interesting to find that provost sources are unanimous in agreeing that the majority of stragglers in the early stages of the battle were not drawn from front-line units. Fifth Army's DPM wrote in his after-action report that 'During the first two days' fighting Battle stragglers from the firing-lines were few and were chiefly those who were genuinely lost and anxious to rejoin their units'.[78] Who, then, were the stragglers that undoubtedly headed for the rear at the beginning of the German offensive? Many of them appear to have been non-combatants. The Germans attacked when Fifth Army was still constructing its defensive positions on the principles (new to the British Army) of 'elastic' defence in depth. In mid-March 1918 approximately 12,200 Italians, 5,200 Chinese, 10,300 POW, 4,500 Indians and 35,800 British were engaged on labouring duties in Fifth Army's rear.[79] When the blow fell on 21 March, these men were spread out over the length and breadth of the army area. In the words of the army's DPM, although Labour companies may have begun the march out of the fighting area in good order, 'they did not remain so for long without straggling towards the rear along the main routes'. Many of these men were insufficiently fit to march in formation and thus fell out and straggled; many of those who had weapons were unable to carry them, and threw them away. A special collecting post specifically for Labour personnel had to be established at Villers Bretonneux. 'From a spectacular point of view', wrote Fifth Army's DPM, 'anyone might well think these men stragglers from the firing lines but the Deputy Provost-Marshal and other Officers well qualified to speak maintained that stragglers from the fighting troops did not get away.[80]

As we have seen, there were some 'teeth-arm' men who fled from the battlefield, but it would seem that the real problems of straggling amongst front-line troops did not set in until they had been in retreat for a number of days, and this seems to have been the result of sheer exhaustion. At the beginning of the battle, most stragglers were simply directed back to their units, and sometimes went back unescorted; 'they didn't get to the Army back areas, nor did they attempt to after receiving their directions'.[81] Later, stragglers had to be rested and fed at straggler posts and taken (sometimes by bus) to central collecting points, and then distributed to various units.[82] Some statistical material has survived which supports the anecdotal evidence that has been cited. The busiest periods for the straggler posts of 8th, 16th, 24th, 50th and 66th Divisions occurred at least six days after the battle began, on 27–30 March. These figures do not tell the whole story, for of these formations 16th, 24th and 66th Divisions were in action from 21 March, but only 24 Division records any figures for the first two days of the battle. Either the other divisions did not collect any stragglers then, which is possible, or their figures are incomplete; but the evidence of 24th Division certainly supports the contention that the worst period for stragglers came only towards the end of March. There were 40 stragglers collected on 21 March, 15 on 22 March, ten on 23 March, six on 24 March, 50 on 27 March and 227 on 30 March.[83] These figures do not necessarily mean that the stragglers belonged to the divisions whose straggler posts collected them, for other corps passed through XIX Corps area.

Naturally, this evidence of the state of British morale in the spring of 1918 should not be treated in isolation. Other factors, such as the numbers of British troops taken prisoner by the Germans and examples of the attackers meeting little resistance from British defenders, should also be taken into account. Nevertheless, an examination of the provost records of the March offensive does not leave the reader with the impression of a beaten army which streamed towards the rear in hopeless rout. In March 1918, the system of straggler posts underwent its first major test, in a defensive battle, since April 1915, and the military police emerged with considerable credit. Later, the lessons learned from the March retreat were applied with success at the battle of the Lys, and subsequently during the victorious advance from August to November 1918.

Effective traffic control arrangements were evolved by the provost branch in parallel with those for straggler control. The CMP was involved in traffic control during the early campaigns of the war to a limited extent, but the first major test came during the battle of Loos, which began on 25 September 1915.[84] The British plan called for two raw formations, 21st and 24th Divisions of XI Corps, to be committed to battle once the crust of the German defences had been broken by Haig's First Army. As these divisions were to be held some miles behind the battle front, the plan called for them to make a long and, in the event, exhausting march before being committed to battle. It was the responsibility of First Army's APM, Major E. R. Fitzpatrick, to ensure that the roads were clear so that XI Corps would be in the right place at the right time.

Fitzpatrick made the best use he could of the limited resources at his disposal, establishing 'control points' at key crossroads and road junctions in the rear area, with divisional and corps APMs stationed at key points and the APMs of I and IV Corps patrolling the main roads in motor cars. In the event, the approach march of 21st and 24th Divisions was subject to unnecessary delays, caused in part by poor traffic control, and their attack was an utter failure. The British official historian concluded that traffic control at Loos was reminiscent of an attempt 'to push the Lord Mayor's procession through the streets of London without clearing the route and holding up the traffic'.[85] The affair became entangled in the plots to replace French as Commander-in-Chief by Haig.[86] The failure at Loos had less to do with overzealous and incompetent military policemen than with poor staff work. The problems experienced at Loos led directly to the birth of effective, modern traffic control in the British Army. As a Guards officer was to write after the war, 'I have always understood that the afterwards excellent system of traffic control was evolved as a result of the lessons of that day'.[87]

By the time of the Somme offensive of 1916, it was well understood that the 'Q' (Quartermaster) staff needed to liaise closely with the APM to ensure that traffic on supply routes was properly controlled.[88] While it would be foolish to claim that there were no failures of traffic control,[89] on the whole the system did work well.[90] In July 1916, for example, 18th Division used 37 yeomanry and MMP on traffic control, in addition to some cyclists to man static traffic posts. 18th Division's provost assumed responsibility for four and a half miles of road in the Bray–Carnoy sector on 23 June. The divisional traffic scheme was relatively sophisticated, including diversionary tracks, roadside bays and a breakdown lorry for the clearance of wrecked vehicles. Most traffic was moved under the cover of darkness. On 6–7 July, 23 guns, 175 limbers and 300 wagons were counted moving east along the road, with horse-drawn traffic mixed in with motor vehicles and columns of marching infantry.[91]

The battles of 1917 saw traffic control arrangements become increasingly sophisticated. Haig, who clearly recognised the importance of traffic control, fought a bureaucratic battle against the War Office in the autumn of 1917 to retain adequate numbers of traffic control personnel.[92] For the offensive against Messines Ridge in June 1917, IX Corps alone employed 14 officers and 433 other ranks exclusively on traffic duties. Each divisional area was divided into two sections, each under a traffic control officer. Each section headquarters was linked by telephone to the others, and to the divisional APM. While some problems did arise, the system was fairly successful.[93] An account of a trench raid by 1/6 Londons in February 1917 illustrates traffic management at a much lower level: two-man control posts, apparently manned by RPs, were established in communication trenches for traffic control, to guide wounded and POW.[94]

The British attack at Cambrai on 20 November 1917 demonstrated that surprise could still be achieved on the battlefield. Tanks were brought up to their start lines by night, without lights.[95] Under these conditions, effective traffic control was vital, and the success on this occasion was repeated when the BEF returned to the offensive at Amiens on 8 August 1918, having contained and survived the German spring offensive. The administrative orders issued by Fourth Army on this occasion encapsulated 'the experience of four years of war'. Naturally, traffic control was given careful attention.[96] By 1918, traffic control was taken very seriously indeed by the British Army. The Traffic Control Officer of 31st Division was told on his first morning in the post, 'If you catch Haig breaking traffic regulations, run him in!'[97] Haig himself, a truly 'provost-minded' commander, paid tribute to the importance of traffic control in his final despatch.[98] By 1918, no army could expect to carry out successful operations without having a system of effective traffic control, and the CMP had a vital operational role which was understood and appreciated at the highest level.

In conclusion, it can be seen that the popular view of the Redcaps in the Great War is inaccurate in many ways. The growth of provost was not simply a response to an increase in disciplinary problems. By 1918, the CMP had expanded the scope of its duties and was performing an invaluable operational role in addition to its traditional one. The growth of the provost branch was paralleled by the growth of other specialist formations with highly specialised tasks, and it should be seen in the context of the development of the BEF from a relatively unsophisticated force into what Peter Simkins has described as 'the largest and most complex single organisation created by the British nation up to that time'.[99]

NOTES

1. This chapter is an expanded version of the author's earlier article, 'British Military Police and their Battlefield Role, 1914–18', published in the now sadly defunct *Sandhurst Journal of Military Studies*, No. 1 (RMA Sandhurst, Camberley, 1990), pp.36–46. The present version draws upon material used in his authorised history of the Royal Military Police, *The Redcaps: A History of the Royal Military Police and its Antecedents from the Middle Ages to the Gulf War* (London: Brassey's, 1994), and he is grateful for the support of the Trustees of the RMP and of the Regimental Secretary, Lt-Col (Retd) P. H. M. Squier. He would also like to thank the following institutions for allowing him to use material in their possession: the Imperial War Museum, the KOYLI Museum, the National Army Museum and the Public Record Office.
2. J. F. Lucy, *There's Devil in the Drum* (London: Faber, 1938), p.50.
3. Hamond Mss, 'Wisdom for Warts, Exuded by an Old Sweat', p.7. The author is grateful to Dr R. Hamond for permission to use this material.
4. J. Brophy and E. Partridge, *The Long Trail* (London: Andre Deutsch, 1965), pp.82, 170. For other examples of unfavourable views of the CMP, see J. Murray, *Gallipoli 1915* (London: New English Library, 1977), pp.38–9, 56; H. Warner Mss, p.462, in IWM.
5. A. Babington, *For the Sake of Example* (London: Leo Cooper and Secker & Warburg, 1983), p.xii.
6. See D. Englander and J. Osborne, 'Jack, Tommy and Henry Dubb: The Armed Forces and the Working Class', *Historical Journal*, Vol. 21, No. 3 (1978), p.599.
7. Ibid., p.595.

8. S. F. Crozier, *The History of the Corps of Royal Military Police* (Aldershot: Gale & Polden, 1951), p.27.

9. For accounts of the work of RPs before and during the war, see J. W. Riddell Mss, IWM 77–73–1; H. Munday, *No Heroes, No Cowards* (Milton Keynes: People's Press, 1981), pp.28–30.

10. H. Bullock, *A History of the Provost Marshal and the Provost Service* (Aberdeen: Milne & Hutchinson, 1929), p.68; A. V. Lovell-Knight, *The History of the Office of Provost Marshal and the Corps of Military Police* (Aldershot: Gale & Polden, 1945), pp.68, 70. For an account of the duties of a garrison policeman in India before the war, see W. H. Davies Mss, in NAM 8201–13.

11. Strictly speaking, the CMP did not come into being until 1926, but the MMP and MFP were often lumped together under the heading 'Corps of Military Police' or 'Military Police Corps' before that date. See *Statistics of the Military Effort of the British Empire During the Great War* (London: HMSO, 1922), p.642; Orders 8 May to 9 Oct. 1914, in Royal Military Police Archives (RMPA), Chichester, Acc.680.

12. (J. M. Grierson), *The British Army. By a Lieutenant-Colonel in the British Army* (London: Sampson Low, 1899), p.77; R. Money Barnes, *The British Army of 1914* (London: Seeley Service, 1968), p.283.

13. Orders 4 and 11 Aug. 1914, in RMPA, Acc.680; Lovell-Knight, *History*, op.cit., p.66.

14. For instance, a party of men from Sheffield City Police enlisted early in 1915: R. C. Brookes, 'The Military Police in the First World War', in *Royal Military Police Journal* (third quarter, 1971), p.16.

15. S. Peel, *O. C. Beds. Yeomanry* (London: OUP, 1935), pp.2–3, 17.

16. War Diary (WD) of APM IX Corps, 9–10 Jan. 1917, in PRO WO154 8; WD of A and Q, 8th Division, appendix, 9 June 1916, in PRO WO95 1681.

17. A. V. Lovell-Knight (ed., *The Corps of Military Police* (Morecambe: Morecambe Bay Printers, 1953), p.37; WD of 16th (Garrison) Battalion KOYLI, 10 March 1917, in KOYLI Museum; Lovell-Knight, *History*, op.cit., p.70; Orders 16 Jan. 1916, in RMPA, Acc.683, and 24 July, 30 Aug. 1918, in RMPA, Acc.684.

18. Englander and Osborne, op.cit., p.595.

19. A. V. Lovell-Knight, *The Corps*, op.cit., p.37; H. S. Rogers application for office of Chief Constable, in RMPA First World War file.

20. *Statistics of the Military Effort*, op.cit., p.642.

21. Statistics are drawn from the *Army List* of May 1915.

22. Lovell-Knight, *History*, op.cit., p.68.

23. Viscount Mersey, *A Picture of Life 1872–1940* (London: John Murray, 1941), pp.255–63.

24. Crozier, op.cit., p.18. For an account written by one such APM, see E. A. McKechnie Mss, in RMPA, Acc.1369.

25. WD of Commandant, Étaples Base Camp, 9–14 Sept. 1917, in PRO WO95 4027.

26. J. M. Winter, *The Experience of World War I* (London: Macmillan, 1988), p.159.

27. WD of APM Lines of Communication, 25 and 29 May 1916, in PRO WO154 114.

28. G. Dallas and D. Gill, *The Unknown Army* (London: Verso, 1985), p.73; 22 June 1916, in PRO WO154 114.

29. 9 Sept. 1917, in PRO WO95 4027.

30. This subject is explored further in the present author's 'The Effect of War Service on 22nd Battalion Royal Fusiliers (Kensington) 1914–18 with Special Reference to Morale, Discipline and the Officer–Man Relationship' (unpublished MA thesis, University of Leeds, 1984).

31. C. Emsley, *Policing and its Context 1750–1870* (London: Macmillan, 1983), pp.151–7.

32. 28 Sept. 1915, in PRO WO154 114.

33. Questionnaire (CSH DO2), and Letter to C. S. Havers (CSH DO8), in RMPA, Acc.1667; H. L. Smyth Diary, 25 Sept. 1915, in RMPA First World War file.

34. Lovell-Knight, *History*, op. cit., p.171; *Soldiers who Died in the Great War*, Part 80, Corps of Military Police (1921), pp.87–91.

35. Crozier, op. cit. p.18.

36. Peel, op. cit., pp.2–3.

37. 'Howard' to D. Williams, 1 and 17 June 1916, Miss D. Williams Mss, in IWM 85–4–1.

38. See *Training and Manoeuvre Regulations 1909* (London: HMSO, 1909), pp.74–5; *Field Service Regulations, Part II* (reprinted London: HMSO, 1911), p.120.
39. *Notes from the Front. Collated by the General Staff* (1914), pp.39–41 (copy in NAM).
40. WD of APM 5th Division, 26th Aug. 1914, in PRO WO154 33; and *Straggler Posts*, p.4, in RMPA First World War file. The latter is a short history of the subject which quotes at length from contemporary documents, most of which have now disappeared.
41. RMPA *Straggler Posts*, op. cit., p.4.
42. R. Blake (ed.), *The Private Papers of Douglas Haig, 1914–19* (London: Eyre & Spottis-wode, 1952), p.79.
43. Lovell-Knight, *History*, op. cit., p.77.
44. *Straggler Posts*, op. cit., p.4.
45. Ibid., p.5; WD of IV Corps General (GS), 10 March 1915, in PRO WO95 721; *Straggler Posts*, op. cit. p.2.
46. *Administrative arrangements during the battle of Loos*, lecture given by Lt.-Col. the Hon. M. A. Wingfield, 16 Jan. 1916, in IWM Misc 134, Item 2072. The author is grateful to Mr Nigel Steel of the IWM for bringing this reference to his attention.
47. *Straggler Posts* op. cit., pp.5–6.
48. Ibid., p.5; Wingfield's IWM *Administrative arrangements*, op. cit., p.4; *Provost Arrangements for Defence Scheme*, XVII Corps, 7 March 1919, in RMPA, Mss 305.
49. See L. Belensky, S. Noy and Z. Solomon, 'Battle Stress: the Israeli Experience', in *Military Review*, Vol LXV, No. 7, pp.29–37.
50. *Straggler Posts*, op. cit., p.5.
51. WD of First Army GS, Appendix D, March 1915, in PRO WO95 154; WD of First Army A and Q, Appendix B, March 1915, in PRO WO95 181; RMPA, Mss 322–425.
52. Lovell-Knight, *History*, op. cit., p.87.
53. *Straggler Posts*, op. cit., p.25; *Provost Arrangement VI Corps*, 4 April 1918, in RMPA, Mss 300.
54. WD of 2nd (G) battalion KOYLI, in KOYLI Museum.
55. *Straggler Posts*, op. cit., p.5; Wingfield's *Administrative arrangements* op. cit., pp.4–5.
56. *Straggler Posts*, op. cit., pp.6–7; WD of 30th Division A and Q, *Report on Operations*, July 1916, and 23 July 1916, in PRO WO95 2315.
57. *Straggler Posts*, op. cit., p.7; WD of APM IX Corps, Appendix III, July 1917, in PRO WO95 8.
58. M. Middlebrook, *The First Day on the Somme* (London; Allen Lane, 1971), pp.94, 221. In fairness to this work, which is in other respects admirable, it should be said that at least one war memoir states that for an attack in August 1916 a battalion appointed battle police and instructed them 'to shoot loiterers': 'Mark VII' (Max Plowman), *A Subaltern on the Somme in 1916* (London: Dent, 1928), pp.58–9.
59. See Babington, op. cit., W. Childs, *Episodes and Reflections* (London: Cassell, 1930), pp. 143–5.
60. WD of 30th Division GS, Operational Order 18, 16 June 1916, Appendix G, June 1916, in PRO WO95 2310; Appendix D in IWM, Sir Ivor Maxse papers, 69–53–7, file 23.
61. J. Terraine (ed.), *General Jack's Diary 1914–18* (London: Eyre & Spottiswode, 1964), p.237; WD of APM 3rd Australian Division, Appendix 3, Aug. 1917, in PRO WO154 78.
62. Letter of F. L. Watson, 20 Aug. 1930, in PRO CAB45 138. For a detailed discussion of the importance of the straggler post system on the Somme, by the Assistant Adjutant and Quarter Master General (AA and QMG) of 2nd Division, see letter of J. P. Villiers-Stuart, 29 Jan. 1937, in PRO CAB45 137.
63. J. Ellis, *Eye Deep in Hell* (London: Fontana 1977), p.187.
64. D. Lamb, *Mutinies: 1917–21* (Oxford and London: Solidarity, n.d.), p.4.
65. Quoted in C. Pugsley, *On the Fringe of Hell: New Zealanders and Military Discipline in the First World War* (Auckland: Hodder & Stoughton, 1991), p. 123.
66. F. P. Crozier, *The Men I Killed* (Bath: new edn, Cedric Chivers, 1969), pp.89–90; Lamb, *Mutinies*, op. cit., pp. 3–4.
67. Gen. Sir George Jeffrys to J. E. Edmonds, n.d. (*c.* 1935), in PRO CAB45 114.
68. *OH 1918*, Vol. 1, p.177.
69. This account of XIX Corps' provost branch during the March Retreat is drawn from *APM*

XIX Corps Provost Diary ... 21st March to 5th April 1918 and the series of *APM XIX Corps Report(s) on Operations ... from 21st March to 7th April 1918*, in *Straggler Posts*, op. cit.

70. *Straggler Posts*, op. cit., p.10.
71. Ibid., p.37.
72. 26 March 1918, in PRO WO154 8.
73. *Straggler Posts*, op. cit., p.33; Lovell-Knight, *History* op. cit., pp.82, 84.
74. A. W. Bradbury Mss, p.5, in IWM.
75. *Straggler Posts*, op. cit., pp.25–6
76. Ibid., p.22. Earlier in the campaign the Guards Division apparently had made use of straggler posts: see RMPA, Mss. 284.
77. H. Gough, *Soldiering On* (London: Arthur Barker, 1954), pp.176–8; J. Keegan, *The Face of Battle* (Harmondsworth: Penguin, 1978), p.176.
78. *Straggler Posts*, op. cit., p.25.
79. W. Shaw Sparrow, *The Fifth Army in March 1918* (London: Bodley Head, 1921), p.17.
80. *Straggler Posts*, op. cit., p.25.
81. Ibid., p.26.
82. For a divisional commander's testimony to the efficacy of the provost arrangements, see April 1918, Appendix F, in PRO WO95 2315.
83. *Straggler Posts*, op. cit., p.37.
84. Unless otherwise indicated, this account of traffic control at Loos is based on documents in PRO WO106 390, *Handling of the Reserves at Loos on the 25th September 1915*.
85. *OH 1915*, Vol. II, p.278.
86. T. Travers, *The Killing Ground* (London: Unwin Hyman, 1987), pp.16–19.
87. Letter, Maj.-Gen. Sir G. Jeffreys, n.d., in PRO CAB45 120.
88. Letter, H. B. Wilkinson, 6 May 1930, in PRO CAB45 138.
89. See letter, L. A. G. Bowen, 31 March 1930, in PRO CAB45 132.
90. See diary, 14 July 1916, in H. Dalton papers I/I 106, in British Library of Political and Economic Science, London School of Economics.
91. IWM, Sir Ivor Maxse papers, 69–53–7, file 23.
92. Haig to War Office, 16 Aug. 1917, in PRO WO32 11355.
93. WD of APM IX Corps, *Report on ... action of 7th June 1917*, in PRO WO154 8. See also *Preliminary Notes on Recent Operations on the Front of the Second Army* (London: HMSO, July 1917), p.6.
94. WD of 1/6 Londons, Appendix III to Feb. 1917, in PRO WO95 2729.
95. J. F. C. Fuller, *Memoirs of an Unconventional Soldier* (London: Nicholson & Watson, 1936), p.204.
96. *OH 1918*, Vol. IV, p.18, and Appendix VII, *Fourth Army administrative arrangements of 6th August 1918*.
97. E. L. Roberts, 'Dirty Work at the Crossroads in 1918', in *Great War Adventures* (undated copy in IWM department of printed books), p. 87.
98. J. H. Boraston (ed.), *Sir Douglas Haig's Dispatches* (London: Dent, 1919), p.341.
99. P. Simkins, *Kitchener's Army* (Manchester University Press, 1988), p.xiv.

CHAPTER FIVE

The Treatment of Casualties in the Great War

Geoffrey Noon

War has always been very destructive of human life and limb, and notoriously so in the case of the Great War, yet a popular conception of the medical treatment in that war is that there had been very little advance on practice since the Crimean or American Civil wars. Amputations on the grand scale are believed to have been the only effective treatment, and the majority of wounded men are believed to have died from wound infections. In fact, however, these assumptions were not even partially true in 1914 and were very far from the truth by 1918.

During previous centuries, the treatment of wounds and disease had changed very little, since medicine had advanced very little during that time; but the years between the Crimean War and the Great War produced dramatic advances in most fields of medicine which were to make a great difference to the prognosis of sick and wounded men during the latter conflict. Before 1914, it was usual for there to be a great imbalance between deaths from disease and deaths from wounds; for example, in the American Civil War there was a total of no less than 24 cases of sickness for every wound received, about two deaths to disease for every one to wounds, and mortality rates stood at around 44 per cent for the wounded and four per cent for the sick (see Table 5.1). In the Boer War there were only slightly better figures, with a total of 13 sick men for every one wounded, and 1.8 deaths from disease to every one from wounds.[1]

During the Great War, however, these ratios changed quite dramatically (see Table 5.2). If not in the US Army, certainly in the British Army worldwide, and particularly on the Western Front, there was a reversal to a total of only 1.3 sick men for every one wounded, one death from disease for every ten from wounds, and mortality rates were around eight per cent for the wounded and one per cent for the sick. These improvements were due not only to great advances made in the treatment of disease, but also to improvements in the treatment of wounds and their complications between 1914 and 1918, and particularly to the efficient organisation of the Royal Army Medical Corps (RAMC).

TABLE 5.1
ANALYSIS OF WOUNDS AND SICKNESS IN THE AMERICAN CIVIL WAR, 1861–62

	Union Army	*Confederates (approx.)*	*Total*
Total wounds	246,712	?	
Fatal wounds	110,070 (= 44% mortality)	94,000	204,070
Total non-battle sick	5,825,480	?	
Fatalities from disease	224,586 (= 4% mortality)	164,000	388,586
Fatal accidents, suicide, etc.	24,872	?	24,872+
Total deaths	359,528	258,000	617,528+

Source: Medicine of the Civil War, US National Library of Medicine, p.9.

TABLE 5.2
COMPARISON OF CASUALTY TOTALS IN THREE WARS

	Total	*Battle Casualties ('Wounds')*	*Non-Battle Casualties*
Union Army in American Civil War, 1861–65	6,097,064	246,712 (4%)	5,850,352 (96%)
British Army in Boer War, 1899–1902	430,876	26,750 (7%)	404,126 (93%)
British Army and Dominion Forces on the Western Front, 1914–18	5,517,455	2,174,675 (39%) (of which 7.6% died)	3,342,780 (60%) (of which 0.78% died)
US Army in Europe, 1917–18	3,781,976	218,213 (6%)	3,563,763 (94%)

Source: Table 5.1 above, and OH of the Medical Services, *Statistics*, pp.14–15 and 270–1.

The statistics published by the RAMC after the war are incredibly detailed, and it is possible to draw comparisons with the Crimean, American Civil and Boer wars, since the figures available for these conflicts are quite extensive – and there are some for even earlier conflicts such as the Peninsular War. Indeed, by 1914, much had been learned by the medical services from the Crimean and Boer wars, not only on the prevention and treatment of disease and on the treatment of wounds, but on the extreme importance of having a properly organised system for the evacuation of the wounded. Further detailed information was also available on the medical services in the American Civil War, particularly in the Union Army of 1864, and this was closely studied.

THE ROYAL ARMY MEDICAL CORPS

The British Army expanded dramatically in size from 1914 onwards, and this was equally true of the RAMC, which was a very small force in 1914, but a very large one by 1918 (see Table 5.3). The expansion led to very great problems both in the recruitment of suitably qualified medical personnel, and in the effect this had on civilian medical practice at home. By January 1918 there were 12,720 medical practitioners in military service, for a total of around six million servicemen, but only 11,482 in civil practice for the remaining home population of 46 million.[2] The output of the few British medical schools was very small by today's standards, and emigration to the various medical services of the Empire was not insignificant. During the war, recruitment of doctors was on a very large scale and this led to some of the civilian work, particularly in large inner-city hospitals, being undertaken by unqualified medical students.[3] There was also a considerable decrease in the number of older consultants available for the civilian hospitals for they, too, were recruited into the forces' medical services in increasing numbers. During the war, over 1,000 doctors were killed: a great waste of a scarce resource.

TABLE 5.3
THE EXPANSION OF THE RAMC, 1914–18 (TOTAL STRENGTH WORLD-WIDE)

	1914	*1918*
Officers	3,168	16,330
Men	13,063	131,099
Trained nurses	2,607	13,218
Total	18,838	160,647

Source: OH Medical Services, *General History*, Vol. 1, pp.44, 153.

RESEARCH AND TREATMENT

During the war, the RAMC instituted a considerable amount of research into such areas as the three key complications of wounds – that is, the effects of shock, blood loss from wounds and the bacteriology of wound infections – often under battlefield conditions. There was even a small group who performed battlefield post-mortem examinations.[4]

The basic research into the detailed understanding of shock consisted of taking a wounded man from the front-line trench, or even from No Man's Land, and escorting him back through the various outposts to the appropriate Casualty Clearing Station (CCS). During this time, his blood pressure, pulse and general clinical observations were checked every few minutes. In this way, a very detailed understanding of the effect of shock was built up. Similar research was carried out into the causation and prevention of many of the prevalent diseases and, later in the war, great efforts were made to produce a rational approach to the detection and treatment of many of the psychological problems which had been identified.

The Analysis of Wounds

A lot had been learned of bullet wounds and their effect during the Boer War; but during that war shell fragments presented much less of a problem than they would in the Great War. It soon became apparent that shell fragments were producing the majority of serious wounds on the Western Front, so research was undertaken to determine just what fragments were produced by the explosion of a shell. German 77mm shells, French 75mm shells and British 18-pounder and 4.5-inch shells were test-fired. The fragments were collected and the shells reassembled so that the size and shape of each fragment could be charted, giving a clear idea of the sort of wound likely to be produced by each fragment. It was found that the German 77mm shell broke into 500 fragments, and the French '75' into 800, because of its lighter casing and larger explosive charge.[5]

After the war the RAMC produced very detailed statistics of casualties, both medical and surgical, admitted to medical units between 1916 and 1920. From the total of 5,635,726 casualties admitted during this time a sample of 18.5 per cent, that is 1,043,643 British casualties, was studied. This covered all units in the United Kingdom, France and Belgium, Italy, Africa, Palestine and Egypt, Macedonia, Mesopotamia, north Russia and India.[6] It was found that 87 per cent of all wounds and 56 per cent of all disease occurred on the Western Front (see Table 5.4).

TABLE 5.4
ANALYSIS OF A SAMPLE OF BRITISH CASUALTIES ADMITTED TO MEDICAL
UNITS WORLD-WIDE, 1916–20

	Wounds	*Injuries and Disease (includes gas)*	*Total*	*Wounds Relative to Total*
Admissions in sample world-wide	206,976	836,677	1,043,653	20%
Admissions on Western Front	180,598 (87%)	463,588 (56%)	644,186 (62%)	28%
Mortality rate	10.2%	0.93%		

Source: OH Medical Services, *Statistics*, pp. 275–6

The analysis of wounds covered such areas as causation of wounds (for example, bullet or shell); regional incidence (for example, arm or leg); nature of wound (for example, contusion, laceration, fracture); geographical area (for example, France, Palestine); arm of the service (for example, infantry, artillery). All this built up a complex and detailed body of statistics, and similar criteria were used in studies of admissions for disease.

The effect of a missile striking the human body (during the Great War) should first be considered. If a shell fragment, say two inches by one inch, strikes a man's thigh, the effects are as follows: it first penetrates the trousers, probably liberally covered with mud and trench detritus; it then penetrates the underpants, unwashed for several days, then the skin, almost certainly covered in septic spots because of the incessant scratching of lice infestation; under the skin it penetrates the subcutaneous fat, severing superficial veins and arteries; it then transects the main mass of muscle, probably severing the main nerve trunk and the large arteries and veins contained in, and beneath, the muscle; on striking the bone, the missile causes this to shatter so that each fragment of bone becomes a subsidiary small missile; the shell fragment will then exit in the same way, making a much larger hole on the way out, with corresponding increase in tissue destruction. The problems of treating such a wound are complex, especially so because of the complications of shock, blood loss and infection.

Shock

Shock may be loosely defined as a condition of bodily weakness resulting from injury or illness which has reduced the volume of fluid or blood in the body. It can vary from fainting to complete collapse. Primary shock comes on rapidly after wounds, and may be transient. It may proceed either directly or, after an interval during which things seem to be normal, to secondary or wound shock, which can be very severe and often difficult to treat. Severe shock is almost always due to blood loss except in certain circumstances such as burns, where there is severe shock but little active blood loss; abdominal injuries where blood loss may be minimal; or coronary thrombosis, where shock may be intense with no blood loss at all.

Quite a lot was known about shock because of extensive and widespread civilian and industrial injuries. Road accidents were common even in 1914, while mines, quarries and foundries were dangerous places in which to work. Some useful information was available from the Boer War, although casualties were on a smaller scale and generally not so severe, being mainly gunshot wounds.

Shock was treated by fluid replacement, mainly using normal saline solution, which had to be made up fresh and could not be stored. Pain relief was usually by morphine injection, although opium products by mouth could be used if the patient's condition warranted it. Today, a group of substances called 'plasma expanders' can be used as a temporary expedient in the treatment of shock and blood loss, if blood is not available. Nothing like that was available during the Great War; but what was available was normal saline containing gum acacia,[7] which worked by expanding the volume and consistency of circulating fluid, thereby temporarily raising the blood pressure. By and large it seemed to work quite well, with very few of the later complications sometimes predicted at the time.[8]

Blood Loss

The circulating fluid volume in the average adult male is about six litres or ten and a half pints. Normally the loss of about a pint of blood in a healthy adult male is barely noticeable; but the complications of shock worsen the effects, and by the time about three pints of fluid have been lost, the results can be severe because there is not enough left to produce a sufficient flow around the body. The symptoms of severe blood loss are partly due to the blood loss itself, and partly due to the body's response to that loss. To compensate for the fluid loss, the pulse becomes faster and weaker, and, inevitably, the blood pressure falls. The body responds by shutting down the circulation to the various organs in order of their importance, starting with the skin, which becomes cold, pale and clammy.

Blood replacement was recognised as being essential early on in the war, but only one surgeon in the United Kingdom was using blood transfusion on a regular basis before 1914.[9] There was some increasing use of blood transfusions as a regular treatment in Canada and the United States by 1914 but this was still on a fairly small scale.[10] At first, direct transfusion was used, passing the blood directly from an artery of the donor into the largest available vein of the recipient. This, of necessity, made its use very restricted.

Indirect transfusion was not possible early on in the war since blood could not be kept, but rapidly clotted. Gradually, a method was developed using citrates and other chemicals, which were inert in the human body, so that blood could be stored for a few days. Experience and improvements in refrigeration made it possible to make blood transfusions more widespread, with a corresponding improvement in the outlook for a wounded man. Improved storage made indirect transfusion possible, that is from donor to storage and then to recipient.

Indirect transfusion was increasing by 1916–17, pioneered at first by Australian and Canadian units in the BEF on the Western Front, but later becoming universal. Blood transfusion was not available any further forward than the CCS until 1917; but by the beginning of 1918 it was available at Advanced Dressing Stations (ADSs). This produced a vast improvement in a wounded man's chances of survival. Blood grouping was in its infancy, and the suitability of blood was tested by a simple agglutination test, depending on the clumping of red cells when the two samples of blood were mixed. From this process four blood groups were defined in what were called 'Moss's tables', which corresponded to the four blood groups used at present. The rhesus factor was unknown at that time; but it did not matter unless the patient was going to have repeated blood transfusions. Under such circumstances, there seem to have been remarkably few adverse transfusion reactions.

At first, blood was given by direct transfusion from a man's comrades; but, as units became more fragmented and storage became possible, this became less of an option. At base hospitals, blood was collected from slightly wounded men, dental patients, men with minor orthopaedic problems and, above all, they seem to have used men with flat feet. It was very popular with the donors, since they usually received two or three weeks' home leave in exchange for a pint of blood.[11]

Wound Infections

These were always a problem in armies, as well as in civilian life; but they were much worse and more widespread on the Western Front than elsewhere. It was far more of a problem in France and Belgium than it had been in the Boer War, or than it would be in Palestine or Mesopotamia. This was because of climatic conditions, the nature of the wounds and the fact that the ground on which the war was fought in France was more hotly contested, intensively cultivated and heavily manured.

Wound infections had been a great problem during the American Civil War, and the reason is not hard to find. The surgeon W. W. Keen recalled, some years later, that 'We operated in old blood-stained and often pus-stained coats ... with undisinfected hands .... We used undisinfected instruments ... and marine sponges which had been used in prior pus cases, and only washed in tap water.'[12] In such circumstances, it is scarcely surprising that nearly all wounds became infected.

Because of the terrible past history of wound infections, a great deal of research was done, by both the British and French medical services, into the bacteriology of wound infections. Numerous groups of organisms were recognised in established wound infections: streptococci and staphylococci were among the most common, with coliform organisms and diphtheroids also being present. The most resistant of all were bacteria of the pyocyaneous and the proteus groups, which tended to occur in wounds which had been infected for a long time. Skin infections were a great problem, often secondary to louse infestation, so that a man with boils, impetigo or septic skin eruptions had very little chance of avoiding infection if he was wounded. Many of the bacteria responsible for wound infections live normally as commensals on the human skin or in the human gut, where they do no harm whatsoever; but they can cause serious infection if they enter an open wound.

As we saw above, a serious problem on the Western Front was that the war was largely fought over intensely cultivated and heavily manured ground. This led to infection of wounds with tetanus, gas gangrene and diphtheroid infections. Most pathogenic bacteria are aerobic – that is, they thrive in the presence of oxygen – but tetanus and gas gangrene infections are caused by anaerobic bacteria, which thrive in the absence of oxygen. They prefer deep wounds with much damaged tissue and cannot survive if a wound is open and well drained so that air can enter it.

To prevent infection from establishing itself, a return to surgical first principles was insisted upon. Wounds were widely excised and all dead and damaged tissue was removed, leaving where possible a large cup-shaped wound which could be easily observed for early signs of infection and easily dressed. The wound was allowed to heal slowly by granulation, which might have taken a long time but gave better results in the long run. By contrast, early suturing of wounds resulted in infection lying bottled-up in the wound, with the formation of abcesses or, worse, the development of gas gangrene. The only anti-bacterial agent available for treating infected wounds was Eusol (Edinburgh University Solution of Lime). This was used for washing wounds and also for soaking dressings in.

Tetanus

Tetanus had been observed in many previous wars, and its effects on mortality rates were well known to military surgeons (see Table 5.5). Tetanus is a disease of cultivated ground caused by an organism known at the time as *Clostridium tetani*. This lives normally in the intestines of domestic animals where it does no harm, but can enter a wound which is contaminated with manured soil. The incubation period is anything from three to 30 days, but is usually between ten and 12 days. The more rapidly the disease is established, the worse the outlook. The organisms affect muscles through their nerve endings, by poisoning with toxins, causing muscular contraction – sometimes localised but more usually generalised. The muscles often first affected are those of the head and neck, hence its old name of 'lockjaw'. Repeated muscular contractions rapidly exhausted Great War casualties with tetanus, and it was impossible for them to take food or liquids. Intercurrent infection, particularly pneumonia, was common if the condition lasted for more than a few days (as it often did). Incubation was much more rapid, and the outlook considerably worse, in very ragged or very septic wounds.

Tetanus was very much a disease of the Western Front. It was negligible in Russia and Italy, unknown in Palestine, and only a few cases were reported in Mesopotamia and Macedonia. Six cases were described from Gallipoli, all of which occurred in patients with very infected trench foot.[13]

In the absence of antibiotics, the only treatments available were surgical excision to prevent it and anti-tetanus serum (ATS). This was developed greatly during the war and given to every wounded man. If tetanus was thought to be a possibility, he was given repeated injections. ATS was reasonably effective in preventing tetanus and in treating established tetanus, but had a high incidence of side effects.

TABLE 5.5
INCIDENCE OF WOUND TETANUS, AS A PERCENTAGE OF ALL WOUNDS

War	Army	Percentage	Mortality
Peninsular War	British:	2%	?
Crimean War	British:	0.2%	?
American Civil War	Union:	0.2%	?
Franco-Prussian War	German:	0.4%	90%
Boer War – no cases reported			
Western Front 1914–18	British:	1.2%	54%

Source: OH Medical Services, *Pathology*, pp. 165–6.

The mortality rate from tetanus dropped from 63.5 per cent in 1914 to 37.9 per cent in 1918. According to the RAMC 1916–20 figures, there were 2,569 cases of tetanus, of which 95 per cent occurred on the Western Front. The overall mortality rate was 54 per cent.[14] The incidence was, in fact, appreciably lower than is popularly supposed.

Gas gangrene

Gas gangrene, like tetanus, is a disease of heavily manured soils. The disease is caused by a group of *Clostridia* organisms, of which the most important was known at the time as *Clostridium welchii*. Like tetanus, the organism lives in the intestines of domestic animals and, more rarely, in humans as well. The incubation period is between one and three days, and is usually of very rapid onset. The infection affects muscles at the site of injury, causing destruction of the small blood vessels in muscle, and of muscle tissue, causing bubbles of gas to form. The disease produces a severe toxaemia so that the casualties become very ill very rapidly. The most common sites for infection were the buttocks, calves and thighs. The further up the thigh the infection became established, then the worse was the outlook, since amputation was the only treatment. Death was very rapid in established cases.

The disease was much less common on the Somme in 1918 than it had been in 1916, since the ground had not been tilled or manured in the intervening period, and exposure to the weather had had some effect on the spores. The *Clostridii* of both tetanus and gas gangrene can form spores which can be dormant in the ground for months, or years, and can be very resistant.

Gas gangrene, like tetanus, was much more common on the Western Front than elsewhere. A serum was developed in an attempt to prevent the onset of the disease, but this had very little effect.[15] Treatment was by prevention –

the wide surgical excision of all wounds, particularly deep and ragged ones, with the wound left open so the air could get in. The limb was amputated at the first sign (often its characteristic smell) of gas gangrene infection. There was an incidence of the disease in wounds of 10–12 per cent of all wounds in 1914–15, but this had fallen to one percent by 1918 owing to improved treatment and transportation of the wounded. The death rate also gradually improved during the war.

Comparing the results of treatment on the Western Front in 1918 and in the north-west Europe campaign of 1944–5 is very instructive. In 1944–45 wounded men were routinely given penicillin by injection and often sulphonamides by mouth as well. Despite the absence of antibiotics in 1918, there was no difference in the mortality rates between the two campaigns.[16] A quotation from a standard surgical textbook published after the Second World War, is apposite: 'Gas gangrene, more than any other complication of wound infection, serves to point the moral that no ancillary methods will make amends for neglect of meticulous primary surgery.'[17]

Consider then the plight of a wounded man – he might lie out in a shell hole for days. He would be suffering from shock, blood loss, infection, malnutrition, frostbite and exposure if cold, or dehydration if hot. If there for several days, he would probably be developing pneumonia as well. The truly astonishing thing is that so many men survived these appalling conditions.

There were particular problems in the treatment of wounds in the Great War, which did not apply during the Second World War or subsequent conflicts. The absence of antibacterial drugs during the Great War certainly made a difference in the treatment of wound and other infections; but that can be overstated. Sulphonamides were first used during the 1930s, and penicillin during the early 1940s. But as the figures for gas gangrene mortality show, these antibacterial drugs would not necessarily have made a tremendous difference to a patient's outlook. Where antibiotics and sulphonamides would have been much more useful was in the treatment of chest and other common infections which produced such a large number of admissions, still with a significant mortality rate, during the Great War. It may well be that, in the long run, two other significant improvements were more important for combat medicine than antibacterial drugs, namely transportation and anaesthesia.

The Transportation of Casualties

Casualty evacuation would improve dramatically by the Second World War, and improve even more thereafter, but on the Western Front it was difficult to move a wounded man on the battlefield, as is well known from the many photographs. There was also a shortage of transport for the rearward evacuation of casualties in 1914 and early 1915, and the inability to handle increasing numbers of casualties adequately led to something of a public out-cry. However, Lieutenant-General Sir Alfred Keogh, a former Director General of the Army Medical Service, was Commissioner of the British Red Cross in France at the outbreak of war. With great energy and vision he put in hand the conversion of a quantity of French rolling stock to ambulance trains, organised and financed by the Red Cross. This produced a rapid and marked improvement in casualty evacuation. Later in the war the various British railway companies produced more and more ambulance trains – for the United States Army as well as for the British – from 1917 onwards, as it became almost a matter of prestige. By this time, Keogh had been recalled to serve as Director General of Medical Services in the War Office, while the existing incumbent, Surgeon-General Sir A. T. Sloggett, was sent to France as Director General there, where he remained throughout the rest of the war.

It was common to need eight men to carry a stretcher in the Ypres salient in 1917, and both bearers and casualties – if they arrived at all – would be exhausted by the time they reached a suitable aid post. Often, because of the great delay in moving a casualty, his shock would be made much worse and infection given a chance to establish itself. There was no helicopter transport to whisk a man away from the battlefield in minutes; neither was evacuation of more seriously wounded men by fixed-wing aircraft possible under battle-field conditions. Moreover, a casualty's problems were not over after his initial stretcher carry. Other methods of transport were scarcely less trying. Neither the handcart with bicycle wheels, nor the flat wagon used on trench tramways had springs; nor did the old horse ambulance that was used in the early part of the war. Travois – simple poles dragged by mules – were used in Salonika, as shown in Stanley Spencer's painting. These must have been even worse, when dragged over rutted tracks, than the old horse ambulance. Motor ambulances were used widely later in the war, but they still had minimal springing. The unfortunate casualties must have been bounced around badly as long as they were anywhere near the battle zone. All in all, the methods of casualty transportation did nothing at all to prevent shock, blood loss or infection.

Each front-line battalion had an establishment of 16 stretcher bearers, initially with half from the RAMC – although these were withdrawn fairly early in the war in order to increase the number of trained personnel avail-able to the field ambulance service. The numbers had to be made up from the battalion's own resources. In battle, it was the custom to increase the number of available stretcher bearers to 32, using bandsmen, pioneers and other such personnel as might be available. The stretcher bearers transported the casualty to the Regimental Aid Post (RAP), under the command of the regi-mental medical officer, where essential first aid was carried out, splints were applied as necessary, and the wounded sorted out as well as possible into groups for treatment (see Figure 5.1). From there, the casualty was moved by the field ambulance (stretcher bearers or light carts) to the ADS. The ADS carried out emergency primary surgery, particularly in arresting haemorrhage. Later in the war, more surgery, and of a more complicated nature, came to be carried out at the ADS, since it soon became apparent that lack of delay was vital for many types of wound.

The next step from the ADS was by Field Ambulance transport (ambulance wagons or cars, or light railway) to the Main Dressing Station ('MDS'); or the casualty made his own way, with or without help, to the adjacent Walking Wounded Dressing Station ('WWDS'). Such casualties who needed further surgery or treatment were transferred by motor ambulance, light railway, lorries or bus to the Casualty Clearing Station (CCS), where most surgery was carried out. The CCS was usually adjacent to a railway siding, and also close to a mobile laboratory and advanced medical stores depot. Later in the war, some CCSs specialised in particular types of wound or gas poisoning.

Those casualties needing further evacuation were then transported by ambulance trains, ambulance barges or motor ambulance convoy to the Advanced Base, or Main Base group of hospitals. These consisted of permanent surgical hospitals and large general hospitals, with all the necessary ancillary services and convalescent units. Any further evacuation would be by hospital ship to the United Kingdom.[18]

Anaesthesia

The use of anaesthetics had not advanced for many years. Despite the fact that surgery had made great strides in the 30 or 40 years before 1914, anaesthesia had not. The anaesthetic agents available were nitrous oxide gas, oxygen, ether, ethyl chloride, chloroform and local anaesthetics, mainly novocaine. Morphine was used for pain relief. The most widely used general anaesthetic was often ether, using a mixture of ether and air given over a Schimmelbusch mask. This is a very safe method of anaesthesia, but induction of the early stages of anaesthesia is very slow: ether produces little muscle relaxation, and is not well tolerated by very shocked patients. Ethyl chloride was tried by inhalation, but although useful for children or dental cases, had no improvement to offer over ether under battlefield conditions, besides being considerably more difficult to use and producing rapid, deep anaesthesia. Chloroform, although much more potent and much more rapid in onset than ether, was considerably less safe and extremely hazardous to use on very shocked casualties. It was little used. Intravenous ether, as a means of rapid induction, was tried but was found to be unsatisfactory.[19]

A great deal of local anaesthesia was used, mainly novocaine, which first became widely used in 1904. Its use was pioneered by Karl Gustav August Bier, Professor of Surgery at Berlin, who later became surgical adviser to the

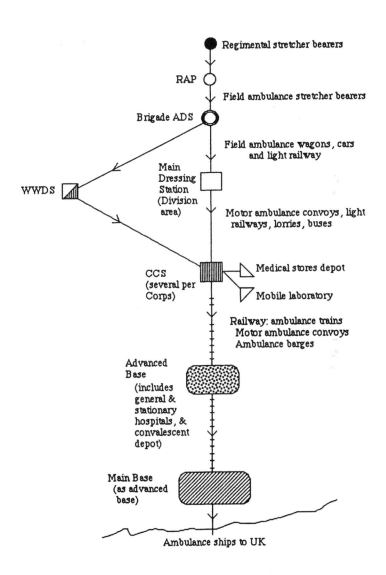

FIGURE 5.1: STAGES IN CASUALTY EVACUATION

German Army. A large number of operations on limbs were done using local anaesthesia, but it also proved useful in chest, abdominal and neurosurgical operations. Spinal anaesthesia was tried, using novocaine to produce anaesthesia of the lower half of the body, but spinal anaesthesia sometimes produces a sudden and severe reduction of blood pressure, which proved extremely hazardous in the presence of severe shock. This method, too, was very little used. Some of the methods used in attempts to anaesthetise badly wounded men would cause great alarm to a modern anaesthetist.

In 1917–18 200 nursing sisters were trained as anaesthetists, using open ether, in order that a like number of anaesthetists working at CCSs and base hospitals could be released, to replace regimental medical officers at the front who had themselves become casualties. The use of nurses as anaesthetists had not been seen before in British medical practice, although it was quite common in the United States and in parts of Europe. Their employment proved of great service, and many of them became very skilful.[20]

Radiology

The use of X-rays was well established in civilian practice by 1914, although there had been numerous casualties among the pioneers because of radiation burns. The machines used at the time were enormous and required their own huge generators. Because of the large bulk of the apparatus, X-rays were available at first only at base hospitals. To move them forward to CCSs required a large fleet of heavy lorries. Later in the war, the equipment became slightly smaller and somewhat less difficult to transport, and by 1918 X-rays were available forward of the CCSs themselves. This speeded up treatment, making a vast difference to the treatment of limb injuries and in finding the location of bullets or shell fragments in a casualty.

The Incidence of Wounds

Wounds to Chest and Abdomen

The low incidence of wounds of the chest and abdomen admitted to medical units (see Table 5.6) indicates how high was the mortality rate from them on the battlefields of the Great War, as the majority never reached a medical unit.

Chest wounds during the Boer War produced a much higher survival rate than anyone had expected. This was because the vast majority were bullet wounds, the fighting was much less intense, casualty evacuation was easier and the climate was more favourable, being mainly warm and dry. The same sort of results occurred in Egypt and Palestine in the Great War, and to a lesser extent in Mesopotamia, for the same reasons. On the Western Front, however, the picture was very different. The vast majority of chest wounds were caused by shell fragments (see Table 5.7), which tended to tear a large hole in the chest.[21] The climate was worse, being conducive to infection, the fighting much more intense and evacuation correspondingly more difficult. The mortality rate from chest wounds was very high, and, probably, the majority never received any medical attention at all. Sauerbruch, the German pioneer of chest surgery, is said to have counted 300 dead on one corner of a battlefield and concluded that 112 (37 per cent) had died of chest wounds – but how and where this happened is not reported.[22]

TABLE 5.6
INCIDENCE OF WOUNDS BY REGION
(From the British 1916–20 sample of medical admissions, excluding gas cases.)

Region	Incidence (percentage)
Head and Neck	16.5
Chest	3.5
Abdomen	2.0
Back	6.0
Upper limb	31.0
Lower limb	40.0
Undefined	1.0

Source: OH Medical Services, *Statistics*, p.279

TABLE 5.7
CAUSATION OF COMBAT WOUNDS

Cause	Union Army of the Potomac, early 1864* (percentages)	British Army, 1916–20 (sample of medical admissions)	
		Total Sample	Without Gas Cases (percentages)
Rifle (or musket)	87	82,901 = 35	39
Bayonet or knife	0.1	684 = 0.3	0.3
Artillery or mortar	6	124,425 = 53	59
Grenade or bomb	–	4,649 = 2	2
Gas poisoning	–	23,626 = 10	–
Other	7	–	–

* Medical statistics of the Army of the Potomac are extensively reported in T. V. Moseley's, unpublished doctoral thesis, 'The Evolution of American Civil War Infantry Tactics' (University of North Carolina, 1967). Note that in other parts of the Civil War the proportion of wounds from artillery was probably considerably higher. The conditions in Virginia in early 1864 were recognised at the time as particularly poor for artillery.

The mortality rate of chest wounds in the American Civil War (Union Army, 1864) was reported as being 87 per cent[23] and in the French Army in the Great War overall, 50 per cent.[24] In the British Army later in the war, certain CCSs specialised in the treatment of chest injuries and, where battle conditions permitted, chest wounds were evacuated to these special units.

This degree of specialisation produced a marked fall in the mortality rate from chest wounds, one unit reporting a mortality rate of 18 percent, and one as low as six per cent.[25] In common with the improvement in the outlook of casualties in general, results improved as the war progressed. The great problem in the treatment of chest wounds in general was that chest surgery was in its infancy in 1914. Few surgeons had any experience, because of the absence of blood transfusions and the primitive state of anaesthesia. Because of these factors, most surgeons were reluctant to attempt chest surgery at all. This makes the improvement during the war even more astonishing, since anaesthesia remained primitive.

On the Western Front, a casualty was three times as likely to die as a result of a shell wound to the chest as of a bullet wound. Death mainly occurred in the first 36–48 hours, from shock and blood loss. If there was survival beyond this point, then infection became a problem; not merely local wound infection but also pneumonia in the collapsed lung.

Abdominal wounds

Abdominal wounds did badly, by and large, for the same reasons as chest wounds, although anaesthesia was somewhat less of a problem. Again, the majority were shell fragment wounds, which caused considerable destruction to the intestinal organs and blood vessels. One surgical unit kept a chart of all abdominal wounds which reached them, showing the location of entry and exit wounds. It was significant that the vast majority of wounds were well clear of the mid-line, where damage to the aorta or inferior vena cava would cause rapid death from exsanguination (total loss of blood). If the patient survived the initial trauma of the abdominal wound, a further complication was peritonitis, that is, inflammation of the membrane lining the abdominal cavity and covering the intestines. This might start at any time within 24–72 hours, depending on the degree of contamination. Nevertheless, a series of 68 post-mortem examinations on men who died of abdominal wounds showed that only three died of peritonitis.[26] The mortality rate from bullet wounds was also significantly lower than that from shell fragments.

During the Boer War, it was the practice to avoid operating on abdominal wounds. The wounded man was treated by bedrest, pain relieving drugs and limited fluids by mouth. If peritonitis occurred, leading to abscess formation, the abscess was drained surgically. The mortality rate, however, was very high.

During the early stages of the Great War the same principle was followed, and abdominal wounds were not operated upon. However, as men were dying of intra-abdominal haemorrhage in large numbers, a change had to be made. A few surgeons in the British Army insisted on rapid evacuation to CCSs, and early operation, from about February 1915. By about May 1915 this practice had become general, but results were still disappointing, with men dying mainly of shock and blood loss. The mortality rate after operation was between 50 and 60 per cent, and even by the end of the war, in most surgical units, this had not improved much, the best figures being about 40 per cent.

It is interesting to compare the results obtained in north-west Europe in 1944–45. One series of 3,579 cases still showed a post-operative mortality rate of 30 per cent.[27] The widespread use of penicillin and sulphonamides reduced the amount of intra-abdominal infection considerably, and also dramatically reduced the incidence of chest infections, before and after operation. This had previously been a great problem, particularly for men with upper abdominal wounds.

In the British series of cases quoted above, 47 per cent of the wounds were caused by shell and mortar fragments and 41.5 per cent by bullet wounds. Bayonet wounds still accounted for only 0.3 per cent similar to the incidence during the Great War.

Wounds of limbs
Great advances were made in surgery during the war, but none more so than in the treatment of limb injuries. Bone grafting became widespread in the treatment of difficult fractures, or where bone was irretrievably destroyed. The use of screws and metal plates was pioneered in the repair of damaged bones, but whereas modern materials are inert and non-irritant to the body, the steel screws and plates used at the time were not, and frequently had to be removed, having done considerable damage to the host bone. They

TABLE 5.8
TREATMENT OF LIMB WOUNDS (FROM THE BRITISH 1916–20 SAMPLE)

Treatment	Incidence
Upper limb without amputation	61,000
Upper limb with amputation	1,100 (1.8% of all upper limb)
Lower limb without amputation	80,000
Lower limb with amputation	3,100 (3.7% of all lower limb)
Total without amputation	141,000
Total with amputation	4,200 (3.0% of total limb wounds)
Grand total	145,200 (= 14% of the sample including 70% of all wounds except gas)

Source: OH Medical Services, *Statistics*, p.279.

usually had to be replaced by bone grafts. The grafts were normally taken from the tibia (the shin bone) by hammer and chisel, whereas modern instruments powered by compressed air are much quicker and less traumatic. Gaps in the bone were filled with chippings from the tibia, and the limbs enclosed in plaster of Paris. This technique was particularly useful in severely damaged bones of the forearm. Prostheses were also made from ivory, and some sheep and beef bones were used in grafting – but these inevitably failed due to rejection by the body.

Because of these techniques, the amputation rate, compared with previous wars, was astonishingly low. The vast majority of injured limbs were saved by surgery (see Table 5.8).

Orthopaedic Surgery and Limb Wounds

In 1914 Liverpool had the only specialised orthopaedic teaching unit in the country, fully and properly equipped, and all subsequent improvements in the British medical services were based on the Liverpool experience. Robert Jones, Professor of Orthopaedic Surgery at Liverpool University became Inspector of Military Orthopaedics in the British Army. The US Army adopted the British procedures, and 21 American orthopaedic surgeons were sent to work under the Inspector of Military Orthopaedics, to be followed by 21 more working in various United Kingdom hospitals.

Advances in orthopaedics during the war were so great that men wounded in 1918 made up only ten per cent of all post-war pensioners. The vast majority of pensioners with limb injuries were from 1915–17. These men had been discharged from the army because of pressure on the medical services from the large number of wounds needing urgent treatment. They did not, unfortunately, receive the full and proper rehabilitation which became the norm later. Some rehabilitation was carried out by the Ministry of Pensions; but precious months and years had by then been lost. By 1918, however, physiotherapy – known at the time as 'medical massage' – and the rehabilitation of injured limbs had become a well-established process. The Almeric Paget Massage Corps became the Military Massage Service during the war. Mr and Mrs Almeric Paget had started it in 1918, following the development of massage and remedial gymnastics from 1894 onwards, and the foundation of an incorporated society in 1900. The Massage Corps developed from a beginning of 50 masseurs in 1914 to 2,000 by November 1918.

Head Injuries

Great advances were made in the treatment of head wounds, almost if not as great as those in orthopaedic surgery. Neurosurgery was in its infancy, with most surgeons reluctant to enter the skull except in extreme urgency. There were very few surgeons working full-time in this field. Two of the great pioneers were Harvey Cushing from Harvard and Sir Victor Hawsley, who was surgical adviser to the British Army and served on the Western Front. Sir Victor Hawsley died while on a visit to Mesopotamia in 1916 but Cushing, after several previous visits, worked in British hospitals from early 1917 onwards, and came into conflict with authority over violations of the censorship rules. Both men did a great deal to improve the standard of surgery on head wounds. The amount of damage to the brain and the location of the injury played a significant part in the outlook of head wounds, the forward part of the brain being of less importance. Infection was also of great importance and, because of the location of the injuries, was more difficult to deal with than infection elsewhere. More than anywhere else, delay in treatment caused problems in head wounds because of the degree of infection that rapidly arose. Nevertheless, the results of treatment of head wounds, considering the difficulties involved, were surprisingly good (see Table 5.9). Most of the men who returned to duty, however, were for any further frontline service, and were employed at bases or on the lines of communication.

TABLE 5.9
WOUNDS OF HEAD, FACE AND NECK
(from the British 1916–20 sample).

Total	34,313	(=3.3% of total sample, and 16.6% of all wounds except gas)
Deaths	2,954	(8.6%)
Returned to Duty	28,153	(82%)
Discharged as Invalids	2,034	(5.9%)
Inadequate Records	1,172	(3.4%)

Source: OH Medical Services, *Surgery*, Vol. II.

Wounds of Blood Vessels

If small enough to be apposed, wounds of blood vessels were simply sutured with very fine sutures. Gaps in blood vessels were bridged by the use of silver (Tuffier's) tubes, which were available at specialist units in from four to six different sizes, to be applied according to the size of the blood vessel to be repaired. These tubes remained patent for between four and ten days before being occluded by clot. They then had to be removed, but sufficient circulation was by then usually available through other blood vessels to the injured part. No anticoagulants were available to prevent blood clotting at the site of operation; but despite this results seem to have been quite good. Silver is inert to the human body, so that it could be used safely in blood vessel wounds. Similarly, plates of silver could be inserted into the skull to bridge any gaps where bone was missing, without the problem of rejection.

The blood vessels most commonly injured were the femoral (thigh), popliteal (knee), brachial (upper arm), axillary (armpit) and the carotid (neck). Only 17.9 per cent of cases developed gangrene due to the loss of blood flow to the injured limb, mainly as a complication of infected, lacerated wounds. Accessibility of the blood vessel was often the greatest problem in treatment, that is the ability to see and hold the damaged artery, since it might retract out of sight.

Injuries to Peripheral Nerves

It was found that 20 per cent of all serious battle casualties showed some injury to important nerve trunks, causing loss of muscular function and loss of skin sensation. In the United Kingdom, specialist hospitals were set up from 1915 onwards for the treatment of nerve injuries, and several were in operation by the end of the war. The latest advances in rehabilitation techniques were widely applied.

Eye Injuries

Injuries to the eye were frequent. Small portable electro-magnets were used to extract small pieces of metal, but since large foreign bodies required a larger magnet (which needed a very large generator) surgery was often preferred. Electro-magnets were used similarly in the treatment of head wounds. Complete removal of the eye was carried out if there was no sight at all remaining in the eye, or in cases of severe infection. Eye infections remained a great problem throughout the war since, owing to the nature of trench warfare, fragments entering the eye were often heavily contaminated. In the absence of antibiotics, the only treatment for severe infections within the eye was removal. A comparatively rare, but much feared, complication was Sympathetic Ophthalmia, in which the unaffected eye also became inflamed. Again, removal of the infected, injured eye was often the only solution. Blows to the head, face or eyes often produced a condition of traumatic double vision, which might respond to the covering of one eye, but it sometimes lasted for several weeks. Whenever possible, even if only a little sight remained in an injured eye and infection and other complications were controllable, the eye was not removed.

Dental Work and Reconstructive Surgery

Dental surgeons were extremely important in the treatment of facial and jaw injuries, as well as in the more traditional routine dental work. The teeth of the average recruit were in a fairly poor state, and fillings and extractions were carried out in large numbers. Dental surgeons were recruited early on in the treatment of injuries of the upper and lower jaws, which were common. Tremendous advances were made in the reconstruction of faces, jaws and other parts of the body by plastic surgery. Bone grafts on metal prostheses were used to build up missing jaws, and the reconstructed areas were covered by skin grafts taken from the chest or elsewhere. Other large areas of skin loss were also covered by grafts, usually tube or pedicle grafts, which might take months of operations. A vast amount was learned, which later proved vital in the advances in plastic surgery that we now take for granted. Very little plastic surgery had been done before 1914, but after 1918 it became a well-established speciality.

Trench Foot

The effects of cold, in the form of frostbite or gangrene, have been recorded in armies from the earliest historic times. Xenophon made various references to the effect of cold in the fifth century BC, during his army's march across Armenia. Trench foot was widespread during Napoleon's campaign of 1812 in Russia, and was common in both the Crimean and American Civil wars.[28] Trench foot is generally considered to be caused by cold, wet and the effects of pressure. These, by restricting peripheral circulation, drastically reduce blood flow, and hence oxygenation, to peripheral tissues, causing tissue death in severe cases. Secondary infection, due to bacterial invasion of the damaged tissues, was a serious complication. The circulation was restricted by boots and puttees. It was common to wear two pairs of socks, so that the boots became too tight and it became impossible to move the toes. The condition usually started on the outer aspects of the toes, the top of the foot, or the heel. The foot became painful and discoloured, either very pale or purplish in colour. It became very cold, with swelling, particularly of the toes. Secondary infection might then cause the condition to progress to gangrene, due to tissue death, leading sometimes to the amputation of the foot. Even slight cases might take several months to recover full function of the foot.

The most important treatment was prevention – by wearing dry socks and comfortable boots. The use of gumboots or thigh waders was encouraged, particularly in wet or muddy trenches. Spare socks were carried, and regular foot inspections were made to pick up the early stages of the condition. Rubbing the feet with whale oil, or one of the foul-smelling ointments provided by the authorities, and dusting the feet with talc also had some effect in prevention. Cold, wet and muddy conditions, however, with prolonged immobility, remained a problem.

Active treatment consisted of elevating the foot, with warmth and gentle manipulation of the foot, toes and ankle in early-identified cases. Sometimes electrotherapy was effective but, by and large, slow natural healing was usual. Trench foot occurred particularly in France and Belgium, but also occurred to a significant degree in Macedonia and Gallipoli. Total admissions for trench foot and frostbite accounted for 6,021 cases in the 1916–20 survey or 0.7 per cent of all admissions – considerably less than is popularly supposed.[29]

Gas Warfare

This is a very involved and complicated subject which will only be considered in general terms here. As for casualties in general, there are many misconceptions about how extensive gas casualties were and how effective gas was as a weapon. As a terror weapon it was very effective; but as a means of inflicting casualties it was much less so. It has been commonly stated that 20–30 per cent of all British casualties in the Great War were due to gas, but there is no foundation for this (see tables 5.7 and 5.10)

TABLE 5.10
BRITISH ARMY GAS CASUALTIES, 1915–18

1915	5.79% of wounds
1916	1.34%
1917	9.29%
1918	18.22%
Total	185,706 (= 9.7% of all battle injuries)
Deaths	5,899 (= 3.1% mortality rate)

Source: OH Medical Services, *Statistics*, p.111.

The gases used as weapons by the Germans, and subsequently by the Allies as well, were of three main groups: asphyxiating gases such as chlorine and phosgene; blistering agents such as mustard gas; and lachrymatory or tear gas such as benzyl bromide and xylyl bromide. Hundreds of gases were developed by both sides during the war, and dozens of them were used, but mainly with little effect. By the end of the war, gas was being released in several ways – by cloud, mortar, special projector and shell, often with multiple fillings. The most effective gas was mustard which, in the British Army, caused eight times as many casualties as all other gases combined, although the mortality rate never exceeded two per cent. The reason for the large increase in British gas casualties in 1918 was the large amount of mustard and lachrymatory gases used in the March and April offensives. The mortality rate for all gases in 1918 was 2.3 per cent, that is 2,673 deaths from a total of 113,764 casualties.[30]

Chlorine was first used on the Western Front by the German Army on 22 April 1915, at 5.30 p.m. on the northern extremity of the Ypres salient, although the initial success was not exploited. Chlorine is intensely irritating to the eyes, nose and throat, causing severe coughing and vomiting. Inhalation produces damage to the lungs which subsequently leads to large amounts of fluid being produced in lung tissue, with death from asphyxia. Chlorine smells strongly of bleaching powder, but phosgene, first used on 19 December 1915, had a smell that was much less strong and was considerably less irritating to the upper air passages. In consequence, more phosgene tended to be inhaled, with greater subsequent damage to lung tissue and more rapid onset of asphyxia.

Mustard gas was first used in the Ypres salient in the summer of 1917, and was known by the French as 'Yperite'. It is a colourless, oily liquid which can persist for months despite climatic conditions, unlike the asphyxiating agents which are quickly dispersed by wind and weather. Because it is oil-soluble, it rapidly penetrates woollen clothing or skin. It produces severe irritation to the eyes, nose and upper air passages, and large blisters on the skin. It also has an effect in breaking down tissue cells, and, in large doses, affects blood-forming tissues. The temporary blindness it caused usually lasted only a few days, but the blisters could take between four and six weeks to heal. Complications were sometimes experienced up to 30 years later, when the old healed injuries to the eye broke down, causing recurrent inflammation. This, in turn, could lead to ulceration and opacity of the cornea (the front part of the eye). In the intervening years, however, problems with the eyes might have been minimal or non-existent. Death from mustard gas was usually caused by inhaling a great deal of the vapour, which produced extensive lung damage.

Lachrymatory gases were used to incapacitate enemy troops in areas which were to be occupied by friendly forces, since unlike mustard gas they were non-persistent after about 12 hours. They were used from late 1915 onwards, especially on the attack fronts of the German spring offensives of 1918.

A great deal of research was carried out, particularly by the British Army, into the prevention and treatment of gas poisoning. As a result of this, the British gas mask was far more efficient than that of any other army. The use of phosgene was foreseen so, when it was first encountered in December 1915, the British gas mask then in use was already proof against it. In contrast, the German Army made very little preparation to protect themselves from gas attacks, as they never expected gas to be used against them on anything like the scale it actually was. The German gas mask was very inefficient and was never properly developed. It seems probable that the RAMC estimate that the German Army suffered more gas casualties than the British and French combined is not far from the truth, although German casualty figures are notoriously difficult to establish with any accuracy. By the end of the war, the British and French armies had a well-established method of treating large numbers of gas casualties, using special units, called 'the Z system'. This was subsequently adopted by the US Army, whereas the Germans had no organisation of comparable efficiency.

It is interesting to note that while gas casualties in the RAMC analysis amounted to 23,626 admissions, in 1916–20, chest infections (that is, bronchitis, pneumonia and bronchopneumonia), which probably had a significantly higher mortality rate, produced in the same period approximately 55,311 admissions in France and Belgium.[31] The climate on the Western Front seems to have been more effective in removing troops from the front line than gas warfare.

The American experience of gas casualties was somewhat different from that of the British and French. Their troops received a thorough training in the possibilities of chemical warfare, and it is likely that the desire to impress the necessity of precautions upon them led to a state of undue nervousness about gas (see Table 5.11). During the war (mainly in its last three months) American troops suffered a far higher proportion of casualties to gas than either the British or French – 31.5 per cent of all battle casualties, yet with a low mortality of less than two per cent.[32]

> TABLE 5.11
AMERICAN ARMY GAS CASUALTIES

	Number of casualties	Percentage of gas casualties
Chlorine	1,843	2.6
Phosgene	6,834	9.7
Arsine	577	0.8
Mustard gas	27,711	39.3
'Gas' unspecified	33,587	47.6
Total	70,552 (=31.5% of a total 224,089 battle casualties)	
Deaths	1,221 (=1.7% mortality rate among gas cases)	

Source: Medical Department of the US Army in the World War, Vol. XIV, *Medical Aspects of Gas Warfare*, p.274.

CONCLUSION

The popular image of the RAMC in its treatment of wounds and diseases, both physical and mental, has not been universally favourable in the more general literature of the Great War. After a somewhat hesitant start owing to the sheer volume of wounds and disease encountered, the RAMC rapidly improved its organisation and training so that by 1918 its results were astonishingly good and represented a clear advance over the practice of 1914. The mortality from all classes of wounds improved regularly and steadily from 1914 onwards, and similar advances were made in the diagnosis and treatment of disease. Modern orthopaedic surgeons, with whom the author worked for many years, have expressed astonishment at the advanced methods in use by 1918, and the excellent results obtained.

Criticism of the French medical services seems to have been common in all ranks of the French Army; but this does not appear to have been echoed by the RAMC. On the contrary, much of the basic research in wound bacteriology, and the classification and treatment of nervous disorders, was done by the French. Co-operation between the two services also appears to have been very good. The greatest problem faced by the French seems to have been the organisation of casualty evacuation. The transport of their wounded apparently broke down completely on a number of occasions. The United States' medical services were able to learn extensively from the experiences and mistakes of the British and French, and seem to have been almost universally good, although their results did not surpass those of their British colleagues. Again, co-operation appears to have been excellent. As for the German Army's medical services, they suffered increasingly during the war from universal shortages, to the extent that by 1918 instruments, equipment and, above all, dressing materials were in desperately short supply. Their unfortunate wounded suffered accordingly.

The casualty lists of the Great War are doleful enough, but would have been very much worse without the efforts of the medical services. Very little has been written about the debt owed to them, and their contribution has never been fully told.

NOTES

1. The principal source for this article is the official (OH) *History of the Great War Medical Services* (12 vol, London: HMSO, 1921–31), written by many authors but most notably Major-General Sir W. G. MacPherson. It includes sections on General History (4 vols), Casualties and Medical Statistics (1 vol.), Hygiene (2 vols), Surgery (2 vols), Pathology (1 vol.) and Diseases (2 vols). The present reference is from the volume *Casualties and Medical Statistics*, pp.270–1

2. OH Medical Services, *General History*, Vol. 1, p.147.

3. Mentioned in the 1949 lectures of the late C. F. V. Smout, Professor of Anatomy in the University of Birmingham.

4. OH Medical Services, *Surgery*, Vol. I, p.443.

5. Ibid., Vol. 1, pp.31–2.

6. Ibid., *Statistics*, p.281.

7. Gum Acacia 6 per cent in 0.9 per cent sodium chloride solution, known as 'Bayliss's gum saline solution'.

8. Mentioned in the 1949 lectures of the late H. P. Gilding, Professor of Physiology at the University of Birmingham Medical School. See also OH Medical Services, *Surgery*, Vol. I, p.102.

9. Ibid., Vol I, p.108.

10. Ibid.

11. Ibid., p.111.

12. *Medicine of the Civil War* (US National Library of Medicine), p.2.

13. OH Medical Services, *Pathology*, p.166.

14. Ibid., p.169.

15. The US Army medical services felt that the anti-gas gangrene serum was very effective, but their mortality rate was approximately the same. See *The Medical Department of the United States Army in the World War*, 17 vols (Washington DC: US Government Printing Office, 1926–29), written under the direction of Major-General M. W. Ireland, Vol. XI, *Surgery*, Part 1, p.279.

16. 40,000 wounds on the 1918 Western Front produced 400 gas gangrene cases (1 per cent), for a mortality rate of 22 per cent and in 1944–5 in north-west Europe there were 287 cases which also had a mortality rate of 22 per cent: OH Medical Services, *Surgery*, Vol. I, p.148; R. M. Handfield-Jones and A. E. Porritt, *The Essentials of Modern Surgery* (Edinburgh: Livingstone, 1951), p.38.

17. Handfield-Jones and Porritt, op. cit. p.37.

18. OH Medical Services, *General History*, Vol. II, p.15ff.

19. The US medical services made widespread use of nitrous oxide and oxygen as a general anaesthetic for almost all cases, claiming that it was safer, even though in general they

tended to have far longer operations than was normal in Britain. They seem to have made less use of local anaesthesia: *The Medical Department of the United States Army in the World War*, op. cit., Vol. XI, *Surgery*, Part 1, p.172.

20. OH Medical Services, *Surgery*, Vol. I, p.178.
21. In the mobile fighting from August 1918 to the end of the war, it was found that the proportion of wounds from rifle and machine gun bullets increased markedly from that obtaining in static trench warfare.
22. OH Medical Services, *Surgery*, Vol. I, p.345.
23. Ibid., p.348.
24. Ibid., p.351.
25. Ibid., p.346.
26. Ibid., p.485.
27. Handfield-Jones and Porritt, op. cit., p.545; OH Medical Services, *Surgery*, Vol. I, pp.477–82.
28. OH Medical Services, *Surgery*, Vol., p.169.
29. OH Medical Services, *Statistics*, p.303.
30. Ibid., p.111.
31. Ibid., p.293; and pp.285, 305 show that the mortality rate was 5.25 per cent.
32. OH Medical Services, *Diseases*, Vol. II, p.497. See also *The Medical Manual of Chemical Warfare* (London: HMSO, 1955), written under the direction of Major-General A. Sachs.

CHAPTER SIX

The Rise of Armour

J. P. Harris

During the Great War the British pioneered military thought on armoured warfare and developed many of its basic tools. They produced not only armoured cars for reconnaissance, heavy tanks for breakthrough and medium tanks for pursuit and exploitation, but bridging tanks, gun-carrying tanks (crude self-propelled guns) and a variant of the Mark V (the Mark V*) tank which was intended partly as an armoured personnel carrier. By 1918 the term 'mechanical warfare'[1] was not infrequently seen in British staff papers and 'armoured forces' was entering circulation.[2] While armour was still a fairly minor factor, even in the run of victories which brought the war to an end, the evidence is strong that tanks saved British and Commonwealth lives, helped maintain the momentum of attacks and sometimes precipitated the surrender of German troops. Though their French allies were not far behind, using substantial numbers of tanks with considerable success in 1918, throughout the war the British were the leaders in the field. The Germans trailed badly, employing tanks for the first time in the spring of 1918 and never on a significant scale in this war.

The rise of armour in the British armed forces in the First World War is a dramatic story. But in telling and analysing it, the historian must be more than usually wary of his traditional foe: hindsight. Everyone now knows that armoured forces played a major part in preventing the entrenched stalemate experienced on the Western Front in 1914–18 from enduring for such a long period in the Second World War. Reading history backwards, it is all too easy to assume that armour was the obvious solution to the Western Front stalemate of 1916–18. After all, did not several of those with the brightest and most original minds – Churchill, Stern, Swinton and Fuller – say so at the time? Some historians have succumbed to the temptation to use the most strident lobbyists for tanks as touchstones of military wisdom in the second half of the First World War, and to assess as reactionary or 'past-oriented'[3] those who regarded their lobbying with scepticism or just with a normal degree of caution. This temptation should be resisted. The tanks of 1916–18 were much more primitive machines and were operating in a different technical environment from those of 1939–45.

The circumstances which brought the tank into existence had been forecast by I. S. Bloch, the Polish banker who had written a six-volume treatise on future war, the condensed English edition of which, entitled *Is War Now Impossible?*, appeared in 1899.[4] On the basis of the advantage to the defender accruing from the firepower of modern weapons, Bloch had predicted a stalemate in the next European war. H. G. Wells had read Bloch and accepted his reasoning. He suggested, in a story written in 1903, that an armoured cross-country vehicle might be a partial solution to the tactical problem confronting the attacking side.[5] Winston Churchill, who could claim the title of father of the British tank with more justice than anyone else, admitted 'The Land Ironclads' as an important source of inspiration.[6]

The briefest of summaries must suffice of how, as First Lord of the Admiralty, Churchill came to be the prime mover in the British genesis of the tank. (It must be remembered that the French came up with the tank concept quite independently.) No armoured fighting vehicle was in service when war broke out and naval use of such vehicles began with the so-called 'Dunkirk Circus' of 1914. The origins of the 'Circus' lay in the temperament of the First Lord – too restless to be satisfied with responsibility for the relatively slack pace of the war at sea. Churchill was concerned (rightly in the long run) that the Germans would use their Zeppelin airships for attacks on British cities. He justified what became the 'Dunkirk Circus' by the need for the Royal Naval Air Service (RNAS) squadrons to have a forward base on the continent to hunt for Zeppelin bases near the Channel coast.[7]

Some of the officers of the RNAS liked fast cars as well as aircraft. Cars were used to supplement air patrols, to help establish forward airfields and to retrieve pilots crashed behind or close to the (still fluid and porous) enemy front. Weapons were soon mounted in the cars and later some crude and apparently ineffective armour was improvised. Before long, with Churchill's approval, the RNAS had established an Armoured Car Division and a centre for design and production at Wormwood Scrubs. Several models were produced, culminating in a Rolls Royce armoured car, based on the Silver Ghost touring car and mounting a machine gun in a revolving turret. By the time this was in production, however, the war had bogged down to such an extent that armoured cars were virtually useless on the Western Front until 1918.[8]

By the end of 1914 Churchill had begun to apply his mind to the problem of trench warfare. In a letter, dated 5 January 1915, to the Prime Minister, H. H. Asquith, Churchill suggested that trenches could be crossed 'quite easily' and barbed wire crushed by 'a number of steam tractors with small armoured shelters in which men and machine guns might be placed, which would be bullet proof. Used at night they would not be affected by artillery fire to any extent.' This proposal in itself bore no fruit. The Prime Minister placed it before the Secretary of State for War, Lord Kitchener, but the latter did not act.[9]

Oddly, a rather absurd proposal for a gigantic wheeled juggernaut, mounting 12–inch naval guns, appears to have been the decisive event in the British genesis of the tank. It was made by an RNAS armoured-car officer, Flight Commander T. G. Hetherington, at a dinner party given by the Duke of Westminster in February 1915. The Duke was also serving in the Armoured Car Division and the dinner was attended by the First Lord. On 20 February 1915, very shortly after this conversation, Churchill set up the Admiralty Landships Committee under the chairmanship of Mr Eustace Tennyson D'Eyncourt, the Director of Naval Construction – a naval architect and a civilian.[10]

In the end, it was the Landships Committee, an Admiralty committee provided with ample public funds on Churchill's sole authority, that employed and directed the engineers who eventually produced a workable tank. The engineers in question were Walter Wilson (a gifted and experienced automotive engineer, serving in the Royal Navy as a lieutenant-commander) and William Tritton and most of the design work was carried out at Lincoln where Tritton was managing director of Foster's, a company that manufactured traction engines. On 16 January 1916, the Tritton–Wilson prototype, subsequently known as 'Mother', made its first move in the works' yard at Foster's. On 29 January 'Mother' was tried out over a model battlefield on Lord Salisbury's estate at Hatfield Park. It performed well enough to be exhibited on 2 February at the same location to a VIP audience including David Lloyd George, the Minister of Munitions, Lord Kitchener, the Secretary of State for War, and representatives of Field Marshal Sir Douglas Haig from GHQ in France. Most of those present were impressed and the production of the Mark I tank was soon in progress.[11]

Mark I tanks were 26 feet long and weighed about 28 tons. They were rhomboidal in shape, with unsprung tracks running round track frames larger than the hull which fitted between them. The shape and track arrangement were designed for negotiating large shell holes, though the tanks still became stuck quite often. The armament was mounted in sponsons – naval-style semi-turrets – at the sides. 'Male' tanks originally mounted two naval six-pounder guns and four Hotchkiss machine guns. 'Female' tanks mounted four Vickers machine guns and one Hotchkiss. Tanks in action sometimes did quite a lot of shooting, though they were very poor gun platforms and probably seldom hit the enemy except at very short range. An effective tactic against machine gun posts was simply to run them over and crush them.

Male and female tanks were ultimately produced in roughly equal numbers. Speed very much depended on the ground. Little over three miles per hour was about the maximimum, even on good going, on the level, though downhill they could sometimes outpace heavily laden infantry – which suggests a dizzy four-plus. All British heavy tanks of this war were very poor ergonomically. The crew of eight got a bone-shaking ride and operated in very high temperatures, in an atmosphere dense with petrol fumes. Steering and changing gear in the Marks I–IV required great physical effort and the participation of most of the crew. These functions were made easier and could be performed by the driver alone in the Mark V, which arrived at the front in the summer of 1918, but the latter vehicle was even worse than the Mark IV in terms of ventilation, and crew fatigue and sickness became even more of a problem.[12]

Ernest Swinton, the Royal Engineers officer, military writer and subsequent Chichele Professor of the History of War at Oxford, whose claim to be the 'originator' of the tank gained widespread credence, actually had little to do with its genesis. He had the right idea very early and wrote one letter on the subject to Maurice Hankey, the Cabinet secretary, on 11 November 1914. Hankey himself wrote a memorandum, sent to the Cabinet just after Christmas, which contains a suggestion for the use of an armoured fighting vehicle that seems to have been inspired by Swinton. Churchill responded positively to this, writing (as already mentioned) to Asquith on 15 January. But given that Kitchener did not respond to the suggestion when Asquith put it before him, this whole chain of events proved to be a dead end.[13] Swinton claimed that he later raised the matter personally with Lord Kitchener on several occasions but, as Swinton also admitted, Kitchener failed to respond. By the time Swinton wrote his first official memorandum on tracked armoured vehicles, which he sent to Field Marshal Sir John French in June 1915,[14] the work of the Landships Committee had been in progress for more than three months. Swinton discovered the existence of this committee only in late July.[15] His claim to have been instrumental in fixing the specification on the basis of which the successful tank was designed is in fact rather dubious. Nevertheless, any analysis of the British Army's tactical thought on the employment of armour must start with him.

In June 1915, the fact about the war that most impressed itself on Swinton's mind was the ability of the Germans to take the offensive successfully on other fronts while holding their own in the west. He concluded that they were defending their positions in Belgium and France with a 'minimum of men', largely owing to their possession of a prodigious number of machine guns. Blasting through successive German defensive positions with high explosive shell was beyond the army's resources in mid-1915. Armoured 'Machine Gun Destroyers' might, he argued, offer a solution. Swinton envisaged the initial use of about 50 of these 'Destroyers' on a front of about three miles with the Destroyers about 100 yards apart. Swinton at this stage did not envisage his Destroyers crushing wire (though in fact that became perhaps the most important function of tanks). He recommended a short preliminary bombardment to break the German wire the night before the assault and 'occasional bursts of rifle fire' to discourage its repair before first light.

'Destroyers' would be targeted wherever possible on previously identified machine gun emplacements which they could eliminate either by fire from the two pounder guns which he envisaged their mounting, or by crushing them. The Destroyers would probably not be able to annihilate the enemy on their own but could reduce dramatically the casualties of the British infantry. The latter would leave their trenches just as the Destroyers reached the enemy's parapet and thus be able to cross the fire-swept zone between the lines 'virtually unscathed'. The British artillery would concentrate on German artillery 'in order to keep down its fire' – the main threat to the Destroyers. There would be no need to bombard the German trenches, which would be reduced by the actions of the Destroyers and the infantry.[16]

Swinton's tactical argument, while containing brilliant elements, was full of weaknesses. No one at GHQ pointed these out, however, and argument centred on the technical rather than tactical feasibility of the proposal. The reaction of the Engineer-in-Chief, Major-General Fowke, was wholly negative. Fowke suggested to French that the construction of an engine such as Swinton proposed was likely to prove impossible, and he seemed disinclined to recommend experiment.[17] French reacted favourably, however, communicating his interest in the idea to the War Office on 22 June.[18] GHQ collectively never offered the slightest opposition to the Machine Gun Destroyer/Landship concept and from February 1916, when Mother was demonstrated, was enthusiastic in its support of the idea.

The effect of French's letter of 22 June to the War Office is not clear and may not have been great. By that time the War Office was already aware of the existence of the Landships Committee and already communicating with it.[19] Details of the latest German field fortifications were taken from GHQ at various times over the next few months and Tritton and Wilson completed their work on the basis of a War Office specification derived from these.[20] When Douglas Haig took over as Commander-in-Chief at the end of 1915, no one at GHQ briefed him on Landships, probably because no one there yet knew much.

Haig was first informed of the Landship concept in a curious memorandum entitled 'Variants of the Offensive' sent to GHQ by Winston Churchill. Having left political office as a result of the failure of his Dardanelles operation, Churchill had arrived on the Western Front in November 1915 as a major. It was entirely characteristic of him that within days of his arrival he should submit to the highest authority a memorandum which, as he put it in his memoirs with equally characteristic grandiloquence, contained 'the conception of a battle and of victory'.[21]

The memorandum was also typical of Churchill in that it contained a certain amount of dross along with its golden nuggets. But when it came to 'caterpillar machines' Churchill had, in one crucial respect, more insight than Swinton. He indicated that one of the main advantages of such machines was their ability to deal with wire without preliminary artillery bombardment (though he was wrong about the method they would use to do so). By forgoing preliminary bombardment, he suggested, a very high degree of surprise could be achieved.[22]

Haig's response was completely positive – a fact worthy of remark. He had just taken over command of the bulk of the British Army in the middle of the biggest and most complex war it had ever fought. He was presented with an eccentric and rather pompous paper from a politician who had left office as a result of the failure of an amateurish venture which had diverted badly needed resources from the crucial front. He might have been forgiven for dismissing such a document. In fact he read it carefully and attached a note to it asking: 'Is anything known about the caterpillar referred to in para 4 page 3?'[23]

Inquiries were made and Major Hugh Elles, a sapper officer based in GHQ's Operations Branch, was sent to London to investigate. In a letter to the War Office on 9 February, Haig indicated that 'the officers who represented me at the trials lead me to the conclusion that the "Tanks" can be usefully employed in offensive operations by the forces under my command'. He mentioned that he had been given to understand that 'thirty or forty at least could be supplied by next May without interfering with the supply of any war material'. Haig wanted at least that number and if possible more.[24] Haig's interest in tanks appears to have been continuous and reasonably active from Christmas Day 1915 until 15 September 1916 when they were first used in action.

A conference held at the War Office on 14 February led to the establishment of a 'Tank Detachment', of the Motor Machine Gun Service of the Machine Gun Corps, to be based and trained at Bisley. Swinton, as an early tank enthusiast, was transferred from the job which he currently held in the Committee of Imperial Defence to take over responsibility for forming and training the new organisation. One of Swinton's main problems over the next few months was the impatience of GHQ to use tanks in action. Haig told Swinton on 14 April that he wanted some tanks in France by the middle of June. It is now obvious that these were wanted for the coming offensive on the Somme. Swinton said that he would try but doubted that it would be possible. In a letter of 26 April, however, he agreed to deliver 75 tanks with crews by the middle of August.[25]

By this stage, Swinton had developed his ideas on tank use somewhat beyond those he had set down in June 1915. He now wanted to use about 90 in an extended line with no more than 150 yards between machines. He thus contemplated an attack frontage of 9,000 yards or about five miles. He wanted the attack to go in just before dawn, slightly ahead of the infantry assault. Though he strongly emphasised surprise, he still did not believe that some preliminary bombardment for wire cutting purposes could be avoided. He did not envisage the tanks working with an artillery barrage, either 'creeping' or 'jumping'. He thought that, if followed up determinedly by the infantry, tanks could force successive lines of entrenchments and achieve breakthrough without close artillery support. He still offered no real suggestion as to how such a breakthrough was to be exploited. He placed very strong emphasis on getting the most out of the tanks at their debut, believing them so vulnerable that their repeated employment would be an 'impossibility'.[26]

In his memoirs, Swinton was to indulge in bitter recrimination against GHQ about the allegedly premature employment of tanks in insufficient numbers on 15 September 1916.[27] Some other writers have tended to echo his tone of righteous indignation in this matter. But two points need to be borne in mind. Firstly, despite his having some good tactical ideas, it is far from clear that Swinton had come up with anything like a formula for decisive victory. Indeed, it is doubtful whether his prescription could even have achieved a significant break-in to a German position. By 1916, German defences were generally so tough that the support of a barrage was vital to assaulting infantry, and Mark I tanks in themselves could not have been an adequate substitute. Secondly, as late as 26 June 1916, GHQ seems to have been prepared to accept most of Swinton's ideas.[28] What caused GHQ ultimately to employ tanks on different principles was mainly repeated disappointment as to the delivery dates for tanks and trained crews.

In August, despairing of having more than a handful of tanks to use on the Somme, GHQ concluded that it must make some use of however many became available during the next few weeks. The idea of attacking with a continuous line of tanks was abandoned. Instead, small groups were to be used to add weight to the assault at points on the frontage where particular difficulty was to be expected.[29]

> The chief obstacle to any infantry advance are the villages, woods, strong points and hidden machine gun positions. No bombardment seems to succeed in obliterating all these places so completely as to present the reappearance of machine guns there as soon as the artillery lifts. The result is that the assault is checked in front of these points and that those elements who continue to advance through the intervals are taken in the flank by machine gun fire.

Tanks were to assist at these locations 'so that they may be overcome simultaneously with the parts where resistance is less'. That opposition should be overcome more or less simultaneously right along the front was extremely important to British tactics at this period. Infantry advances were closely geared to an artillery fire-plan which could not be altered once the attack had started. The barrage (whether creeping or jumping) moved ahead at a prearranged rate and everything depended on the infantry keeping close behind it. Thus GHQ intended that 'numbers of tanks should be tasked to deal with each of these pivots of defence. They should be loosely supported by bodies of infantry told off for the purpose.' These would advance under cover of the tanks, to

> clean up behind them, and eventually consolidate the locality when taken.... Each Tank attack will be a definite operation against a limited objective allotted to a selected number of Tanks and a selected body of infantry all under one Commander. In certain cases a pair of Tanks supported by a platoon might suffice.

Adding weight to the assault at selected points was not, in principle, a stupid way of using a small number of tanks. But unless they had really intimate infantry support, tanks were eventually found not to be at their best in villages. (They could not shoot into windows above the ground floor and their top armour was weak, leaving them vulnerable to grenades.) They were also, as Swinton had already warned, of very little use in woods, where they tended to become 'bellied' on tree stumps.

GHQ does not appear to have taken seriously the view, strongly stated by Swinton, that tanks would stand little chance of success after their first employment. To Haig and his staff the tank was merely one new weapon among several which this war had produced. As with the other weapons, the best methods of using the tank could, in their view, only be worked out by trial and error.[30] In the present writer's opinion, this was a more realistic and valid approach than Swinton's.

The briefest of sketches of the actions of the tanks on 15 September 1916 and on subsequent occasions during the remainder of the Somme battle must here suffice. By mid-September, there were three companies of tanks in France but all the personnel were inadequately trained and one company was so poorly trained as to be incapable of taking the field. There were also numerous technical hitches, owing to minor design faults and to the machines not being adequately run in. Fifty tanks had been sent to France with the two companies actually employed on 15 September and a further ten had been delivered as reserves. Only 49 machines were fit for duty on 15 September and 13 of those broke down before crossing the start line. Thus only 36 machines saw action.[31]

The attack of 15 September was essentially a conventional infantry assault, employing nine divisions, prepared by an intensive three-day preliminary bombardment and supported by a creeping barrage. The tanks were spread out across the front operating in small groups, or, owing to the breakdown of many machines, in some cases individually. The intention was for the tanks to keep ahead of the infantry. There were so few tanks, how-ever, that it would have been absurd to dispense with the proven technique of a creeping barrage. As usual, it was considered vital for the infantry to stay close to the latter. In order to avoid hitting the tanks with British shells, however, 'lanes' 100 yards wide through the barrage were left open for the tanks.

Given that many tanks failed to cross their start lines and that others fell behind, these lanes were in many cases deadly to the infantry, who were left exposed to German machine gunners within them. The poor training of the tank crews resulted in some completely losing their sense of direction and firing on their own infantry. Steering was also poor and, despite the 'lanes', some tanks apparently wandered into the British barrage. The whole attack achieved very limited results, the maximum penetration being less than two miles and only about six square miles being gained altogether.

The best results were obtained by 41st Division in the centre of the XV Corps front. This division was exceptionally well endowed with tanks, being allocated ten, of which seven managed to start. Three tanks appear to have reached the village of Flers. As far as this objective (almost one mile from the start line) they were accompanied by infantry who secured and held the village. The infantry advance petered out at that point, however, and only two unsupported tanks got as far as the village of Gueudecourt, about two miles beyond the start line, where they were knocked out by German batteries.[32]

The tank's debut could not realistically be regarded as an unqualified success – though that is how it was hailed in most of the British press. But neither could it be dismissed as an unmitigated failure. Despite the poor training of their crews, tanks had managed to advance further than any infantry (though they did not survive for long without infantry support) and in some parts of the front they had been of genuine help in subduing trenches and strongpoints. In some cases, the appearance of tanks had greatly frightened the Germans, inducing flight or surrender. At other points, however, it seems that German gunners, even when tanks approached very close to their positions, kept their nerve and engaged them like any other target. Very few tanks were fit for action on 16 September. Apparently only three did any actual fighting, but these played a considerable part in disrupting a German counter-attack.

After 16 September, there was a lull in the Somme battle. When, on 25 September, Fourth Army renewed its offensive it appears to have employed only 12 tanks. Their performance varied greatly. The following day one tank distinguished itself in an attack by 21st Division on a major position known as the Gird Trench. This tank made a important contribution (fully attested by the infantry) to the seizure of the position and the capture of 370 German prisoners for small loss to the British. The XV Corps report on the operation stated: 'What would have proved a very difficult operation, involving probably very heavy losses, was taken [sic] with the greatest ease entirely owing to the assistance of the tank.'[33]

Hitherto, tanks had by no means received universal acclaim from the infantry and it might be thought that they badly needed this sort of tribute. Actually GHQ had already decided in their favour. Haig had met Swinton and Albert Stern (former secretary of the Landships Committee and then in charge of tank production at the Ministry of Munitions) at his advanced headquarters at Busquesne on 17 September.[34] He pronounced that though tanks had not achieved all that had been hoped of them, they had saved many lives and fully justified their existence. The same day Kiggell, Haig's Chief of the General Staff, wrote to Field Marshal Robertson, the Chief of the Imperial General Staff (CIGS),. in exactly the same terms: 'Consider that the utility of the tanks has been proved. It has been established that the magnitude [sic] of the success on the 15th in certain localities was directly attributable to the employment of tanks.'[35]

Major General Butler, Haig's Deputy Chief of Staff, recommended at a conference on tanks, apparently held at the War Office on 19 and 20 September 1916, that a further 1,000 should be ordered. Butler also indicated GHQ's intention to aim at expansion to five Tank Brigades – one for each of the British Armies in France – each brigade to consist of 144 front line tanks plus 72 spares. Though never fully attained in practice, this intended scale of provision was extraordinarily generous for a new engine of war which had given only a fairly modest proof of its capacity. There were indications that the Heavy Branch, Machine Gun Corps (as it was now termed) was expected to develop into a corps in its own right. Analogies were being drawn with the Royal Flying Corps – the latter already regarded as an élite, vital to the operations of the BEF.[36]

By October 1916, GHQ had already decided that the Heavy Branch should be redesignated the Tank Corps,[37] though the new title was not actually granted for several months. Earlier still, the decision was made to appoint Lieutenant-Colonel Hugh Elles to command the tanks in France. Elles was a natural choice. As one of Haig's representatives at the Hatfield Park demonstration, his favourable opinion had played a major part in the creation of the Heavy Branch. He was also a good choice. Though his intellectual endowment appears to have been unremarkable, Elles had courage, good humour and the capacity to inspire subordinates. Some of the latter had the technical expertise and others the vision which Elles himself lacked. The headquarters which Elles established in the château of Bermicourt near St Pol, just north of the road from Montreuil to Arras, became one of the main centres of ideas on the employment of armour.[38]

In the meantime, GHQ formulated its own doctrine. On 5 October Kiggell completed 'Notes on the use of Tanks',[39] taking into account the lessons of the recent fighting on the Somme. This document is remarkable for its balanced assessment of the new weapon and offers a useful corrective to the post-war writings of Swinton and Fuller, which imply that it was only the obscurantism of higher authority that prevented the tanks winning the war by the middle of 1917.

Though he argued that in 'the present state of their development they must be regarded as entirely accessory to the ordinary methods of attack, i.e. to the advance of Infantry in close co-operation with Artillery', Kiggell gave tanks full credit for what they had been able to accomplish. He by no means exaggerated their vulnerability. If anything he underplayed it. He made no mention of the problem of 'bullet splash' – fragments of bullets penetrating tanks through gaps between the armour plates and through eye-slits, inflicting extremely painful, if seldom fatal, wounds. He noted that, although tanks were very vulnerable to artillery while static, they were far less likely to be hit while moving. Once they got close to enemy positions, moreover, they attained relative immunity from indirect fire and the Germans had not yet started deploying field guns forward for specific use in an anti-tank, direct fire mode. Overall, the number of tanks actually knocked out by enemy artillery had been very small in relation to the number that had simply broken down. Kiggell did not minimise the difficulties of mounting operations with the Mark I, however. The ideal was that, in an attack, the majority of the tanks should reach the enemy front-line trench about 50 yards ahead of the infantry. But this was difficult to achieve in practice. The main problem was that the pace of tanks was extremely sensitive to ground.

> Downhill, over easy going they can move faster than the infantry. Up-hill or over difficult ground they move slower. If they start any appreciable time before the infantry they will probably bring down the enemy's barrage before the infantry has got away. If they do not start sufficient time ahead of the infantry the latter will soon pass them unless the ground is very favourable to the Tanks. If they are moving any appreciable distance ahead of the infantry there is an immediate complication as regards the barrage which it is essential the infantry should move close to.

Tanks, in GHQ's analysis, were of most use to the infantry where the start line for the attack was not more than 350 yards from the trench to be assaulted. In these circumstances, if the ground was favourable, the tanks could start moving at the same time as the infantry and still reach the enemy trench ahead of them. If the ground was less favourable or the distance to be covered greater, then allowing the tanks to start a minute or two earlier might still be possible without bringing down the enemy's defensive barrage soon enough to prevent the infantry leaving their trenches. Otherwise it might be better, Kiggell implied, to accept that the infantry would arrive at the enemy's first line before the tanks. At their existing stage of development, tanks were 'merely accessory to the combined action of Infantry and Artillery' and it would not be justifiable 'to take any risk of interfering with that combination or of bringing about the failure of the infantry attack through not affording our men the protection of an artillery barrage or bringing down on them prematurely the enemy's barrage'.[40]

Over the next few months, a remarkable collection of individuals assembled at Elles' headquarters in Bermicourt. Among these, perhaps the most original minds were the technical adviser, F. Searle, and the General Staff Officer 1, J. F. C. Fuller. Searle appears to have been the most mechanically knowledgeable of the people at Bermicourt and was to a great extent responsible for a gradual improvement in the reliability of tanks and for several technical innovations of considerable tactical importance. Fuller was the principal theoretician.

Because he was such a prolific, vigorous and lucid writer, historians have arguably paid more attention to Fuller than his true significance during the war warrants. For one thing, the headquarters at Bermicourt was by no means the sole source of ideas on tank use.[41] (The Cambrai, Hamel and Amiens operations all seem to have had their origins in headquarters belonging to infantry formations, and by 1918 the War Office and the Supreme War Council were independently generating ideas on the use of armour.) Bermicourt and the advanced headquarters, which Bermicourt established from time to time to supervise preparations for major battles, were in fact largely administrative and logistical centres. Though capable of giving technical and tactical advice, Elles and his staff did not themselves make decisions on the conduct of operations. In battle tanks came under the command of the infantry formations to which they were attached. Elles and Fuller, moreover, did not always agree. There is evidence that whereas Elles was aware of Fuller's intellect he was less sure of his judgement[42] and there was sometimes good reason to doubt the latter.[43]

A brother officer at Bermicourt noted that Fuller wrote 'reams and reams about training, plans of campaign, organization and schemes for the use of tanks.'[44] It is surprising how little really critical analysis these 'reams and reams' have been subjected to by historians. Throughout the war Fuller had a tendency to exaggerate the powers of the tank. His first major staff paper on tank use indicates a failure to recognise their limitations in terms of both protection and mobility which is so staggering as to make one wonder how much time (if any) he actually spent riding in them, even behind the lines. (There is no record that he ever went into battle in one.) His claim in a staff paper of February 1917 that they could negotiate 'practically any ground'[45] was simply not true. Tanks routinely sank into soft mud, got stuck in big shell holes and became bellied on tree stumps.

Throughout 1917, the Heavy Branch/Tank Corps underwent a slow but steady expansion, having a total of nine battalions by the Battle of Cambrai in November 1917. For most of the year, while sometimes useful tactically, tanks had no major effect on the course of operations and only barely justified the major effort expended upon them in terms of production, maintenance and manning. Several reasons may be put forward for this. For one thing, as Fuller tacitly admitted in a 1917 lecture, the Mark I was obsolescent by the time it arrived at the front. It had been designed to deal with the shallow German field fortifications of mid-1915. By the time it saw active service in September, the much greater depth and sophistication of German defences posed serious difficulty.[46] The problems of mechanical unreliability and limited cross-country mobility have already been noted. In addition, a type of German small arms ammunition – 'K' ammunition, which could be used in ordinary rifles and machine guns – proved very effective against Mark I tanks.[47]

The first British offensive effort of 1917 was the battle of Arras, which began on 9 April. There were so few tanks available that they could hardly be taken into account as a factor in the planning of the offensive. Tanks were not used in the attack on the first-line objective but were to move forward at zero hour and to join the infantry for the assault on the second-line positions. They were employed in relatively small groups to give the infantry assault added weight at selected points, very much according to the doctrine which Kiggell had laid down in the previous October.

In other respects, the tank story on 9 April 1917 was very much the same as on 15 September 1916. A high proportion of the tanks involved, which were a combination of Mark Is and Mark IIs (only a very minor adaptation of the Mark I), failed to arrive at their start lines because of mechanical breakdown and other problems. Of those that did arrive, some performed useful service but had little influence on the course of the battle, the general pattern of which was that the infantry successfully stormed the German forward positions, which had been thoroughly smashed by the preliminary bombardment, but had great difficulty in making an impression on more rearward positions and could not achieve a breakthrough.[48]

Despite the very modest achievements of tanks at Arras, GHQ resolutely kept its faith in their potential. Haig wrote to the War Office on 5 June 1917 expressing the opinion that

> events have proved the utility of Tanks both as a means of overcoming hostile resistance and as a means of reducing casualties in the attacking troops and I consider that sufficient experience has now been gained to warrant the adoption of the Tank as a recognized addition to the existing means of conducting offensive operations.

Haig took a definite interest in the technical development of the new arm. In addition to helping fix specifications for the next generation of heavy tanks – the Mark Vs, finally available in summer 1918 – GHQ welcomed the idea of the Medium or Chaser tank (already under development at home) and helped fix specifications for an 'ideal' Chaser.[49]

The greatest British offensive effort of 1917 was made in Flanders. It had been in contemplation since January 1916 and was conducted in two distinct stages – a preliminary operation to secure the Messines–Wytschaete ridge, mounted on 7 June, and the main effort further north, the infantry assault for which began on 31 July. The former operation is usually known as the 'Battle of Messines', the latter as 'The Third Battle of Ypres' or 'Passchendaele'.

The Messines operation, planned by the Second Army staff under General Plumer, had been in preparation for over a year. It was initiated by the explosion under the ridge of 19 gigantic mines, containing between them a million pounds of high explosive. This was followed by an infantry assault behind a creeping barrage supported by some 68 Mark IV tanks. (The Mark IV was not essentially very different from the Mark I but was better armoured and proof against the German 'K' ammunition.) There were three main reasons for the very limited role given to tanks in this operation. First, when Second Army began planning it, there were virtually no tanks available. Second, Plumer and his staff were confident that they had perfectly adequate means of effecting the limited result intended without them. Finally, the ground was grossly unsuitable.[50]

The part actually played by tanks was minor and their record mixed. According to the Heavy Branch's own statistics only 19 of the tanks rendered any assistance at all to the infantry. The advance was made over ground which had been heavily shelled for months and was badly cratered, and it was uphill. In most cases, the tanks simply could not keep up with the infantry advance. Forty-eight of the tanks taking part became ditched or bellied at some stage. A further 17 broke down mechanically during the course of the day, though some were repaired and returned to action.

The above statistics might make the tanks at Messines appear to have been completely useless, but that was not so. One tank led the successful assault on the heavily fortified village of Wytschaete and the firepower of two disabled machines played a part in the breaking up of a German counter-attack the following morning.[51] The most pro-tank commentator would have had to admit that the tank achievement at Messines had been limited, but this operation was not planned with them in mind and there was hope that they would be able to play a more significant role when one was.

The first half of 1917 had been somewhat disappointing for the Heavy Branch. Yet no institutional catastrophe came its way. GHQ continued to show patience and goodwill. On 27 July 1917, about seven weeks after Messines but before the start of the main part of the Flanders offensive, the Heavy Branch Machine Gun Corps was, by Royal Warrant, formally established as the 'Tank Corps'. The tank's status as a new arm was thus fully recognised and the large expansion earlier agreed upon continued, albeit slowly. It was the late summer of 1917 which was the nadir of the tanks' reputation in the British Army. By August, during Passchendaele, such derogatory remarks were being made about their potential by both corps and army headquarters that, in view of the deepening manpower crisis, the continued expansion of the corps was jeopardised and cuts appeared to be a possibility.[52] Indeed, despite the rather dramatic achievement at Cambrai on 20 November, in which the corps played a significant role, the manpower crisis did lead to a small reduction in its establishment at the end of the year.[53]

The first infantry attack of the Third Battle of Ypres began at 3.50 a.m. on 31 July. The preliminary bombardment had begun on 16 July and was originally supposed to last only ten days, but plenty of shell was available and Gough eventually secured Haig's agreement to a six-day extension. Fifth Army's offensive was supported by 3,091 guns. Four and a quarter million shells were fired up to and including the first day of the infantry assault. All three Tank Brigades then on the Western Front were brought to Flanders to take part – a total of 216 tanks, although only 136 were used on the first day, starting behind the infantry. Unable to catch the infantry up, the tanks played no part in the assault on the first-line objective and a mere 19 were able to play any part in the attack on the second line.

Though the first day of this offensive was much less catastrophic than the first day of the Somme – some gain of ground being made all along the front and heavy losses being inflicted on the Germans – its long term prospects were greatly reduced by the torrential rain which began falling that afternoon. It rained for four days continuously and the ground became a quagmire. Thus, by the beginning of August, Tank Corps Headquarters had come to the conclusion that the tanks could be of little further use in the Flanders campaign. On 2 August Elles suggested to Headquarters Fifth Army that those tanks still surviving – 42 had been written off on the first day – should be kept for use *en masse* on more suitable terrain.[54]

GHQ was initially reluctant to pull the tanks out of the Flanders battle and used the occasional successes they achieved there, despite the generally appalling conditions of ground, as justification for delay in so doing.[55] It finally acceded to a formal request by Elles on 7 September to withdraw five battalions. The main reason stated for the withdrawal was the need to conduct training, which was virtually impossible in the Fifth Army area, but Elles also indicated that there were possibilities for the use of tanks on both the First Army and Third Army fronts, to the south of the Ypres area.[56] GHQ approved Elles' request in terms which suggest that the possibility of a major tank operation later that autumn had been under discussion for some time. Elles was told to 'earmark and hold available for use in mid-October as many tanks as may be required for that operation'.[57] A Third Army scheme for an attack in the neighbourhood of Albert towards Cambrai was eventually adopted.

The contemporary record does not altogether support the interpretation favoured by Fuller, Liddell Hart and several subsequent historians that the Cambrai offensive grew out of a proposal put forward by Fuller in August for 'tank raids' – hit and run attacks using tanks and infantry with air support but without preliminary artillery bombardment. Fuller's and Liddell Hart's versions are that this astute idea was taken over by higher authority and blown up into a project for a much larger and ultimately unworkable offensive.[58] Elles had a commendable preoccupation with secrecy and little was committed to paper at Tank Corps Headquarters until a late stage in the planning process. After the battle had started, however, Elles wrote down his recollection of its genesis. He thought the scheme for the Cambrai offensive came from Third Army. General Sir Julian Byng, its commander, had been turning it over in his mind for some time before summoning Elles in September. In Elles' words:

> The plan was Sir J. Byng's, the choice of place his too. He also pro-pounded the scheme of attack without preliminary bombardment. ...
>
> The plan was much enlarged subsequently and not perfected till late October.
>
> Only myself and Hardress-Lloyd [commander of 3rd Tank Brigade] knew of the project – Fuller and Searle were not told till mid-October and the rest not till 23 October.[59]

If the basic Cambrai battle plan had been generated within Tank Corps Headquarters it is difficult to believe that Elles would not have seized the credit for that organisation. The fact is that Bermicourt, and Fuller in particular, had no monopoly on the generation of ideas for tank use. Moreover, to look at Cambrai as essentially a 'tank battle' is misleading. The innovation which made Cambrai possible was the technique of the 'silent registration' of artillery. This permitted the preliminary bombardment to be dispensed with, which, in turn, allowed surprise to be achieved while still offering the infantry effective fire support from zero hour. But there was still one problem – the enemy wire. Great belts of this covered the Hindenburg and Hindenburg Support Line positions in front of Cambrai. Without a pre-liminary artillery bombardment the wire could not be gapped adequately. Third Army needed tanks mainly for crushing paths through wire.[60] Indeed, the Third Army plan does not appear to have placed reliance on tanks for any other task.

Tank Corps Headquarters, which established an advanced post at Albert, worked at a feverish pace between the conclusion of its planning conference on 26 October and the start of the operation on 20 November. In addition to the problems of logistics and secrecy, there were a number of technical difficulties which the corps had to overcome in time for the attack. The most crucial was that the main trenches of the Hindenburg Line position were too wide for tanks to cross. A solution was worked out by Searle and his staff. Each tank carried a massive, tightly compressed bundle of sticks, known as a 'fascine', which could be released from inside the tank, blocking the trench and allowing the tank which released it and others following to pass. Preparing and affixing the fascines was a monumental task in itself which had to be carried out at Tank Corps workshops at Erin, near Bermicourt, before the tanks were entrained for Albert.[61]

Less than two German divisions held the six-mile stretch of front attacked on 20 November 1917. The German artillery in the area was exceptionally weak, there being only 34 guns at zero hour in the sector attacked.[62] At dawn on 20 November, approximately 350 tanks led five infantry divisions of Third Army's III and IV Corps into the attack. That morning was, by Western Front standards, one of exceptional offensive success. Aided by a thick mist as well as by artificial smoke[63] used as part of the jumping barrage, the British overran the main Hindenburg position along the whole stretch attacked. The Support Line was attacked in the second half of the morning and that too was captured along most of the frontage. At some points, four miles had been gained by the end of the day, something not attained in four months at Third Ypres.

As with most Western Front offensives from the autumn of 1914 onwards, the impetus was lost after the first day. It is debatable whether the Cavalry Corps had a fleeting opportunity to penetrate into the German rear areas on 20 November. If so, it was certainly not seized. The tanks took heavy casualties on the first day and, as always happened, their crews were generally rendered incapable after several hours in action by the physical effort of operating the vehicles, combined with the effects of high interior temperatures and carbon monoxide poisoning. Some tanks were scraped together to participate in infantry assaults on subsequent days but these attacks lacked the cohesion and element of surprise achieved on 20 November.

On 27 November, General Byng decided that tanks were likely to be of little further use in this battle and that they should be withdrawn from the salient which they had helped to create. Nevertheless, 23 tanks of 2nd Tank Brigade, already withdrawn from the salient itself but not far removed from the battlefield, were able to participate in a counter-attack from Gouzeaucourt in the direction of Villers–Guislain and Guislain Wood which played an important part in stabilising the situation on 30 November, the day of the major German counter-offensive.[64]

The Battle of Cambrai was effectively a draw. Gains made by the Germans in the counter-attack of 30 November over and above the recapture of terrain lost since 19 November, virtually equalled the gains which the British were able to retain. In terms of prisoners and guns taken, there seems to have been roughly equivalent results. After a gloriously promising start, therefore – church bells were rung in England in celebration of victory for the first time in the war – the battle ended in disappointment and a considerable amount of recrimination.[65]

In the aftermath of Cambrai, there was vigorous debate on the future of the tank in the BEF. It must suffice to say here that two factors overshadowed it: a deepening manpower crisis and the growing realisation that the Allies would, for the first half of 1918, lose the initiative on the Western Front and be forced to make the transition to the defence. Despite its success of 20 November 1917, GHQ and the War Office decided to restrict the expansion of the Tank Corps, at any rate for the time being.[66] Tanks could not in themselves hold ground and how useful they were likely to be once the British Army assumed the strategic defensive was largely a matter of conjecture. The main role for the tanks decided upon by GHQ was that of counter-attack. The success of 23 tanks of 2nd Tank Brigade against the German counter-offensive of 30 November at Cambrai was thought to offer some hope that they might be useful in that role, and it was also the role for which Bermicourt argued.

Only the most cursory summary of tank operations in the period of the German spring offensive can be provided here. The offensive began on 21 March on the fronts of British Fifth and Third Armies. The height of the crisis (21–26 March) saw the virtual collapse of command and control in the Fifth Army sector and considerable disarray in Third Army. Most of the tanks were held too far back to influence the first day's events and the disintegration of the over-extended Fifth Army was well-advanced by the end of that day.[67]

Thereafter, the tanks under the command of these armies were either used in rather hurried, disjointed and small-scale counter-attacks or not used at all. None of the new Mark V heavy tanks had yet arrived. The Mark IVs were so slow and lacking in manoeuvrability that German storm troops could sometimes do as they were trained to do with static centres of resistance – by-pass them and continue the advance regardless.[68] While some tank counter-attacks did cause the Germans casualties and delay, Major Hotblack, the Tank Corps' intelligence officer, came to the conclusion that its whole policy on the defensive use of tanks had been misconceived. Rearguard action rather than counter-attack should, he believed, have had the main emphasis. The mobility of the Mark IV tank was too low to enable it to be a flexible instrument of counter-stroke and both tank and infantry reserves had been held too far back.[69]

Tank losses in the March retreat were heavy, but more and better tanks were on their way to the front. Some of the relatively fast (eight miles per hour maximum) and mobile Medium A 'Whippet' tanks had already arrived in time for the German offensive and predictably had proved more effective in the counter-attack role than the Mark IVs. The Mark V tanks, which began to arrive as the front stabilised in early summer, looked almost exactly like the Mark IVs, but were mechanically rather different. They were slightly faster and a good deal more manoeuvrable. Steering demanded much less physical effort on the part of the crews. For the first time, the driver could steer the tank unaided. Ventilation, however, was worse than in the Mark IV and, consequently, crew endurance remained severely limited.[70]

British tanks achieved some real successes in the last months of the war. During the 'Hundred Days', between the opening of the Battle of Amiens and the end of active hostilities on 11 November, the Tank Corps was inundated by demands for its help.[71] A precursor of the Hundred Days' successes was the little battle of Hamel, planned by General Sir Henry Rawlinson and his Fourth Army staff. In reality, the success there on 4 July was mainly a result of a high degree of surprise, combined with overwhelming artillery firepower employed in the counter-battery role and in the form of a very intense creeping barrage. Despite the ecstasies into which Fuller goes about this success in his memoirs,[72] it is not clear whether the 60 Mark V tanks of 5th Tank Brigade, while undoubtedly of some assistance, played a crucial part.

Nevertheless, at Hamel, as historians Robin Prior and Trevor Wilson have pointed out, Rawlinson appears to have hit on a winning method which was to work repeatedly over the next four months.

Artillery superiority, surprise (achieved by extraordinary security precautions and by the silent registration of the artillery), neutralisation of enemy artillery (by counter-battery from zero hour), slow moving and very concentrated creeping barrages including smoke, wire gapped at zero hour by shells with the No. 106 Fuse, a degree of air superiority which helped make artillery superiority effective: these were the main ingredients of the successful recipe. Tanks were a very welcome extra, but still an optional one. Rawlinson, whose Fourth Army was in the van for much of the Hundred Days, was reasonably pro-tank but never saw tanks as the principal instrument of victory. In the planning of Amiens he originally intended to use six battalions of heavy tanks (196 machines), 30 supply tanks and 48 Whippets, less than half the number eventually employed. Fuller talked him into using almost the whole corps. When the great attack was mounted on 8 August, the large number of tanks used (including 324 heavy fighting tanks and 96 Whippets) certainly contributed to the ease with which some Germans were induced to surrender and helped keep British and Commonwealth casualties down. But such a large number of tanks was probably not essential to victory.[73]

Edmonds, the official historian, indicated regret that tanks were never again used on the same scale as at Amiens. The same lamentation has been raised by several subsequent historians, some of whom have attempted to use this as an indictment of GHQ.[74] But any such charge is dubious, to say the least. The main thing was to defeat the German Army as quickly and as efficiently as possible. In the Hundred Days the war, though still slow-moving by the standards of some campaigns of the 1939–45 period, was too fast for the tanks. Really major tank operations like Cambrai or Amiens, which used most of the corps on a single axis, were extraordinarily difficult to mount and took weeks of preparation.[75] The Allied victory in the Hundred Days, on the other hand, was achieved by mounting successive blows rapidly in different parts of the front, giving the enemy no respite. To have deliberately slowed operations in order to allow most British tanks to be concentrated at one place would have been ludicrous – tanks simply were not that important. Their concentration would not have conferred sufficient advantage to offset the loss of offensive momentum. If the tempo of operations were maintained, on the other hand, by the time the tanks had been concentrated, the front would probably have moved away.

Even when acting relatively dispersed, the tanks experienced great difficulty in keeping up with the action. As the report of 4th Tank Brigade on operations between 27 September and 17 October put it:

> During a battle of movement it becomes an interesting problem and a new experience, moving Tanks forward daily to keep in touch with the battle area in case they are wanted by the Corps to which they were allotted.
>
> Corps and Divisional Plans could not be settled till late in the evening for the following days [sic] operations – it was therefore well-nigh impossible to think of getting Tanks up by dawn to precede the Infantry attack.
>
> The daily movement of Tanks tested the endurance of crews, and mechanical troubles had to be dealt with on the spot under conditions which, as far as the time available went, were quite different to what the crews had been accustomed to before.[76]

So great was the stress the tanks were under that 4th Tank Brigade practically pleaded for the infantry not to use more than they really needed[77] – a contrast to the traditional litany of complaint against penny-packeting. Further evidence of the difficulties tanks were having with mobile warfare comes from 5th Tank Brigade. After an operation on 18 September in support of the assault on the Hindenburg Line, the Brigade reported that 'Exhaustion was again prevalent and after a hard action there is no doubt that the crews must have 48 hours in which to recuperate'. A high tempo of operations was clearly quite out of the question, a point reinforced by the Brigade's response to a Tank Corps Headquarters questionnaire about crew endurance:

When a tank is in good condition with a new engine, favourable weather, not exposed to hostile shelling or very severe fighting, the crew may be counted upon for 12 hours in action after leaving the line of deployment.

The average time is, however, about 8 hours, but very hot weather, hard fighting and engines requiring overhaul considerably lessen this period.

In the action of 23 August some crews were physically ill after 2 hours' fighting. These Tanks had done a bit of running and it had been impossible to overhaul the engines. Consequently the exhaust had warped and joints became loose, and the Tank was full of petrol fumes. Three men were sent to hospital, one of them in a critical condition.[78]

It is remarkable how different in tone are the statements from the Brigade headquarters conducting operations in the Hundred Days from the theoretical papers put out by Fuller and others earlier in the year.[79] It is clear that any notion of dramatic breakouts and pursuits, or of the tank as a major war-winning weapon, are pure fantasy as far as 1918 is concerned. Tanks could barely keep up with the relatively hectic pace of operations in which the infantry were engaged. It is difficult to believe that 1919 would have seen a complete tactical revolution.

In fact, though there was no operation on the Cambrai or Amiens scale, tanks were by no means always used in driblets after 8 August. Tank Corps' records show six occasions on which more than 50 and three on which more than 100 were used.[80] But there was a price for this intense activity. As Tank Corps Headquarters reported to GHQ:

The fighting strength of the Tank Corps on 8 August was approximately 7,200 of all ranks with 500 semi-trained reinforcements.

Battle casualties to personnel for the period [8 August–20 October] amount to:

Officers	*Other Ranks*
561	2,627

...Casualty figures are high but it should be noted that anti-Tank defence stiffened considerably from August 21st.[81]

At over 40 per cent these casualties were probably proportionally in excess of those of the infantry for the same period. Prior and Wilson have demonstrated that true battle casualties for the Fourth Army (the spearhead Army for much of the time) in the Hundred Days were quite low compared to earlier periods of intense fighting in this war. In the case of the BEF as a whole, much confusion has arisen between battle casualties and victims of the influenza pandemic who were also listed as 'casualties'.[82] Elles makes it clear, however, that he is discussing only battle casualties. The fact that Tank Corps' battle casualties were so high in the period, despite the general decline, is indicative of the continuing vulnerability of tanks as well as the increased attention the Germans were paying them. The more seriously the Germans took tanks, the less realistic it was for the British to regard them as a panacea – not that many senior commanders in the field were tempted to do so.

Tanks were a First World War innovation of great future importance. History, however, ought not to read backwards. The types of tank available to the BEF in 1918 were sometimes very useful but hardly indispensable, and by no means revolutionary in their impact on war.

NOTES

The author thanks the Trustees of the Liddell Hart Centre for Military Archives for permission to quote from several documents.

1. See for example, *Tank Programme 1919*, Section XIV, undated but apparently early 1918, PRO WO 158/865; and *Tanks and Mechanical Warfare*, 14 May 1918, PRO WO 158/827.
2. Director General Tank Corps to DCIGS, 1 June 1918, Minute 1, PRO WO 158/827.
3. This phrase is used in T. Travers, *How The War Was Won* (London: Routledge, 1992), p.32.
4. On Bloch's influence on Wells see W. Warren Wagar, *H G Wells, Journalism and Prophecy 1893–1940* (London: Bodley Head, 1964), p.71.
5. H. G. Wells, 'The Land Ironclads', in *The Complete Short Stories of H G Wells* (London: Ernest Benn, 1966), pp.115–38.
6. Minutes of Proceedings of Royal Commmission on Awards to Inventors (henceforth *Minutes of Proceedings*), 7 Oct. 1919, p.6, para. 2, Tank Museum, Bovington.
7. Ibid., p.6, para. 6.
8. B. Liddell Hart, *The Tanks*, 2 vols, (London: Cassell, 1959), Vol. I, pp. 18–20.
9. *Minutes of Proceedings*, 7 Oct. 1919, pp. 7–8, Tank Museum.
10. ibid., 7 Oct. 1919, p.8, paras, 33–7.
11. Liddell Hart, op. cit., pp.30–53.
12. On the Mark I tank see Fuller's 'The History, Organization, Tactics And Training of Tanks', March 1917, section on History of Tanks 1916, TS/8, Fuller Papers, Liddell Hart Centre For Military Archives, King's College London (henceforth LHCMA). On Mark I's ability to outpace infantry going downhill see Kiggell's 'Notes On The Use Of Tanks', 5 Oct. 1916, PRO WO 158/832. For a general guide to the technical side of British tanks in the First World War see D. Fletcher, *Landships* (London: HMSO, 1984), *passim*.
13. *Minutes of Proceedings*, 7 Oct. 1919, p.8, paras, 33–7.
14. Swinton to GHQ, 'The Necessity For Machine Gun Destroyers', 1 June 1915, Swinton, Tank Museum.
15. A. Stern, *The Tanks 1914–16: The Logbook Of A Pioneer* (London: Hodder & Stoughton, 1919), pp.40–1, and Swinton, *Eyewitness* (London: Hodder & Stoughton, 1932), pp.160–2.
16. Swinton, 'The Necessity For Machine Gun Destroyers', op. cit.
17. Document B, undated but obviously June 1915, Swinton Papers, Tank Museum.
18. French to War Office, 22 June 1915, Document F, Swinton Papers, Tank Museum.
19. On 16 June 1915, General Scott-Moncrieff, the Director of Fortifications and Works at the War Office sent a letter to the Landships Committee stating 'the view of the General Staff' on the subject of landships and this was read out at a meeting on 22 June 1915, 'Landships Committee Progress Report', 23 June 1915, Stern Papers 1/C/2, LHCMA.

20. Liddell Hart, op. cit., p.40–2.
21. W. S. Churchill, *The World Crisis, 1915* (London: Thornton Butterworth, 1923), p.86.
22. 'The Variants Of The Offensive', 3 Dec. 1915, PRO WO 158/831.
23. Liddell Hart, op. cit., p.48.
24. Haig to War Office, th Feb. 1916, PRO WO 32/5754.
25. 'Recommendations of Conference held at the War Office on 14th February 1916', WO 32/5754; Swinton did not last long as the head of the 'Heavy Section' in Great Britain. He was replaced in October 1916 by Brigadier-General F. Gore Anley. Anley, in turn, was replaced as Administrative Commander Heavy Branch by Major-General Sir John Capper in May 1917. Relations between the British end of the 'Tank Corps' (as it became) and the HQ established at Bermicourt in France seem to have been consistently awkward.
26. Swinton, 'Notes On The Employment Of Tanks', Feb. 1916, Stern Papers 1/C/2, LHCMA.
27. Swinton, op. cit., pp.294–9.
28. 'Digest of Decisions Reached at a Conference on the 26th June 1916', PRO WO 32/5754.
29. 'Preliminary Notes On The Tactical Employment Of Tanks', August 1916, PRO WO 158/835.
30. Ibid., para. 9.
31. Liddell Hart, op. cit., pp.70–1.
32. Ibid., pp.71–5.
33. Ibid., p.77.
34. Ibid., p.79.
35. Kiggell to Robertson, 1/14/40, Robertson Papers, LHCMA.
36. 'Recommendations for the Expansion of the Heavy Section (Tanks), Machine Gun Corps', Put Forward by Major-General Butler, Deputy Chief of the General Staff, France, At a Conference Held on 19 and 20 Sept. 1916, PRO WO 158/836.
37. GHQ to AG, QMG etc., Sept. 1916 (exact date not entered on carbon copy held at PRO), PRO WO 158/836.
38. Elles' appointment to command the tanks in France was announced to the Armies by GHQ on 29 Sept. 1916, PRO WO 158/863. On Elles and Bermicourt see *HQ Tanks*, a privately printed booklet almost certainly by Captain Evan Charteris who served the Tank Corps in the office of historian, 355.486.86:92 (Charteris), Tank Museum.
39. 'Notes On The Use Of Tanks', AdvGHQ, 5 Oct. 1916, PRO WO 158/832.
40. ibid.
41. Great Britain had no shortage of imaginative theorists of tank use. Some of these were civilians like the naval architect, Eustace Tennyson D'Eyncourt, who had been chairman of the Landships Committee. Long after this committee had been wound up, D'Eyncourt was sending memoranda to Haig about tank tactics. See, for example, D'Eyncourt to Haig, 22 Aug. 1917, BCI/12, Fuller Papers, LHCMA. Ideas for the employment of tanks in specific instances also came from divisional, corps and army staffs and commanders.
42. Elles' frequent assertions to Fuller – 'No, Boney, you are wrong', 'You are wrong Boney' – are noted by Charteris in *HQ Tanks*, op. cit., 15.
43. Witness Fuller's statement in February 1917 that tanks could traverse 'practically any ground', see Note 45. See also R. Prior and T. Wilson, *Command On The Western Front* (Oxford: Blackwell, 1992), p.307, on Fuller's ideas on tank cavalry co-operation at Amiens.
44. Charteris, op. cit., p.4.
45. Training Note No. 16, Tank Operations (1) Character of Tank, TS/6, Fuller Papers, LHCMA.
46. Fuller's 'History, Organization, Tactics and Training of Tanks', section on History of Tanks 1916, TS/8, Fuller Papers, LHCMA.
47. Liddell Hart, op. cit., pp.102, 107.
48. C. and A. Williams-Ellis, *The Tank Corps* (London: Country Life, 1919), pp.48–62.
49. Haig to War Office, 5 June 1917, PRO MUN 4/2791.
50. Williams-Ellis, op. cit., pp.63–9.
51. 'Messines, Details Of Assistance Rendered By Tanks', undated, PRO WO 158/858.
52. Liddell Hart, op. cit., p.115.
53. 'Tank Corps Organization' (possibly an account prepared for the Corps history), p.18, PRO WO 158/804.

54. Liddell Hart, op. cit., p.114.
55. Haig to Sir Eustace Tennyson D'Eyncourt, 27 Aug. 1917, BCI/13, Fuller Papers, LHCMA.
56. Elles to the General Staff at AdvGHQ, 7 Sept. 1917, BCI/4, Fuller Papers, LHCMA.
57. Colond Tandy, General Staff to Tank Corps HQ, 11 Sept. 1917, BCI/5, Fuller Papers, LHCMA.
58. Fuller, *Memoirs of an Unconventional Soldier* (London: Nicholson & Watson, 1936), pp.169–81; Liddell Hart, op. cit., p.132.
59. General Elles' 'Notes On The Battle Of Albert' (undated) BCI/3, Fuller Papers, LHCMA. This document was confusingly listed in the index to the Fuller Papers in the LHCMA as relating to the Battle of Albert, 21–22 August 1918. From the context in which the document was found in the Fuller papers, as well as from the text of document itself, this was evidently wrong. The document reference is now being changed.
60. Official History (OH), 1917, Vol. 3, pp.13–15.
61. Williams-Ellis, op. cit., p.103.
62. M. Farndale, *History of the Royal Regiment of Artillery; Western Front 1914–18* (London: Royal Artillery Institution, 1986), p.220.
63. MGO (Sir William T. Furse) to CIGS (Sir William Robertson), 17 Dec. 1917, para. 2, BCII/42, Fuller Papers, LHCMA.
64. 'Preliminary Report on Tank Corps Operations with Third Army', 20 Nov. 1 Dec. 1917, TCOIV/16, Fuller Papers, LHCMA.
65. OH, op. cit., pp.273–5.
66. 'Tank Corps Organization', p.18, PRO WO 158/804.
67. On the role allotted to the tanks during preparations to meet the German Spring Offensive see CGS, GHQ (Lawrence) to Armies and the Tank Corps, 13 Feb. 1918, PRO WO 158/832, and 'Record of a Conference of Army Commanders' at Doullens on Saturday, 2 March 1918, PRO WO 158/864. On the tanks' performance in the March battles see Liddell Hart, op. cit., pp.162–3.
68. Liddell Hart, op. cit., p.167.
69. Report by Hotblack, 2 April 1918, Fuller Papers, Tank Museum. On the weakness of the Mark IV in 'open warfare' see 'Preliminary Report Of Operation Of The Tank Corps', 27 March 1918, and Elles to Capper, 29 March, B7, Fuller Papers, Tank Museum.
70. On tank losses and on the role played by the Medium As in the March fighting see Elles to Capper, 29 March 1918, and 'Summary Report Of Operations Of The Tank Corps', 27 March 1918, B7, Fuller Papers, Tank Museum. On the Mark V see Williams-Ellis, op. cit., p.124.
71. Elles to CGS, GHQ forwarding 'Summary of Tank Actions', 8 Aug. to 20th Oct. 1918, TCOIV/28, Fuller Papers, LHCMA.
72. Fuller, op. cit., p.291.
73. On Hamel and the 'Formula For Success' see Prior and Wilson, op. cit., pp.292–300; on the planning for Amiens see pp.301–8. On statistics for actual tank use at Amiens on 8 August see Liddell Hart, op. cit., p.171.
74. Travers, op. cit., p.144.
75. The Cambrai battle was conceived in August. The Tank Corps first briefed the majority of its officers on 25 and 26 October (Fuller BCI/15, Fuller papers, LHCMA). The operation was launched on 20 November. Preparations for Amiens took about three weeks. The logistical complexities were considerable. Each of the three Tank Brigades used required a reserve of 80,000 gallons of petrol, 20,000 pounds of grease and 20,000 gallons of oil. Prior and Wilson, op. cit., pp.302 and 318.
76. 'Report on Operations', 4th Tank Brigade, 27 Sept. 27 to 17 Oct., 1918, TCOIV/2, Fuller Papers, LHCMA.
77. Ibid.
78. 5th Tank Brigade, 'Report on operations of 18th September with Australian, III and IX Corps', 15 Oct. 1918, TCOIV/7, and 'Supplementary Report', 1 Sept. 1918, appended to 5th Tank Brigade 'Report on operations of 8–15 August with the Australian Corps', TCOIV/5, Fuller Papers, LHCMA.
79. See Fuller, 'The Tactics Of The Attack As Affected By The Speed And Circuit Of The Medium D Tank', 24 May 1918, B.62, Fuller Papers, Tank Museum, and Captain Stephen

Foot's paper on A Mobile Army, 24 April 1918, quoted in Stephen Foot, *Three Lives* (London: Heinemann, 1934), pp.345–9.

80. 'Summary of tank actions 8th August–20th October 1918', TCIV/28, Fuller Papers, LHCMA.

81. Elles to CGS, GHQ, 29 Oct. 1918, para. 5, TCOIV/28, Fuller Papers, LHCMA.

82. Prior and Wilson, op. cit., p.391.

CHAPTER SEVEN

Cavalry and the Development of Breakthrough Doctrine

Stephen Badsey

Whatever its other points of interest, the study of the Western Front in the Great War seldom presents the opportunity for a good laugh. But one of the few which may be almost guaranteed comes when the issue of British cavalry operations is raised. A firm consensus exists, and has grown in strength since the Great War itself, that the cavalry was in all respects useless. Its soldiers spent their time safely in the rear, wasting rations and playing cards, or else engaged in futile mass charges in close order against machine guns, only to be mown down and massacred. It really is a case of 'damned if you do and damned if you don't' for the cavalrymen – they are either passive spectators to the fighting, or its most reckless and incompetent victims.

This record of criticism is constant, from contemporary memoirs of the Western Front by infantrymen, or above all tankmen, who poured scorn on what one veteran of Cambrai called 'our medieval horse soldiers',[1] through to modern studies of the doctrines and strategy of the British Army of the Great War period, and particularly of the career of Douglas Haig, which are content to take the uselessness of the cavalry for granted. To cite only a few distinguished cases, Professor John Gooch has argued, in *The Plans of War*, that Haig's pronouncement while Director of Staff Duties in 1909 that cavalry 'must keep close to the other arms who attack the infantry and prepare the way for the decisive action of the cavalry' (which might in other circumstances be thought a reasonably balanced judgement) shows 'an ominous faith in the effectiveness of cavalry' and therefore 'served to cement into strategic thought an outmoded doctrine'.[2] Professor Tim Travers' *The Killing Ground* (while not actually having the word 'cavalry' in its index) describes Haig at Aldershot Command before the war seeking to professionalise the Army by the creation of a common doctrine 'while at the same time clinging to traditional ideas about morale and cavalry'.[3] In similar fashion, while the sympathetic biography by John Terraine seeks to defend Haig by denying that he should be called a 'cavalry general', Dr Gerald de Groot's more critical recent biography sees the basis for the disastrous attempts at breakthrough operations on the Somme and in the Ypres salient, as opposed to a more sensible strategy of limited offensives, in what Lloyd George called the 'ridiculous cavalry obsession' of Haig and his staff.[4] This assumption that 'cavalry generals' were necessarily incompetent is an exclusively British phenomenon. No such criticism has been levelled against such notable former cavalrymen as Pershing, Langle de Cary and Brusilov; or on the German side against von der Marwitz, who defended Cambrai with such effectiveness in November 1917 (possibly the only Western Front battle in which the Army commanders on both sides were cavalrymen).

The belief that Haig and his staff paid too much attention to the cavalry is fuelled by another consensus, that the British maintained too much of it on the Western Front, where it consumed supplies and wasted shipping. Historians from Sir Basil Liddell Hart to Professor Norman Stone have chuckled over the absurdity that in the course of the Great War the British shipped to France a greater tonnage of horse fodder than ammunition, in the process using more shipping than was sunk by German submarines. The explanation for this which is equally familiar is that, as A. J. P. Taylor put it in his *The First World War*, 'most of the generals were cavalrymen'.[5] It is common ground that what Winston Churchill in *The World Crisis* called 'large masses of cavalry' were maintained by the British on the Western Front only through 'the absurd misconceptions of the staff'[6] in believing that they could ever be used.

This conventional viewpoint, however prevalent it may have become, represents, at best, a half truth. There was a role for the British cavalry on the Western Front, of a kind, and its performance was by no means a comical disaster. First, the myth that the cavalry did nothing on the Western Front, or that the life of a cavalryman was a safe billet, may be dispensed with reasonably easily. The War Office's *Statistics of the Military Effort of the British Empire During the Great War*, although both incomplete and sometimes self-contradictory, give some interesting indications of what the cavalry was doing between 1914 and 1918. At its strongest, in early 1915, the British cavalry force on the Western Front numbered about 25,000 men and horses, of which some 19,000 were cavalrymen (line cavalry, yeomanry and household troops rather than supporting arms such as sappers and signallers attached to cavalry formations). According to the *Statistics* between August 1914 and November 1918 these cavalrymen suffered 4,421 dead and 14,630 other casualties, not including officers. In fact, the cavalry had the highest proportion of killed to other casualties of all the fighting arms, with the Tank Corps having the lowest. Nor was the life of a cavalry officer a soft option. In the infantry, and in the British Army as a whole, the ratio of officer casualties to those of the 'other ranks' (the contemporary term for privates and NCOs) was broadly equal to the proportion of officers in the army. In the cavalry, however, the proportion of officer casualties was more than double the average, at almost one to every nine other ranks' casualties, giving a total loss for the cavalry on the Western Front of about 21,000 all ranks. The only fighting arm with a higher officer casualty ratio than the cavalry, and by far the most dangerous arm for officers to serve with, was (curiously) the Tank Corps again, with an officer casualty ratio of some four times the average.[7]

In absolute terms, to be sure, the life of a cavalryman in the Great War was more than twice as safe as that of a tankman, and incomparably more safe than that of an infantryman. In all theatres, casualties to cavalrymen accounted for just over one per cent of all casualties suffered by the fighting arms of the British Army. But, in extreme cases, the level of casualties in cavalry regiments in battle could easily rival those of infantry battalions. By the end of First Ypres, the 9th Lancers had lost three-quarters of their officers, the 18th Hussars had been reduced to just over a third of their strength and the 11th Hussars to just over half strength. The battles of March 1918 cost the 5th Lancers and the 3rd Hussars over a quarter of their men, while the Scots Greys lost half of theirs.[8] While casualties are not evidence of achievement, they must be taken as evidence of activity. The cavalrymen were clearly doing *something* during those four years.

A possible explanation is that the cavalry actually suffered its casualties charging machine guns. Perhaps so, but like many other things known about the Western Front, this old cliché vanishes like smoke when attempts are made to pin down cases of it actually happening. Cavalry were certainly not bullet proof, and Haig has been ridiculed for writing in his *Cavalry Studies* of 1907 that modern bullets had little stopping power against horses. Nevertheless, however remarkably, Haig was more accurate than his detractors have realised. Veterinary tests of the period, and combat experience both during the Second Boer War of 1899–1902 and the Great War, confirmed that horses do not suffer to any great extent from reaction shock. Unless the bullet was lucky enough to hit a major organ or a leg bone it would not bring down a charging horse at anything more than almost point-blank range. Stories from the period of horses collapsing in death from wounds *after* a successful charge are surprisingly common.[9] Like the infantry, the cavalry were far more likely to be stopped on the Western Front by artillery or barbed wire – a device invented, after all, to restrict the movement of animals – than by the machine gun.

What might be called 'the cult of the machine gun' in relation to beliefs about the Western Front has emerged from many sources. But the idea that machine guns rendered cavalry useless seems to owe its respectability largely to the (now slightly notorious) British Official Historian, Brigadier-General Sir James Edmonds. To take just one example of several, in his *Official History* of operations on the Western Front in 1918, Edmonds quotes with approval the remark of an American officer, 'you can't have a cavalry charge until you have captured the enemy's last machine gun.' Twenty pages later in the same volume is an account of a successful charge by the Canadian Cavalry Brigade (then part of the 3rd Cavalry Division) which captured 230 prisoners, three artillery pieces and 40 machine guns.[10] This achievement was in no way unique for the last year of the war. On the first day of the Battle of Amiens, 8 August 1918, the 7th Cavalry Brigade (also part of the 3rd Cavalry Division) captured over 300 prisoners, including a successful charge by the 7th Dragoon Guards at the Bois de Cayeux which took 40 prisoners, two artillery pieces and ten machine guns, at a cost to the regiment of five killed and 43 wounded. Indeed, the total casualties for the entire Cavalry Corps over four days of battle at Amiens were 887 men and 1,800 horses, which by the standards of infantry losses on the Western Front was remarkably low.[11]

Various reasons have been advanced for Edmonds' hostility towards the cavalry, which seems to have been based at least in part on personal dislike of Haig and Allenby following his experiences sharing an Army Staff College course with them. He certainly never lost an opportunity in the *Official History* to criticise the cavalry or belittle its achievements, describing the remarkable cavalry exploitation between 8 and 10 October 1918 on Fourth Army front, which netted over 500 prisoners, as something which the infantry could have done for themselves at less cost.[12] One certain contributing factor was that Edmonds, as himself a Royal Engineer, believed that the adoption at an early stage of engineer siege techniques to the Western Front, rather than a breakthrough strategy, would have led the British to victory sooner and at less cost. While the merits of such limited 'bite and hold' attacks against a strategy of breakthrough have been subject to much recent analysis, historians have accepted almost without enquiry the fundamental idea, fostered by Edmonds, that breakthrough was impractical because of the cavalry's essential uselessness.[13]

As the historian John Terraine pointed out in 1980, the belief that the British Army on the Western Front was handicapped by large masses of cavalry will not pass even the most straightforward test of statistics. The British began the Great War with a single cavalry division on the Western Front, expanded in October 1914 into a Cavalry Corps of three divisions. This force, together with two Indian cavalry divisions which arrived in France in November 1914, formed the BEF's main mounted component on the Western Front until March 1918, accounting at its strongest for between two and three per cent of the total BEF strength in men, and six per cent in horses. On the last day of the war, the active strength of the British cavalry in France and Belgium was 13,984 men, compared to 13,594 for the Tank Corps and 53,634 for the Machine Gun Corps. It is quite true that the BEF consumed approximately 5.9 million tons of horse fodder during the war, compared to just over 5.4 million tons of ammunition. But the overwhelming majority of horses required by the BEF served as haulage and transport animals for the Royal Artillery, Royal Engineers, the Army Service Corps and, of course, the infantry, a total of 449,880 horses and mules in August 1918.[14] That Liddell Hart, who had served as an infantry officer on the Western Front, could foster such an error is surprising to say the least.

The idea that cavalrymen as a group played a disproportionate role in the command of the BEF and the direction of the British war effort may also be called into question. Certainly, both the commanders of the BEF, Sir John French and Sir Douglas Haig, had either begun or served the bulk of their regimental careers in cavalry regiments, as had the Chief of the Imperial General Staff (CIGS) from December 1915 to February 1918, Sir William Robertson. In addition, of ten officers who at various times commanded the five British Armies on the Western Front five were cavalrymen: Haig, Allenby, Byng, Gough and Birdwood (who had also served with the infantry and the Indian cavalry). Equally certainly, the presence of these men in high command cannot be accounted for by mere chance or statistical probability, since the proportion of cavalry in the regular British Army before 1914 was approximately eight per cent of all regular troops. But it is also hard to substantiate the view that the common denominator of having begun their careers in the cavalry either linked these very different men together, or can be held responsible for the positions to which they rose during the war. Far from their forming a united cavalry *bloc*, the antagonism between Haig and Allenby, or Allenby and Gough, is well known. A more likely common factor is that many of the senior commanders who came to prominence in the Great War had backgrounds in socially exclusive or high status regiments, including the Army commanders Horne (Royal Horse Artillery) and Rawlinson (Coldstream Guards), and Robertson's replacement as CIGS, Henry Wilson (Rifle Brigade), as well as those who had served in cavalry regiments. Good social connections were required at the top of the British Army in the Great War, the most significant exception being Plumer of Second Army (York and Lancaster Regiment), who was at least an Old Etonian.

Once away from the very highest echelons, the number of cavalrymen holding high commands in the Great War was no greater than might have been predicted from a statistical average of the officers available, as an analysis of the *Army List* for the war years shows. By the end of the war, only one of the BEF's 19 Army Corps (not including the Australian and Canadian Corps) on the Western Front was being commanded by a pre-war cavalryman (plus, unsurprisingly, another commanding the Cavalry Corps), and two more commanding infantry divisions. Of 18 cavalrymen holding the rank of major-general on the same date (of which seven were Staff College graduates and four had served in another arm during their careers), the majority were employed on staff or non-combatant duties. Even so, the most prestigious staff grouping in the BEF, the first echelon of Haig's head-quarters, contained just 22 cavalrymen out of 326 officers.[15]

Away from the very highest ranks, the percentages of lieutenant-generals and major-generals in the army by the end of the war who had begun their careers in the cavalry were eight and a half per cent and seven per cent respectively, or just about the proportion of cavalry in the pre-war army. The only blip on the graph is the rank of temporary lieutenant-general, of which 27 per cent were cavalrymen, or nine officers. Including all officers of the rank of major-general or above, 31 officers were cavalrymen out of 331 in total – hardly an army dominated by cavalrymen. Admittedly, there was a single case of promotion from major in 1914 to temporary lieutenant-general by 1919, and he was a cavalryman. But this was the extraordinary G.T.M. Bridges, who had been British military attaché to four European courts before the Great War, who helped negotiate the American contribution to the war effort in April 1917, whose military career continued after the Armistice in such politically sensitive areas as White Russia and Ottoman Turkey (despite losing a leg at Passchendaele), and who was in all respects a quite exceptional man. The image presented in C.S. Forester's novel *The General* of 1936, still cited in factual works on the Great War, of the typical Western Front corps commander as a narrow minded, pre-war regimental cavalry major promoted above his abilities, has simply no basis in fact.[16]

Even at the level of high command, it is hard to find evidence in the statistics of promotion to support the belief, held by some officers even before the Great War, in some kind of a 'cavalry conspiracy' over and above the military patronage characteristic of the late-Victorian and Edwardian army. It is actually untrue that success in the Second Boer War in any way advanced the careers of cavalrymen as a group rather than those of other officers. If anything, the evidence is slightly the other way. In 1914, the only cavalrymen to hold significant positions in the BEF were French, Haig and (unsurprisingly again) Allenby as commander of the Cavalry Division. The only cavalryman to hold the rank of full general was Haig, and there were, in addition, three cavalrymen out of 27 lieutenant-generals, and eight out of 114 major-generals, or seven per cent again. In so far as it had any existence, the 'cavalry conspiracy' consisted of Field Marshal Sir John French and General Sir Douglas Haig, and there is little to suggest that either surrounded himself with cavalrymen in preference to other officers. In addition, while at Aldershot Command both men had gained more experience of commanding infantry and all-arms formations than any other officer in the BEF except Sir Horace Smith-Dorrien. Since the 'cavalrymen' are often singled out among Western Front commanders for their ignorance of infantry or artillery tactics, it should be noted that Smith-Dorrien had also made his reputation as a regi-mental officer in commanding irregular mounted troops, as had Rawlinson, Wilson and Plumer.

However ironic it may seem, the cavalry officers of the Great War who reached high rank on the Western Front may have owed their rise very largely to the simple fact of survival. Although hardly for want of trying, all the cavalry divisional and brigade commanders survived the First Battle of Ypres (although one was invalided sick during the battle), so putting an effective block on promotion within the cavalry above regimental level for the next three years. Allenby, as commander of the newly formed Cavalry Corps, went on to command an Army (and later the Egyptian Expeditionary Force), as did two of his divisional commanders, while the third divisional commander and two brigade commanders went on to command Army Corps (not all of them on the Western Front). But while officers with command or staff experience were at a premium in the expanding army of 1915, regardless of their arm of service, it was clearly not army policy to appoint cavalry lieutenant-colonels to command infantry brigades. A cavalry regimental commander who survived First Ypres would have done slightly better than average to have received any promotion at all by the end of the war, almost invariably to non-operational duties or staff work rather than command. It was actually less likely that a lieutenant-colonel commanding a cavalry regiment in 1914 would rise to command even a cavalry division than that his brigade commander would secure command of an Army Corps or his divisional commander of an Army. In every case but one of a cavalry regimental commander being promoted, his successor was simply the senior major of the regiment or of another cavalry regiment inheriting the post by seniority.

It is highly likely that the retention of the same commanding officers, together with the *comparatively* low casualty rates, enabled the cavalry regiments to keep their pre-war character much longer than the regular infantry battalions of the BEF, something commented on by senior officers as late as 1917. However, the stagnation in promotion prospects within the cavalry also led to a steady haemorrhaging of good officers away from the cavalry to other arms, both by junior officers accepting transfers and by other ranks being commissioned, since it was common British Army practice that newly commissioned officers were moved to another regiment. It was characteristic of the army of the period that the extent of this loss was largely determined by the attitude of individual regiments and their commanding officers. While the 11th Hussars was proud that 20 of its NCOs and privates were commissioned during the war, the 1st Life Guards managed to avoid commissioning a single man.[17] But despite the considerable variations between regiments, the overall trend was that, throughout the war, promotion at junior level was significantly more likely for officers transferring away from their cavalry regiments than for those who stayed behind. Contrary to the common perception, these officers did not all join the Royal Flying Corps – only about five per cent of its officers had started their careers in the cavalry.

Nevertheless, by January 1918 there were 14 former cavalrymen ranking as squadron commanders, and five as wing commanders. Cavalrymen were in fact more likely to join the Tank Corps, making up 15 per cent of its officer corps by the war's end.

There remains the argument that the cavalry on the Western Front was in some way small but deadly, that despite the weakness of the British cavalry force, its very existence as an arm of exploitation led a British high command dominated by cavalry officers into planning battles around its use, in the false belief that a breakthrough on the Western Front could be achieved. This argument should be viewed sympathetically, since it contains a grain of truth – but only a grain. In order to assess its strengths it is first necessary, rather than accepting without investigation the ideas fostered by Edmonds and the cavalry's detractors, to review the actual organisation and tactics of the British cavalry both before the Great War and as they evolved on the Western Front.

Largely through its experience of colonial warfare in the late-nineteenth century, and particularly the Second Boer War, the tactics of the British cavalry were, by 1914, years ahead of those of its continental rivals. While the French still had 12 regiments of armoured cuirassiers with breastplates, armed only with sword and pistol, and the Germans continued to practise charges of divisional size on a regular basis, the British cavalry was a very different sort of arm. In appearance, thanks to the reforms of the Haldane era, the cavalryman of the BEF closely resembled an infantryman on horseback, with a virtually identical khaki uniform, and with much the same weapons. In 1914 the cavalrymen, like the infantry, carried the Mark III SMLE rifle, and they could hold their own with it even in the legendary BEF. There were occasional cases before the war of cavalry regiments winning regional shooting contests. Some regiments made it a point of honour to have no third-class shots, and at least one good shooting regiment, the 14th Hussars, had an actual majority of marksmen.[18] The rifle was carried in a saddle holster (indeed, the curved bolt and shortened wood-enclosed barrel of the original Mark I SMLE of 1904 had been designed with the cavalry in mind), counterbalanced on the other side of the saddle by the 1908 pattern sword. Lancer regiments carried their lances into battle, although Dragoon and Dragoon Guard regiments, which had at the end of the nineteenth century carried the lance for the front rank only, had largely discontinued the practice by 1914. Cavalry regiments, like infantry battalions, were equipped with two Vickers machine guns. In fact, the cavalry had received these one year earlier than the infantry, in 1912, to replace the heavier Maxim gun, and the proportion of machine guns and field guns in the British cavalry division of 1914 was higher than in the cavalry divisions of any other belligerent.[19]

In the years between the end of the Second Boer War and the start of the Great War the tactics of the British cavalry had been the subject of major reforms, and of an intense and sometimes vitriolic dispute over the respective merits of dismounted firepower and the mounted charge. Recent historiography has interpreted this dispute as a meritorious attempt at reform under Lord Roberts as Commander-in-Chief, followed soon after by what has been described as 'a cavalry counter-reformation' under French as CIGS.[20] An alternative explanation sees the debate not in simple terms as reform challenging reaction, but as a dispute between two rival interpretations of Roberts' period of command in South Africa, in which the balance of truth lay rather more with French than with Roberts. Regardless of this, the actual result was, as all commanders were agreed by 1914, not a return to outmoded tactics but a cavalry force trained to a very high standard in both mounted and dismounted action. The cavalry was capable of effective dismounted skirmishing, of open order charges in troop and squadron strength against infantry and artillery, and of some quite sophisticated tactics of fire and movement, including the taking and holding of ground by 'galloping' the position – rushing it mounted and then dismounting in place – a technique which had developed in South Africa itself, and of which Haig was an enthusiastic champion.[21]

The drawback to these relatively new ideas on tactics were that they were over-ambitious. They were difficult to explain to some of the more traditionally minded officers, and there were occasional (and entirely justified) complaints on exercise of cavalry trying to charge uphill against entrenched infantry. There was also an understandable and deep scepticism among officers of the infantry and artillery about the cavalry's faith in itself and its new tactics, and a reluctance to use it. 'No one seemed to know what to do with it', lamented Major George Barrow (later deservedly famous for his command of 4th Cavalry Division in Palestine in 1918) of manoeuvres in India just before the Great War, 'and got out of the difficulty by giving it a free hand'.[22]

For scouting and protection purposes, each of the six infantry divisions of the original BEF had its own mounted contingent, consisting of a squadron of cavalry (two squadrons until spring 1914) together with a cyclist company. But the BEF's main concentration of cavalry was in the single cavalry division of four brigades, each of three regiments, plus an independent fifth brigade which in practice tended to tag along. This cavalry division was supposed to be the main scouting force and collector of intelligence on enemy movement for the BEF in advance or retreat (although, astonishingly, it had no intelligence officer until Allenby appointed one unofficially on mobilisation in 1914), as well as its decisive arm of attack in an encounter battle. But by 1914, it was accepted doctrine that once a set-piece battle was joined the cavalry should wait in reserve behind the main battle line for the infantry to create a break. 'This may not happen, remember,' as an article in the *Cavalry Journal* put it, 'for three or four days!'[23] The cavalry, capable of acting independently with its own firepower, would then 'ride for the *G* in Gap' (an expression deriving from the British Army's 'bingo' system of map reading, replaced in 1915 by the grid system),[24] break through, and sustain itself on a raid many miles behind the enemy lines.

The problem was that the cavalry division was simultaneously too large and too small for its conflicting roles as both the BEF's eyes and its fists. It was too unwieldy for effective scouting or raiding, and because there was only one of it, there was a reluctance to risk it against what were certain to be superior enemy numbers in battle. Edmonds claimed to have asked Haig before the war why four brigades were needed instead of the more usual three, and to have been told that four brigades were essential for the close order charge against another cavalry division – two brigades in the front line, one in the second line and one in reserve. Haig may have said it, but this is probably just one of Edmonds' stories. The real reason was that the Treasury would not sanction the cost of a second divisional headquarters and supporting troops for the cavalry, despite requests before the war.[25] In practice, during the first of the BEF's operations in August and September 1914, the cavalry functioned first as one five-brigade division and then increasingly as two separate divisions, one of three and one of two brigades. This organisation was made official in October 1914, when the supporting troops for the second and third cavalry divisions were created together with the Cavalry Corps headquarters.

Paradoxically, for an arm which prided itself on aggressiveness and 'cavalry spirit', the cavalry began its career on the Western Front with a major defensive victory in covering the retreat from Mons. From the very first encounters, the British cavalry displayed a massive superiority in small-unit actions over the three divisions of the German II Cavalry Corps opposing it, including the celebrated dismounted defensive battle at Néry on 1st September. The ability of the cavalry to dominate its enemies in scouting and patrol work prevented the Germans from pressing the BEF during the retreat from Mons, and in fact made the whole manoeuvre possible. Despite the famous observation that Admiral Jellicoe at Jutland was the only man who could have lost the war in an afternoon, Allenby in 1914 could have easily lost it, at least for the British, in ten minutes. If he had wrecked his cavalry in an ill-judged mass charge, he would have left the BEF vulnerable to German raiding forces and in no state to play its decisive role in the Battle of the Marne. The one exception to days of continuous unhampered march for the BEF was Allenby's confession in the early hours of 26 August to Smith-Dorrien that he could not screen II Corps properly, since two of his cavalry brigades under Gough had lost contact with the main force and were no longer under his command, forcing Smith-Dorrien to stand and fight at Le Cateau.[26] This was the single failure in an otherwise exceptional performance by the cavalry. If the BEF had been forced to fight a Le Cateau every day, it would have disintegrated very quickly.

The cavalry's record on information gathering was, however, very much less impressive. It frequently found itself in front of the divisional cyclists in the retreat and behind them in the advance, while most of the crucial strategic reconnaissance for the BEF came, unexpectedly, from aircraft. Haig, who had a gift for finding fault with everyone but himself, was also unimpressed with what he felt to be the limited plans for the cavalry, positioned behind his own I Corps for the advance from the Marne, and by the apparent lack of urgency shown by its commanders.[27] Although this opinion has been disputed, Haig was probably right. The cavalry, like the rest of the BEF in 1914, was a perfect miniature. Its tactics and battlefield performance could hardly have been faulted, but the art of how to employ it operationally or strategically, of how to take risks with confidence with units of divisional size or greater, was missing from the high command. This is a little hard to understand from Sir John French, given his own superb handling of the Cavalry Division in South Africa in 1900. The explanation may be found in the influence of Henry Wilson, Vice-Chief of Staff of the BEF in 1914, who throughout his career had shown little faith in the cavalry or understanding of its use, and who certainly believed that during this period he was dominating French.[28]

As proof, if it were needed, of its generally high battlefield standards and professional competence, the cavalry – now reinforced to three divisions – finished 1914 at First Ypres with the one tactic for which it was theoretically untrained, by holding seven miles of trenches as orthodox infantry against repeated attacks by II Bavarian Corps. This was a remarkable achievement. At full strength, a cavalry regiment of the period mustered about 600 men and horses, divided into three squadrons, each of four troops. A cavalry division was not only considerably smaller than an infantry division, but required nearly a quarter of its strength as horse-holders. Dismounted, it could muster the firepower only of an infantry brigade, or about the equivalent of an understrength infantry division for the whole Cavalry Corps. 'You have done the finest thing cavalry have done in history', the survivors were told after the battle, 'as you had an Army Corps against you', leading a subaltern to record modestly that 'for a matter of fact we only did what the infantry always do, except for the fact that we had no supports or big guns.'[29] For the cavalry of even 20 years before, such an achievement would have been absolutely unthinkable. But, in fact, the greatest successes of the cavalry were still in the future.

In November 1914, the British Cavalry Corps was joined by the Indian Cavalry Corps of two divisions, which remained behind on the Western Front when the Indian Corps was withdrawn at the end of 1915. The two Indian cavalry divisions were a little larger than the British divisions (with four squadrons to a regiment rather than three larger squadrons in the British pattern), and followed the normal structure of the Indian Army of one British and two Indian regiments in each brigade. Of 31 British regular cavalry regiments in 1914, 22 served with the three British cavalry divisions, which were brought up to strength in November 1914 by the addition of five yeomanry regiments, and six served with the Indian cavalry divisions. The remaining three British regiments were stationed in India in 1914, of which two joined Indian cavalry brigades in Mespotamia in the course of the war, and one (the unfashionable 21st Lancers) saw no active war service at all. As well as rounding out the cavalry divisons, the yeomanry also began to take over the role of divisional cavalry for some of the infantry divisions, with the squadrons being grouped together from 1915 to form corps cavalry regiments (although the squadrons often remained detached with individual divisions). This arrangement of corps cavalry regiments, three British cavalry divisions and two Indian cavalry divisions on the Western Front remained broadly constant until March 1918, the exception being that in June 1916 one of the Indian cavalry brigades was detached for duty in Mespotamia, being replaced by the Canadian Cavalry Brigade. Officially designated as Mounted Rifles, the Canadians were in all respects identical to British cavalry, being commanded by the fire-eating J. E. B. Seely, an experienced British yeomanry officer who had been forced to resign as Secretary of State for War in May 1914 over the Curragh Incident. The only other significant change was that in November 1916 the 1st and 2nd Indian Cavalry Divisions were renamed the 4th and 5th Cavalry Divisions respectively.

The cavalry were used once more dismounted to hold the front line during the emergency of Second Ypres in April 1915. Otherwise, because British doctrine required a breakthrough and a defeated enemy before committing the cavalry, they did in fact spend 1915 largely sitting behind the lines waiting for the infantry to make a gap, which singularly failed to happen at either Neuve Chapelle in March or Loos in September. Instead, throughout the year, corps cavalry were employed as orderlies, snipers, working parties, traffic controllers and on similar duties, while the five cavalry divisions worked to keep their horses fit and alive outdoors in all weathers – in itself a full time occupation. Also, to their disgust, as well as serving dismounted in the trenches, the cavalry were required as labour parties to dig them. 'No doubt this was necessary work,' one officer complained, 'but nothing could have been devised to dampen the spirits of cavalrymen more.'[30] Both the morale and the standards of the cavalry declined progressively. Haig was equally disgusted, on visiting the Indian Cavalry Corps headquarters in early 1915, to find that its commander really was playing cards with his staff.[31]

Following Loos, one of French's last decisions before his replacement by Haig was that during winter, when it was hardest to keep the cavalry's horses fit outdoors, they should instead be moved to permanent indoor stables, and a single Dismounted Cavalry Division should be formed from the Cavalry Corps, to help hold the trenches along with the infantry until the better weather of the spring. Haig confirmed this decision, and the cavalry became equipped with the panoply of trench warfare, including bayonets, hand-grenades and, from early 1916, steel helmets and Hotchkiss automatic rifles. From then on the Dismounted Division, one division among many, shared the infantry's routine experience of the trenches each winter until the end of the war, distinguished only by the habit of many cavalry officers of wearing spurs and riding boots no matter how unsuitable the conditions. As the better weather came each spring, the cavalrymen were reunited with their horses to take their place as part of the BEF's reserve.

Although for the British cavalry on the Western Front 1915 was largely a wasted year, it did keep its main pre-war reason for existence, the possibility of a mounted breakthrough. Most of the other combatant nations of the Great War had rejected the idea of massed cavalry action, following the experience of 1914. The French attached an infantry regiment of three battalions to each of their cavalry divisions, and employed them until the end of the war as a source of mobile firepower. The Germans also, concluding as early as September 1914 that 'the dismounted cavalryman should be able to fight exactly as an infantryman; cavalry charges no longer play any part in warfare' reorganised their cavalry divisions as, in effect, mobile infantry brigades.[32] To this extent, the argument that the British high command was guilty of a 'cavalry obsession' is valid – of the major belligerent nations, the British alone continued after 1914 to plan as if the mounted action of the cavalry still had a part to play in war. However, the only commander on the Western Front who held consistently to this belief throughout the war was Douglas Haig himself.

The first of the doubters was Henry Rawlinson, who after Neuve Chapelle, confided to his friend Henry Wilson that Haig had looked for too much. Rawlinson continued:

> He expects to get the cavalry through with the next push, but I very much doubt if he will succeed in doing more than kill a large number of gallant men without effecting any great triumph. I should be content with capturing another piece out of the enemy's line of trenches and waiting for the counter attack. I am not a believer in the cavalry raid, which even if it comes off will not effect very much.[33]

Rawlinson also complained about the 'cavalry generals' to Kitchener, and even indirectly to the King. This was by no means a disinterested position, since Rawlinson had himself been heavily criticised for the losses suffered by his IV Corps at Neuve Chapelle, and excused himself by arguing that both Haig and French had insisted on continued attacks in order to get the cavalry though, the evidence for which is very slight indeed.[34] Nevertheless, this is the first clear record of a fundamental disagreement between Rawlinson and Haig on the value of cavalry, and on breakthrough operations against 'bite and hold' tactics, which was to bedevil both their relationship as commanders and British battle planning on the Western Front to the very end of the war.

Slowly or quickly, the other senior British officers on the Western Front also came to the same conclusion – that the use of cavalry on the battlefield was impractical. By the time of Loos, even French seems to have given up all idea of a cavalry breakthrough – or at least he had given Haig that impression. Haig's own thinking had advanced only as far as doubling the pre-war estimates by expecting a wearing-out fight of 'five or six days' before 'a strong Reserve of all arms' could be committed.[35] By the Battle of Arras in April 1917, even Byng had rejected all belief in the offensive power of cavalry and the possibility of a breakthrough. 'We gave up that catchword some time ago', he wrote to his fellow cavalryman Philip Chetwode, who was serving in Palestine.[36] Haig's last remaining supporter among his Army commanders in seeking ways to employ the cavalry appears to have been Hubert Gough, although the planning for the first stages of Third Ypres in July 1917 suggests that he also had given up the idea of a cavalry break-through by then. The same profound lack of faith in the cavalry was also exhibited by William Robertson as CIGS, who whatever his original arm of service, was by 1916 preoccupied with sustaining a mass army in which infantry and artillery were by far the most important priorities.

In the course of the war, no new British regular cavalry or Indian cavalry regiments (of which there were 39, mostly serving in India) were created, and the only source of fresh mounted regiments for the British was the yeomanry of the Territorial Force. In 1914 there were 54 yeomanry regiments (plus three mounted regiments of the Special Reserve and one more, the Welsh Horse, founded on the outbreak of war), 42 of them organised into 14 mounted brigades. Most regiments included a small number of rifle-armed cyclists who, for various reasons, could not provide their own horses. On mobilisation in 1914, those yeomanry regiments which were not sent to France were consolidated into the 1st and 2nd Mounted Divisions, the former including a four-battalion cyclist brigade. The 1st Mounted Division functioned largely as a training unit, sending a brigade to Gallipoli in 1915 and two more to Egypt in 1916. The 2nd Mounted Division was sent dismounted to Gallipoli in August 1915, was progressively reinforced up to a strength of five brigades, and was then broken up in Egypt in January 1916. Two brigades were sent to Salonika, and two others to Palestine, where they helped form the Imperial Mounted Division and the ANZAC Mounted Division, alongside Australian and New Zealand troopers. In 1917, the Imperial Mounted Division was expanded to form both the Yeomanry

Division and the Australian Mounted Division, and consolidated together with the ANZAC Mounted Division into the Desert Mounted Corps. The Australian cavalry, of which there were five brigades, were officially designated as Light Horse, and the single New Zealand brigade as Mounted Rifles. Although intended to act as dismounted skirmishers, in practice these troops were virtually identical to British cavalry in training and tactics, particularly after being issued with swords in early 1918, and performed some notable mounted charges. It was the yeomanry and the imperial forces, rather than the regular cavalry, who would demonstrate the continued effectiveness of cavalry in their remarkable mobile operations in Palestine in 1917 and 1918.

In Britain, the yeomanry had expanded by spring 1916 to form three divisions, although all were largely devoted to training troops for other theatres, and one was very incomplete. However, in June 1916 Robertson ordered their conversion to cyclist troops. Haig naturally protested that he was being robbed of his mounted reserve on the very eve of the Somme, while one regiment in a spirit of mockery and frustration erected a tombstone 'Sacred to the Memory of Spurs'.[37] Most of the yeomanry in Britain had disappeared by November, although a few regiments escaped conversion for almost a year. In January 1917 an entire infantry division, the 74th (Yeomanry) Division – the famous 'broken spur' division – was formed in Egypt from unattached yeomanry regiments collected there, and later fought both in Palestine and on the Western Front. In the summer of 1917, those yeomanry which had survived as corps cavalry regiments also began conversion to cyclists or infantry.

At the same time, Robertson adopted a policy of reducing the regular cavalry in France, each time despite Haig's protests. However, this was clearly not entirely Robertson's own decision. From early 1916, the CIGS began to come under pressure from the War Committee (later the War Cabinet) to reduce the number of cavalry in the BEF, on the general argument that they were of no value and that the cost in shipping to transport supplies to them was too great. Perhaps predictably, the loudest demands for withdrawing the cavalry, or at least wintering them in Britain (from which they would have been unlikely to return) came from the Secretary of State for War, David Lloyd George. Robertson passed this pressure on to Haig, who strongly resisted either suggestion. Even King George V himself, on a visit to the Western Front in June 1916, was induced to raise informally with Haig the issue of whether his cavalry could be reduced in numbers or sent elsewhere.[38] As already mentioned, the result was the removal of a brigade from the 2nd Indian Cavalry Division two weeks before it was intended by Haig to play a major role in the opening of the Somme offensive.

Thereafter, Robertson's actions in seeking to reduce Haig's cavalry went far beyond any realistic saving in manpower or shipping, and suggest either a particular antagonism between Robertson and Haig on this issue, or an attempt to use the cavalry as a bargaining counter. Perhaps the most bizarre episode occurred in July 1917 when the commander of the 4th Cavalry Division (the old 1st Indian) returned from leave to find that one of his three British regiments had been ordered home without his knowledge, to be replaced by an Indian regiment.[39] By this time, all the regular cavalry regiments were noticeably below strength, and the number of reserve cavalrymen training in Britain had dropped to about 5,000 troops, or a third of the notional reserve figure. Finally, in November 1917, Robertson stopped cavalry recruiting altogether, and it was not resumed for the rest of the war. In consequence, the number of cavalrymen and yeomen serving at home, throughout the Empire and in all theatres of war dropped from a high point of 140,452 men in July 1916 to 75,100 in November 1918.[40]

From the very start of his command of the BEF, Haig was anxious to prove both that a breakthrough operation was possible and that the cavalry could play a role in it, against the scepticism of many of his own Army commanders and, at best, the indifference of the CIGS. To add to his problems, the cavalry was steadily losing some of its best officers and NCOs, and was itself steadily declining both in quality and in quantity, with little prospect of making up its numbers. Placed in a position of either using his cavalry or losing them altogether, Haig therefore undertook, in early 1916, a major revision of the pre-war doctrine that the cavalry should wait behind the infantry for the line to be broken, and then exploit to a considerable distance beyond it. In January he informed his Army commanders that 'The first gap will probably not be wide enough to pass great forces through, even if they were immediately available; while small forces, however mobile, pushed through beyond supporting distance would, under the existing conditions, certainly be held up, and eventually enveloped by superior numbers'. Haig's solution was that 'The operations to be undertaken will entail both attack and defence, mounted and dismounted, and the closest co-operation between the cavalry and the other arms will be essential'.[41]

In March, as well as forming a new Fourth Army under Rawlinson for his forthcoming offensive, Haig broke up the two Cavalry Corps and disbanded their headquarters. Instead, a special force known as the Reserve Corps was formed under Hubert Gough, and renamed the Reserve Army in May. Placed directly under GHQ control, the intended role for the Reserve Army in the forthcoming Somme offensive was to be held back when Rawlinson's Fourth Army attacked, but to be close enough to the front to fight its way forward, rather than wait for a perfect gap. As Haig instructed Rawlinson in April, 'Opportunities to use cavalry, supported by guns, machine guns etc., and infantry should be sought for, both during the early stages of the attack and subsequently'.[42] If this method of attack worked, GHQ's most optimistic forecast called for the cavalry to advance only as far as Bapaume before turning back to attack the enemy trenches from the rear, an advance of just ten miles and a far cry from the plans for deep cavalry raids of earlier years. Haig impressed on Gough the need to improve the standard of the cavalry for this operation. 'Above all,' Haig wrote, 'he is to spread the "doctrine" and get cavalry officers to believe in the power of their arm when acting in co-operation with guns and infantry.'[43]

What exactly this meant in terms of organisation and training, and how radical a departure Gough's force represented from pre-war cavalry and infantry tactics is, at this distance, hard to assess. Edmonds' *Official History* is quite silent on the subject, hardly giving the Reserve Army a mention before the start of the battle. Gough's own account in his memoirs is thoroughly confused, stating at one point that the object was 'to create a striking force of all arms – with cavalry predominating' and at another that his orders were 'to advance through the centre and raid Bapaume'.[44] There was certainly no clear written doctrinal statement from Haig to Gough. The issue is further complicated by the fact that the command, structure and nature of Gough's force became the subject of a serious dispute between Rawlinson and Haig. What is known is that from April 1916, after Gough's additional appointment by Haig as Temporary Inspector General of Training of Cavalry Divisions, the cavalry divisions began to take the mounted troops (the divisional cavalry, cyclists and, in some cases, armoured cars) of infantry divisions for special training courses lasting about two weeks. The cavalry divisions themselves also undertook special training in how to cross trench lines rapidly with regimental- or brigade-sized forces. No combined training appears to have taken place below divisional level, and the co-operation which Gough envisaged was entirely among divisions. In June, an infantry division which had been already earmarked for the Reserve Army, the 25th Division, spent two weeks training in mounting an attack on the enemy's third line of trenches after the first two lines had been captured and breaking out into open country, culminating in a rehearsal exercise watched over by Gough (interestingly, it was also at this time that the 25th Division adopted a horseshoe as its divisional sign). By 16 June, plans existed to attach II Corps of three infantry divisions to the Reserve Army, which then consisted only of the 1st and 3rd Cavalry Divisions and the 2nd Indian Cavalry Division. This training and structure clearly suggest that the embryo Reserve Army plan was for the 25th Division to exploit any success by Fourth Army, closely followed by two or more of the cavalry divisions (probably with 2nd Indian Cavalry Division in front) and then by the infantry of II Corps following up.[45]

In one sense, Gough's Reserve Army harked back to the Napoleonic concept of a General Reserve which Haig had learned at the Staff College, while 'the intelligent co-operation of the three arms' had become an army cliché long before the Great War. But in another sense, Haig's concept of an all-arms striking force clearly pointed the way to the future of mobile war-fare. However, the idea was also very ambitious. A cavalry division on the Western Front occupied nearly ten miles of road space, and needed to be held at least that distance behind the front to be safe from enemy artillery before the initial attack. Bringing these reserve forces through the chaos of the rear areas and destruction of the battlefield demanded techniques of staff work, traffic control and an understanding of large-unit warfare which the British Army in 1916 was only just beginning to grasp.

The main reason that the exact nature of Haig's plan for the Reserve Army is hard to discern is that it was thoroughly sabotaged by Rawlinson as commander of Fourth Army. On 21 June, after repeated attempts, Rawlinson at last secured Haig's agreement that Gough's force should come under Fourth Army rather than GHQ. Next day, II Corps was taken away from Reserve Army, leaving it only with the three cavalry divisions, while Rawlinson explained to his corps commanders that, although Haig insisted on the presence of the cavalry in the attack plan, he did not expect them to be used. For the day of the attack, two of the three cavalry divisions would be assembled about five miles behind the British front, but they were only to advance through the centre in the wake of two reserve infantry divisions if the German front collapsed completely. To emphasise the point, Rawlinson's orders stipulated that on no account should the cavalry hamper the attack by using roads needed for the infantry or artillery.[46] When the battle began on 1 July, Rawlinson quite simply ignored the Reserve Army, leaving it without orders. At midday, despite having just been informed of the successful capture of Montauban by XIII Corps, Rawlinson decided that there was no chance of an exploitation and stood the Reserve Army down, refusing even to commit XIII Corps' reserve division. Gough, together with his chief of staff, waited all day at Fourth Army headquarters in ignorance of what was happening, not prepared to interfere.[47]

Yet, at almost exactly the time that Rawlinson was deciding not to use the cavalry, the chance for an exploitation was there, on the British right near Montauban and Mametz, where, in contrast to the rest of the front, the attack had met with some success. This was spotted by Haig at GHQ, who telegraphed to his wife at 10.55 a.m.: 'Very successful attack this morning – captured portion of enemy second line on a front of 8,000 yards – we hold the hills about Longueval and hope to get the cavalry through – all went like clockwork.'[48] Haig was, as so often, optimistic. The furthest British advance on 1 July reached more than a mile short of the ridge at Longeuval. It is also probably a factor that the advance came where Rawlinson least expected it. Believing that the German line was strongest on the right, he had set the first day's initial objective for the infantry attack there (the 'Green Line') as the German second line of trenches, rather than the third line as in the centre and left. Gough also expected the breakthrough to come in the centre. However,

Haig's observation suggests strongly that he was unaware of Rawlinson's change to his plans for Reserve Army.

What would have happened had Rawlinson used the Reserve Army as Haig intended must remain a matter of speculation. Reviewing the map of the Somme battlefield, or the ground as it exists today, it does not strain credulity to suggest that if held close to the original Fourth Army front and moved forward at midday, 25th Division and 2nd Indian Cavalry Division between them might have gained another mile or two in company with 9th (Scottish) Division, the XIII Corps reserve, past such places of later horror as Delville Wood and High Wood to the British third objective (the 'Purple Line') which was the greatest advance expected that day. Instead of the confused scramble of individual battalions which actually took place, the next two or three days' fighting might even have taken the fresh troops of the Reserve Army (which by then would have numbered at least three cavalry and four infantry divisions) perhaps two more miles, a distance which it would ultimately take the British Army on the Somme until 20 November to cover, with staggering losses. Those who agree with Rawlinson that the cavalry was valueless would regard this speculation as ludicrously optimistic. Whether the Reserve Army concept of an all-arms force would have succeeded remains one of the great 'what ifs' of warfare. Two things are hard to understand from the episode. One is why no attempt was made to continue the experiment, the other is why Haig took no direct action against Rawlinson – something which in more general terms continues to puzzle historians.

Following the fiasco of 1 July, Rawlinson was left in no doubt of the importance that Haig placed on using the cavalry, and a different tone appears in his own diary, anxious to use the cavalry but doubtful of the chances of doing so. The assault by Fourth Army on High Wood which followed on 14 July only showed the pointlessness of holding the cavalry too far in the rear, and the staff-work difficulties of bringing it forward once the attack had started. Following the success of his night attack, Rawlinson called at 7.40 a.m. for the 2nd Indian Cavalry Division to exploit forward. The division began to move from its assembly area at 8.20 a.m., but by midday the German artillery, which was its main target, had already begun to withdraw. 'Oh! if we could get the cavalry through to charge them!' Rawlinson lamented.[49] It was not until nearly 7 p.m. that two regiments of the leading brigade, the Secunderabad Cavalry Brigade, crossed the British front line and went into action. In a fine piece of co-operation, while two infantry battalions charged into High Wood itself and captured its southern corner, the two cavalry regiments, the 7th Dragoon Guards and 20th Deccan Horse, delivered a simultaneous charge south of the wood which broke into the unfinished German Switch Line defences, killing or capturing over 60 of the enemy. Finally, driven back a short distance to a defensible position, the cavalry dismounted and dug in. Failing to receive infantry support during the night, they pulled back with their prisoners in the early hours of the morning, having taken about 100 casualties.[50]

Two things are noteworthy about this charge, the only significant British mounted attack on the Western Front between 1914 and the Battle of Cambrai, other than the fact of its success. The first is that with only two regiments advancing in line it was too weak to maintain momentum. The second is that the cavalrymen were not so much shot down as pinned down after their initial charge had spent itself, being able to keep the ground that they had already gained, but unable to push on further. It did not take much military imagination to realise that if two regiments could charge success-fully for 1,000 yards into unprepared German defences, a further two brigades arriving early enough in the day could have continued the charge by a further 1,500 yards to the east, so taking the German positions at Longueval and Delville Wood in the rear and obviating the need for a further month's hard fighting. The problem of using the cavalry effectively in the conditions of 1916 was not one of tactics or its vulnerability to machine guns, but of staff-work and of what today would be called cybernetics – of how to get a large enough force of cavalry through early enough in the day to make a difference before night fell, at a time when communications beyond the front line depended on nothing better than dispatch riders, aeroplanes, kite balloons and homing pigeons, together with the ubiquitous flag morse and runners.

Delays on the approach, resulting in the cavalry arriving too little and too late, would be the pattern for the next two years, making a vicious circle that with every failure there was less reason for the other arms to expect the cavalry to achieve anything next time. There was even a strong suspicion that the infantry could have taken High Wood themselves during the day but had been forced to wait for the cavalry at Rawlinson's insistance, resulting in a further bloodbath before the wood was finally taken two months later.

On 7 September the Cavalry Corps was reformed under Lieutenant-General Sir Charles Kavanagh, including all five cavalry divisions. Four days later, Kavanagh met Rawlinson to discuss the employment of the cavalry in the forthcoming battle of Flers-Courcelette, and how to solve the problem of getting the cavalry up in time. Rawlinson records that they agreed that 'the leading regiment must settle the moment for the cavalry to go through', a significant advance in doctrine. But Rawlinson's own views, recorded on the day before the attack, reveal that although he was prepared to entertain the idea of the cavalry being of some use after the experience of 14 July, he had either not grasped Haig's all-arms concept, or had rejected it. 'I think that there is a fair chance of getting the cavalry through,' Rawlinson wrote, 'but I am a little anxious lest Kavanagh should act prematurely and thus compromise the action of the other arms, particularly the artillery which would have to cease fire.'[51] Once more, the cavalry received no orders from Fourth Army on the day of the attack.

An ironic footnote to the discussion of the cavalry's role on the Somme comes from Siegfried Sassoon's *Memoirs of an Infantry Officer*, describing a march past Rawlinson as Army Commander before the battle. 'He had taken the salute from four hundred officers and NCOs of his Army', Sassoon wrote with some bitterness. 'How many had been killed since then, and how deeply was he responsible for their deaths? Did he know what he was doing, or was he merely a successful old *cavalryman* whose peace-time popularity had pushed him up to his present perch?'[52] (emphasis added). By 1916, the belief that all the army's ills were the fault of the cavalry and of cavalry generals was so well established that Sassoon could take it for granted. The error of calling Rawlinson a cavalryman remains surprisingly common among otherwise careful modern historians of the Great War.[53]

The year of Arras and Passchendaele went by, leaving the cavalry with little to show except a steady deterioration both in their numbers and in the quality of their junior leadership. Meanwhile, both Robertson and the War Cabinet continued to press Haig to reduce his cavalry force in the light of the German unrestricted submarine warfare campaign, begun in February 1917. Haig's sensitivity towards the deteriorating quality of his cavalry force, his anxiety to justify its existence in battle and the increasing impossibility of replacing its losses are all reflected in the manifestly contradictory orders which he gave the Cavalry Corps for its role in Arras. 'They should be carefully handled so that their value may remain unimpaired,' Haig ordered; 'it is essential that the Cavalry Corps should be in a condition to deliver an effective blow against the enemy in battle; this moment has not yet arrived.'[54] To order the cavalry to attack and at the same time not to take casualties was simply not possible.

For Arras, two of the cavalry divisions were held in reserve with First Army and Fifth Army. The Cavalry Corps, consisting of two cavalry divisions, one infantry division and the remaining cavalry division in corps reserve (a structure similar to that planned by Gough for the Reserve Army before the Somme, but without the additional infantry corps), was placed under Third Army command. The orders issued by Allenby as commander of Third Army show that he had a much better understanding of how to use the cavalry than Rawlinson. For the first day's attack on 9 April, Kavanagh's two leading cavalry divisions were drawn up in positions north-west and south of Arras respectively, with the heads of their columns less than 4,000 yards from the British front line. Allenby's orders were that if his main attack by VI Corps succeeded in breaking through the German defences, a distance of about 5,000 yards to the Green Line, the Cavalry Corps could then exploit for a further 5,000 yards to the line of the River Sensée, which it would hold until relieved by the infantry, and then advance for a further bound of 5,000 yards in the direction of Cambrai to complete an all-arms advance of some eight miles. The main drawback to the plan was that, because of the shallowness of the British front before Arras, the cavalry divisional columns would have to pass through the town before coming into action. Also, in the light of Haig's orders, Allenby made it clear that the cavalry was not to be used unless the first infantry attacks achieved total success. 'The enemy may bring up his reserves and show a strong battle front about the Green Line or in front of it,' Allenby predicted with unsurprising accuracy. 'In this case the Cavalry Corps will not advance.'[55]

With the strong German resistance to Third Army's initial attack, and the driving sleet and snow in which the battle was fought, it was not until the third day that the cavalry got a chance to come into action. Two brigades of the 3rd Cavalry Division were put through in support of an infantry attack, enabling three of their regiments to capture the village of Monchy-Le-Preux from the Germans in a surprise 'gallop' attack. It was an enterprising piece of work but, although soon reinforced by the infantry, the two brigades sustained over 600 casualties in holding the village against German counter-attacks. Byng, who commanded the Canadian Corps at Arras, confessed that 'it seems rather a pity to lose all these chaps who were perfect cavalrymen for the sake of a village which is a complete shell trap for the British side'.[56]

For Third Ypres even Haig gave up the idea of a cavalry exploitation on the first day – at least temporarily – in his anxiety to husband the cavalry for their decisive advance later in the battle. The cavalry was intended to take part only after its first phase, the seizing of the Staden–Passchendaele ridge, which ultimately occupied the whole of the autumn. In preparation for the second phase the cavalry began in September, on Haig's orders, to train in co-operation with tanks as well as infantry, but the chance to use the two arms together never came. Once again, the cavalry were left waiting around behind the lines.

The cavalry's next opportunity, the Battle of Cambrai of November 1917, is still surrounded by too much mythology, most of it generated by partisan supporters of the tank, to allow a simple description either of the battle or of the cavalry's role in it. The questions of what the battle was meant to achieve and of why it was launched so late in the year and without reserves have never been satisfactorily resolved. What is clear, however, is that in terms of staff-work and all-arms co-operation the battle was a shambles on the British side. On its first day, 20 November, *four* separate corps headquarters, III Corps, IV Corps, the Cavalry Corps and the Tank Corps (the last unofficially), all issued contradictory orders to the leading cavalry and infantry brigades. The Tank Corps version of co-operation was reduced to 'we go straight in and sit on the Germans until the cavalry come'.[57] Interestingly, Haig recommended to Byng, now commanding Third Army, the employment of 'detachments of all arms, lightly equipped' to lead the attack,[58] a revival of his ideas from before the Somme; but Byng ignored the suggestion. The result was almost a case-study in an unco-ordinated battle plan which thoroughly deserved to fail.

It is a reflection of the poor planning for Cambrai that on the right of the battlefield the attack was launched in front of one of the few obstacles on the Western Front that was genuinely impassable for cavalry, the St Quentin–Escaut Canal. 'Horses can cross almost anything,' Brigadier-General Seely, commanding the Canadian Cavalry Brigade, pointed out, 'they can even swim broad rivers, as they have often done in war. But the one thing they cannot get over, unless they can bridge it, is a canal with sheer-sided banks. They can get in but they can't get out.'[59] Incredibly, Byng's orders called for III Corps, led by the tanks, to seize the crossings over the canal south of Masnières with the intention of passing the whole Cavalry Corps – less the 1st Cavalry Division, which was to cover its inner flank by moving between Marcoing and Fontaine – through this tiny bottle-neck, and ride in a giant arc clean around Cambrai from south-east to north-west to regain the British line. It was a comparatively simple matter for the Germans defending the canal to destroy the bridges as the tanks approached with the infantry and cavalry behind them.

The result was an unmitigated and frustrating failure for the cavalry. One of Seely's Canadian regiments, the Fort Garry Horse, found an undefended footbridge and got one squadron across with half an hour of daylight left, only to have the commander of 2nd Cavalry Division (apparently on the advice of an infantry brigade commander) refuse permission for any further reinforcement to follow. Cut off behind enemy lines, the squadron charged through the German rear areas before stampeding their horses with nightfall. Only 50 men recrossed the canal that night. Further north, between Marcoing and Masnières, the 7th Dragoon Guards also got a squadron across one bridge, but had to fall back under enemy fire. In the centre, the failure of IV Corps to clear Flesquières resulted in the 1st Cavalry Division also getting just one squadron into action. Belonging to the 4th Dragoon Guards, this delivered a successful charge near Cantaing, retiring with over 70 prisoners for the loss of seven men and 15 horses. But that was all. The commander of IV Corps was convinced that a gap had been there and that the cavalry had missed it, and entered a formal complaint against 1st Cavalry Division after the battle. The cavalrymen were deeply humiliated. In confidential reports to Haig, officers blamed the failure partly on poor co-operation with the other arms, but chiefly on the promotion block which had forced good officers out of the cavalry, and on their generally poor morale and lack of faith in them-selves[60]

In the German counter-attack which followed Cambrai, the cavalry was used once more in its familiar emergency role, as dismounted firepower to plug the British line. On 1 December, however, a dreadful incident took place, born of the immense frustration felt by senior cavalry officers at their failure a few days earlier. The Mhow Cavalry Brigade, fighting dismounted in support of the 1st Guards Brigade, was ordered to make a mounted attack against the German positions, apparently at Kavanagh's personal insistence and over the protests of its divisional and brigade commanders. This was an exercise in futility to rival the worst experience of the infantry on the Western Front. After a charge by the 2nd Lancers (Gardner's Horse) had been pinned down, the 6th Inniskilling Dragoons sent an unsupported squadron forward into uncut wire in an attempt to gallop the Villers Guislain ridge. Blasted by artillery, machine-gun and rifle fire, the squadron was virtually wiped out, losing 112 men and 187 horses for no result.[61]

The cavalry's failure at Cambrai also brought the question of its continued presence on the Western Front to a head. By this stage of the war the cavalry issue had become, for Lloyd George in particular, little more than another weapon with which to attack Haig; and Robertson, who was struggling to survive politically as CIGS, and was finally replaced by Wilson in February 1918, gave Haig no support at all. Haig's desperation at the prospect of losing his cavalry is reflected in the arguments with which he defended them in front of the War Cabinet on 7 January, stressing their value in defensive operations and even describing the cavalry as 'resembling highly trained mobile infantry rather than the old cavalry arm',[62] something which would have been anathema to him before the war.

Rejecting this special pleading by Haig, the War Cabinet ordered a major cavalry redeployment with the stated aim of reinforcing the cavalry in Palestine and reducing the amount of shipping needed to supply the Western Front. In a complicated juggling act of troop movements, the two Indian cavalry divisions in France were broken up, and their Indian regiments, together with one divisional headquarters, were sent to Palestine, where they were reformed by breaking up the Yeomanry Division to provide the British troops and a second headquarters. In return, nine yeomanry regiments in Egypt and Palestine were formed into five machine gun battalions and sent to the Western Front, where the three Household Cavalry regiments, together with six yeomanry regiments (including two of corps cavalry which had somehow survived so far) were marked for conversion to cyclist or machine gun battalions. The three British cavalry divisions were reorganised, with the Canadian Cavalry Brigade joining the 3rd Cavalry Division. (Perhaps significantly, the only yeomanry regiment to survive with the cavalry was also the most socially prestigious, the 1st Queens Own Oxfordshire Hussars as part of the 2nd Cavalry Division.) The net result was 19 fewer regiments of cavalry in France for two more in Palestine – hardly the substantial reinforcement for the Egyptian Expeditionary Force that Lloyd George claimed in his memoirs. This redeployment deprived Haig of almost half of his mobile reserve for the forthcoming German offensive of March 1918, while so much shipping was needed to bring it about that no net saving on ships was made.

The Household Cavalry and yeomanry had already surrendered their horses, and the Indian cavalry had embarked at Marseilles, when the German offensive began on 21 March – a fact for which Gough never forgave Robertson. In the emergency, the yeomanry regiments (with one exception) reclaimed their horses and joined in with the regular cavalry, providing an effective mobile defence for the retreating Third and Fifth Armies based on small dismounted fire teams together with occasional mounted charges of troop or squadron strength. The most famous mounted attack of the battle (largely because of Seely's skill as a self-publicist) was delivered by a squadron of Lord Strathcona's Horse of the Canadian Cavalry Brigade, which charged to recover Moreil Ridge in front of Amiens from the Germans on 30 March.[63] To argue whether such a small cavalry force played a significant role in halting the German offensive is to miss the point that the essence of the British defence was all-arms co-operation, in which the cavalry played a vital part by providing mobile firepower. Haig and Gough were certainly convinced that a principal reason for the German defeat was their failure to employ their own cavalry as an arm of exploitation. There were cases of British battalions retreating in virtual panic at totally unfounded rumours of German cavalry attacking.

For the remainder of the war, the Household Cavalry, as lorry-borne machine gunners, provided the fire support for cavalry divisions which had regained something of their prestige and their confidence since the dark days of Cambrai. Haig worked to revitalise the cavalry, breaking the promotion jam by removing two divisional and six brigade commanders, and only narrowly rejected the idea of removing Kavanagh himself as Cavalry Corps commander. Haig stressed the training of the cavalry troop under its leader as the basic tactical unit, and on leadership from the front in the attack. This planning paid off in the Battle of Amiens, before which Haig insisted that Rawlinson find a major role for the Cavalry Corps. Rawlinson's solution was to draw partly on Haig's improvements to the cavalry, partly on the experience of Arras and later battles, and partly on his own previous experience of mounted troops before the Great War. For the first day of the battle, 8 August 1918, the cavalry divisions were drawn up in their assembly areas as dispersed brigades rather than in divisional columns, with each brigade area about 8,000 yards behind the front, and the difficult staff-work problems of bringing them up and passing them through the infantry early enough were finally solved. An hour after the first infantry attack, the cavalry brigades were in position only 2,000 yards behind the original front and ready to go through.

The first objective for the cavalry was set as the old Amiens outer defence line, which ran from Le Quesnel northwards to the River Somme at Bray, a distance of, at most, five miles from the original British line. Edmonds in the *Official History* criticises the cavalry for advancing only as far as this objective, and not attempting to press on a further four miles south-west to its second objective at Chaulnes until late afternoon, by which time the strengthening German defences had made the advance impractical. However, the Fourth Army account, which is confirmed by the cavalry divisional war diaries, states that the cavalry was to advance through the infantry to secure the Amiens outer defences, but then hold them until the arrival of the infantry before pushing on once more.[64] This use of mounted troops to 'gallop' a position and secure it was familiar from previous battles and had, of course, been part of Allenby's plan at Arras, but had never been attempted before on such a scale. It was also highly reminiscent of similar mounted 'gallops' by British mounted troops against defended Boer positions during the Second Boer War, including those undertaken by the 8th Mounted Infantry under the (then) Lieutenant-Colonel Henry Rawlinson. In effect, Rawlinson had integrated the cavalry into his usual 'bite and hold' scheme in order to double the size of the 'bite' from 5,000 to 10,000 yards, enough to take it through the German defences.

The cavalry's success on 8 August put its value on the Western Front beyond dispute. All the first line of objectives were taken by early afternoon, together with 1,300 prisoners. Successful mounted charges were delivered by the 5th Dragoon Guards of the 1st Cavalry Brigade (one against a train-load of surprised Germans) and the 7th Dragoon Guards of the 7th Cavalry Brigade, although an attempt by the Canadian Cavalry Brigade to 'gallop' Beacourt Wood, defended by three German infantry battalions, was unsuccessful. Even Rawlinson admitted that the cavalry had done 'splendid work', while Fourth Army's war diary pays tribute to 'the cavalry and infantry co-operating admirably'.[65]

The only significant criticism of the cavalry after the battle came from the tankmen, resulting from the failure of co-operation between the cavalry and the new Whippet medium tanks, which had otherwise also had a very successful day. The problem was that the Whippets could not keep up with the cavalry in the advance, but tended to surge ahead on their own when under fire. This reflected more a lack of faith on both sides, and the difficulties of co-ordinating an all-arms battle, rather than any inherent weakness of the cavalry or its tactics. Indeed, the difficulty of how to co-ordinate other arms with armour has become one of the great military problems of the twentieth century, and has never been solved with complete satisfaction to the present day.

From Amiens onwards, a major problem for Haig was trying to convince his sceptical Army commanders that this time he was right and the war could be won quickly. On finding that for Third Army's attack on 21 August Byng had planned to use only a brigade of cavalry, Haig told him 'that the Cavalry

Corps is now 100 per cent better than it was at Cambrai. He must use the cavalry to the fullest extent possible.' Haig also instructed his Corps commanders to 'reinforce where we are winning, not where we are held up!' – the classic catchphrase of successful exploitation tactics.[66] Even corps cavalry were temporarily reintroduced by attaching a regiment to each corps involved in the attack, while a brigade of infantry in buses was added to the lorried machine guns of the Household Cavalry to turn the Cavalry Corps into a true all-arms formation. By this date, however, the cavalry was a steadily wasting asset, and on 1 September the Cavalry Corps was pulled back into reserve to keep it up to strength in case the German front should collapse altogether. With the malice characteristic of someone who, in his own eyes, was never wrong, Haig wrote to Henry Wilson as CIGS that 'Our shortage of cavalry is daily becoming more noticeable, and there is no doubt that your predecessor committed a serious error in sending off to Palestine two cavalry divisions last February. I hear that they are doing little or nothing there.'[67] This remark was almost ludicrously untrue, as Haig would find out a few days later when Allenby's thunderbolt of mobile warfare shattered the Turkish forces in Palestine.

Major exercises were mounted for the Cavalry Corps in September to test its co-operation tactics, including the use of overflying aircraft machine-gunning the ground only a few yards ahead of the charging cavalry – something for which Haig had high hopes, and which later became standard practice for British airmen co-operating with White Russian cavalry in the War of Intervention. The Cavalry Corps was used once more, on 8 October on the Fourth Army front in its final successful breakthrough near Le Cateau, before being withdrawn to rest two days later. Thereafter, individual regiments and brigades were used across the front to spearhead the British advance through to the Armistice. By this date the entire Cavalry Corps, at under 14,000 men and horses, was not very much stronger than the original Cavalry Division of 1914. In fact, the War Cabinet had only narrowly decided in June not to reinforce Haig by sending the Australian Mounted Division from Palestine to France. The final irony about the cavalry on the Western Front was not that there was too much of it, but that at the end of the war there was actually not enough.

In summing up, it is clearly a mistaken judgement to describe the cavalry on the Western Front as a failure. But although it played a greater part in victory than is usually realised, its success was of a middling sort. Its two greatest achievements were defensive operations covering retreats, rather than glorious forward movements, and its tactical innovations and contribution to the last great offensives of 1918 fade into insignificance compared with those of the artillery, infantry or engineers. Nevertheless, it is certainly wrong, given the success of cavalry operations in Palestine and Mesopotamia, and also in Poland and Russia in the years immediately following the Great War, to argue that those who continued to believe in the value of the cavalry alter 1918 were either misguided or short-sighted. A true replacement for the cavalry, in the form of a practical genuinely fast tank, did not exist in the Great War or for some years thereafter. Horsed cavalry became obsolete only when mechanical armoured vehicles, which were less vulnerable to fire, became as manoeuvrable over all terrain, easier to maintain and cheaper to keep. This was far more a long-term technological and even social phenomenon than an issue of military tactics. It happened in western Europe in the inter-war period, but not in eastern Europe until after the Second World War, and in some parts or the world it has not actually happened yet.

Finally, there is the interesting problem of the alternative past. What would have happened if Haig had asserted his authority over Rawlinson before July 1916, as he did before August 1918, and the Reserve Army had been used as he intended? In September 1944, it was considered worth while to risk three airborne divisions in Operation Market-Garden to end the Second World War before Christmas. The result was the disaster at Arnhem, the notorious 'bridge too far' in which the leading division was virtually wiped out. But what would have happened if the cavalry divisions of the Reserve Army, organised and positioned as Haig had intended, had been risked by Rawlinson on the late morning of 1 July 1916? Would the British Army have been spared the rest of the Somme – perhaps even Passchendaele too? We shall never know.

TABLE 7.1
THE BRITISH CAVALRY DIVISIONS OF THE GREAT WAR

THE WESTERN FRONT

August 1914

The Cavalry Division
  1st Cavalry Brigade
  2nd Cavalry Brigade
  3rd Cavalry Brigade
  4th Cavalry Brigade (incl. the composite Household Regt)
  5th Cavalry Brigade (independent) – attached to the Cavalry Division in August 1914

November 1914

THE CAVALRY CORPS
  1st Cavalry Division
    1st Cavalry Brigade
    2nd Cavalry Brigade
    9th Cavalry Brigade (incl. one yeomanry regt)*
  * This brigade joined the division in April 1915

2nd Cavalry Division
3rd Cavalry Brigade
4th Cavalry Brigade (incl. one yeomanry regt)
5th Cavalry Brigade

3rd Cavalry Division
6th Cavalry Brigade (incl. one yeomanry regt)
7th Cavalry Brigade (incl. one yeomanry regt)
8th Cavalry Brigade (incl. one yeomanry regt)

THE INDIAN CAVALRY CORPS

1st Indian Cavalry Division
Mhow Cavalry Brigade (incl. one British line regt)
Lucknow Cavalry Brigade (incl. one British line regt)
Sialkot Cavalry Brigade (incl. one British line regt)

2nd Indian Cavalry Division
Ambala Cavalry Brigade (incl. one British line regt)
Secunderabad Cavalry Brigade (incl. one British line regt)
Meerut Cavalry Brigade (incl. one British line regt)*
* This brigade left the division in June 1916.

September 1916

THE CAVALRY CORPS

1st Cavalry Division
1st Cavalry Brigade
2nd Cavalry Brigade
9th Cavalry Brigade (incl. one yeomanry regt)

2nd Cavalry Division
3rd Cavalry Brigade
4th Cavalry Brigade (incl. one yeomanry regt)
5th Cavalry Brigade

3rd Cavalry Division
6th Cavalry Brigade (incl. one yeomanry regt)
7th Cavalry Brigade (incl. one yeomanry regt)
8th Cavalry Brigade (incl. one yeomanry regt)

4th Cavalry Division
Mhow Cavalry Brigade (incl. one British line regt)
Lucknow Cavalry Brigade (incl. one British line regt)*
Sialkot Cavalry Brigade (incl. one British line regt)
* The British line regt with this brigade was sent to India in 1917.

5th Cavalry Division
Ambala Cavalry Brigade (incl. one British line regt)
Secunderabad Cavalry Brigade (incl. one British line regt)
Canadian Cavalry Brigade

March 1918

THE CAVALRY CORPS

1st Cavalry Division
1st Cavalry Brigade

2nd Cavalry Brigade
9th Cavalry Brigade

2nd Cavalry Division
3rd Cavalry Brigade
4th Cavalry Brigade (incl. one yeomanry regt)
5th Cavalry Brigade

3rd Cavalry Division
6th Cavalry Brigade
7th Cavalry Brigade
Canadian Cavalry Brigade

A Household Cavalry Composite Brigade of motorised machine gunners formed the Cavalry Corps reserve.

EGYPT AND PALESTINE

April 1917

THE DESERT COLUMN

The ANZAC Mounted Division
22nd Mounted Brigade
1st ALH Brigade
2nd ALH Brigade
NZ Mounted Brigade

The Imperial Mounted Division
2nd Mounted Brigade
6th Mounted Brigade
3rd ALH Brigade

All 'Mounted' brigades are British yeomanry, except for the New Zealand Mounted Brigade. ALH brigades are Australian Light Horse. The composition of both divisions seems to have changed frequently.

July 1917

THE DESERT MOUNTED CORPS

The ANZAC Mounted Division
1st ALH Brigade
2nd ALH Brigade
NZ Mounted Brigade

The Yeomanry Division
6th Mounted Brigade
8th Mounted Brigade
22nd Mounted Brigade

The Australian Mounted Division
3rd ALH Brigade
4th ALH Brigade
5th Mounted Brigade

7th Mounted Brigade and the Imperial Camel Corps Brigade were independent as part of the Desert Mounted Corps reserve at this date.

September 1918

THE DESERT MOUNTED CORPS

The ANZAC Mounted Division
  1st ALH Brigade
  2nd ALH Brigade
  NZ Mounted Brigade

The Australian Mounted Division
  3rd ALH Brigade
  4th ALH Brigade
  5th ALH Brigade

4th Cavalry Division
  10th Cavalry Brigade
  11th Cavalry Brigade
  12th Cavalry Brigade

5th Cavalry Division
  13th Cavalry Brigade
  14th Cavalry Brigade
  15th (Imperial Service) Cavalry Brigade

The cavalry brigades were all composed of one yeomanry regt (from breaking up the Yeomanry Division and the mounted brigades) and two Indian cavalry regts (sent from France), except the 15th, which was three Indian regts maintained by the ruling princes of their respective states.

GALLIPOLI

August 1915

2nd Mounted Division
  1st Mounted Brigade
  2nd Mounted Brigade
  3rd Mounted Brigade
  4th Mounted Brigade
  5th Mounted Brigade

September 1915

2nd Mounted Division
  1st Composite Brigade
  2nd Composite Brigade
  1st Scottish Horse Mounted Brigade
  1st Highland Mounted Brigade

In December 1915 this division was withdrawn to Cairo and reorganised back to its original structure. In January 1916 it was broken up as follows:

1st Mounted Brigade – renumbered 22nd Mtd Bde, served with ANZAC Mtd Div., Yeomanry Div., renumbered 12th Cavalry Bde and reorganised, served with 4th Cavalry Div.

2nd Mounted Brigade – renumbered 6th Mtd Bde, served with Imperial Mtd Div., Yeomanry Div., renumbered 14th Cavalry Bde and reorganised, served with 5th Cavalry Div.

3rd Mounted Brigade – renumbered 7th Mtd Bde, served in Salonika (independent), returned to Egypt June 1917, renumbered 10th Cavalry Bde and reorganised, served with 4th Cavalry Div.

4th Mounted Brigade – renumbered 8th Mtd Bde, served western Egypt and with Yeomanry Div., renumbered 11th Cavalry Bde and reorganised, served with 4th Cavalry Div.

5th Mounted Brigade – served western Egypt, renumbered 13th Cavalry Bde and reorganised, served with 5th Cavalry Div.

MESOPOTAMIA

November 1918

The Imperial Mounted Division
6th Indian Cavalry Brigade (incl. one British line regt)
7th Indian Cavalry Brigade (incl. one British line regt)
11th Indian Cavalry Brigade (incl. one British line regt)
This has no relationship at all to the original Imperial Mounted Division in Palestine. The three brigades were independent until virtually the end of the war.

THE HOME FRONT

August 1914

1st Mounted Division
Eastern Mounted Brigade
1st South Midlands Mounted Brigade
2nd South Midlands Mounted Brigade
Notts and Derby Mounted Brigade

September 1914

1st Mounted Division
Eastern Mounted Brigade
South Wales Mounted Brigade
Welsh Border Mounted Brigade
North Midlands Mounted Brigade
Cyclist Brigade (four battalions from TF infantry regts)
2nd Mounted Division
1st South Midlands Mounted Brigade
2nd South Midlands Mounted Brigade
Notts and Derby Mounted Brigade
London Mounted Brigade

May 1915

1st Mounted Division
1st South Wales Mounted Brigade
Welsh Border Mounted Brigade
2/1st South Wales Mounted Brigade

2/1st North Midlands Mounted Brigade

2nd Mounted Division
1st Mounted Brigade
2nd Mounted Brigade
3rd Mounted Brigade
4th Mounted Brigade
This division was sent to Gallipoli in August 1915.

2/2nd Mounted Division
2/1st Notts and Derby Mounted Brigade
2/1st South Midlands Mounted Brigade
2/2nd South Midlands Mounted Brigade
2/1st London Mounted Brigade

April 1916

1st Mounted Division
1st Mounted Brigade
2nd Mounted Brigade
3rd Mounted Brigade
4th Mounted Brigade
These have no relationship to the brigades of the same number which fought with 2nd Mounted Div at Gallipoli and were renumbered later in Egypt. In July 1916, the division was converted to cyclist troops and renamed **1st Cyclist Division**. In November 1916 the division was broken up.

3rd Mounted Division
2/1st Notts and Derby Mounted Brigade
2/1st South Midlands Mounted Brigade
2/2nd South Midlands Mounted Brigade
2/1st London Mounted Brigade
This division was previously 2/2nd Mounted Div. In July 1916 (after 1st Mounted Div. had become 1st Cyclist Div.) it was renamed **1st Mounted Division**. In September 1916 it was converted to cyclist troops and renamed **The Cyclist Division**.

4th Mounted Division
13th Mounted Brigade
14th Mounted Brigade
15th Mounted Brigade
16th Mounted Brigade
This division was created in March 1916. In July 1916 it was converted to cyclist troops and renamed **2nd Cyclist Division**. It was broken up in November 1916.

January 1917

The Cyclist Division
1st Cyclist Brigade
2nd Cyclist Brigade
3rd Cyclist Brigade
4th Cyclist Brigade
This was the old 2/2nd Mounted Div./3rd Mounted Div./1st Mounted Div. It served at home until the end of the war.

NOTES

1. Major Philip Hammond, 'F' Battalion, Tank Corps, quoted in Robert Woolcombe, *The First Tank Battle, Cambrai 1917* (London: Arthur Barker, 1967), p.85.
2. John Gooch, *The Plans of War. The General Staff and British Military Strategy c. 1900–1916* (London: Routledge & Kegan Paul, 1974), p.117.
3. Tim Travers, *The Killing Ground. The British Army, the Western Front and the Emergence of Modern Warfare, 1900–1918* (London: Unwin Hyman, 1987), p.5.
4. John Terraine, *Douglas Haig. The Educated Soldier* (London: Leo Cooper, 1963), p.21. Gerard De Groot, *Douglas Haig 1861–1928* (London: Unwin Hyman, 1988), p.234. David Lloyd George, *The War Memoirs of David Lloyd George* (London: Odhams Press, 1938), Vol. 2, p.2038.
5. A. J. P. Taylor, *The First World War. An Illustrated History* (London: Hamish Hamilton, 1963), p.20. B. H. Liddell Hart, *History of the First World War* (London: Pan edn, 1972), p.35. Norman Stone, *The Eastern Front 1914–1917* (London: Hodder & Stoughton, 1975), p.49.
6. Winston S. Churchill, *The World Crisis 1911–1918* (London: 4-Square edn, 1960), p.583.
7. *Statistics of the Military Effort of the British Empire During the Great War 1914–1920* (London: HMSO, 1922), pp.65–6, 207–8, 245–9 (hereafter *Statistics of Military Effort*).
8. E. W. Sheppard, *The Ninth Queen's Royal Lancers 1715–1936* (London: Gale & Polden, 1939), p.255. Charles Burnett, *The Memoirs of the 18th (Queen Mary's Own) Royal Hussars 1906–1922* (Winchester: Warren & Son, 1926), p.74. L. R. Lumley, *History of the 11th Hussars (Prince Albert's Own) 1908–1934* (London: RUSI 1936), p.188. Ralph Legge Pomeroy, *History of the Scots Greys (The Second Dragoons) August 1914–March 1919* (London: privately printed, 1938), p.149. J. R. Harvey and H. A. Cape, *The History of the 5th (Royal Irish) Regiment of Dragoons from 1689 to 1797 and afterwards The Fifth Royal Irish Lancers from 1858 to 1921* (London: Gale & Polden, 1923), p.410. Walter Temple Willcox, *The 3rd (King's Own) Hussars in the Great War (1914–1919)* (London: John Murray, 1925), p.257.
9. See Douglas Haig, *Cavalry Studies* (London: Hugh Rees, 1907), p.8, and the criticisms by J. F. C. Fuller in introduction to Leon Wolff, *In Flanders Fields* (London: Longman & Green, 1958), p.xiii, James Marshall-Cornwall, *Haig as Military Commander* (London: B. T. Batsford, 1973), p.65, and Basil Collier, *Brasshat. A Biography of Field Marshal Sir Henry Wilson* (London: Secker & Warburg, 1961), p.96. But see also Report A1294 'Report on Experiments with Various Bullets against Animals 1902', War Office Library 'A Papers' held in the main library of the British Ministry of Defence, London; Frederick Smith, 'The Effects of the Lee-Metford Bullet on the Bones of Horses', *Journal of the Royal United Services Institute*, Vol. 38 (1894), pp.41–50; G. T. Denison, *Modern Cavalry* (London: Thomas Bosworth, 1868), p.182; and R. M. P. Preston, *The Desert Mounted Corps* (London: Constable, 1921), pp.80–4.
10. J. E. Edmonds (gen. ed.), *The History of the Great War based on Official Documents, Military Operations* (London: HMSO, various dates) (hereafter *Official History*), *France and Belgium 1918*, Vol. V, pp.196 and 216. See also John Ellis, *The Social History of the Machine Gun* (London: Crosset, 1975), pp.111–48, and John Terraine, *The Smoke and the Fire. Myths and Anti-Myths of War* (London: Leo Cooper, 1992), pp.130–42. For Edmonds see Brian Bond, *The Victorian Army and the Staff College 1854–1914* (London: Eyre Methuen, 1972), pp.158–69 and Travers, op.cit., pp.10–11.
11. Archibald Montgomery, *The Story of the Fourth Army in the Battles of the Hundred Days, August 8th to November 11th 1918* (London: Hodder Stoughton, n.d.), pp.44–6. *Official History, France and Belgium*, Vol. IV, pp.53 and 158. J. M. Brereton, *A History of the 4th/7th Royal Dragoon Guards1685–1980* (Catterick: privately printed, 1982), pp.338–9. Ralph Legge Pomeroy, *The Story of a Regiment of Horse, Being the Regimental History from 1685 to 1922 of the 5th Princess Charlotte of Wales's Dragoon Guards* (Edinburgh: Blackwood,1924), Vol. I, pp.325–8.
12. *Official History, France and Belgium*, Vol. V, p.235. Montgomery, op.cit., p.200.
13. Two important recent works on British higher command in the war, Tim Travers, *How the*

War Was Won. Command and Technology in the British Army on the Western Front 1917–1918 (London: Routledge, 1992), and Robin Prior and Trevor Wilson, *Command on the Western Front. The Military Career of Sir Henry Rawlinson 1914–1918* (Oxford: Blackwell, 1992), are sadly flawed by following Edmonds in this matter.

14. Terraine, *The Smoke and the Fire*, pp.161–6. *Statistics of Military Effort*, pp.65–6, 207–8, 249, 400, 484–5, 521.

15. These figures are taken from a comparison of the monthly *Army List* (London: HMSO) between January 1915 and January 1918. See also 'Composition of the British Armies in France, 1 February 1919', Acc.3155.220j, Papers of Field Marshal Earl Haig, held in the National Library of Scotland (hereafter Haig Papers).

16. C. S. Forester, *The General* (London: Penguin, 1936). See Norman Dixon, *On the Psychology of Military Incompetence* (London: Jonathan Cape, 1976), p.307, and Charles Messenger, *The Art of Blitzkrieg* (London: Ian Allen, 1976), p.11, for the wide acceptance of Forester's version as fact. See also Tom Bridges, *Alarms and Excursions* (London: Longmans, 1938).

17. Richard Brett–Smith, *The 11th Hussars (Prince Albert's Own)* (London: Leo Cooper, 1969), p.232, and R. A. Lloyd, *A Trooper in the Tins* (London: Hurst & Blackett, 1938), p.75.

18. J. Gilbert Browne and E. J. Bridges, *Historical Record of the 14th (King's) Hussars, Volume II, 1900–1922* (London: RUSI, 1932), pp.251 and 272. Edward L, Spears, *The Picnic Basket* (London: Secker & Warbur, 1967), p.77. Lumley, op. cit. p.10.

19. H.V.S. Charrington, *Where Cavalry Stands Today* (London: Gale & Polden, 1927), p.25.

20. De Groot, op. cit., p.94. Brian Bond, 'Doctrine and Training of the British Cavalry', in Michael Howard (ed.), *The Theory and Practice of War. Essays Presented to Captain B. H. Liddell Hart on his Seventieth Birthday* (London: Cassell, 1965), pp.97–125. E. M. Spiers, 'The British Cavalry 1902–1914', *Journal of the Society for Army Historical Research*, Vol. 57, No. 230 (1977), pp.71–9. Richard Holmes, *The Little Field Marshal, Sir John French* (London: Jonathan Cape, 1981), pp.151–65.

21. Stephen Badsey, 'Mounted Combat in the Second Boer War, *Sandhurst Journal of Military Studies*, No. 2 (summer 1991).

22. George de S. Barrow, *The Fire of Life* (London: Hutchinson, 1941), p.130.

23. 'Eques' (pseudonym), 'Cavalry on the Battlefield', *The Cavalry Journal*, Vol. 3, No. 10 (1908), p.143.

24. Shelford Bidwell and Dominick Graham, *Fire-Power, British Army Weapons and Theories of War 1904–1945* (London: Allen & Unwin, 1982), pp.102–8. The same book, pp.32–4, has some enlightened and neglected things to say about the British cavalry before 1914.

25. Edmonds quoted in Brian Gardner, *Allenby* (London: Cassell, 1965), p.75. Zara Steiner, *Britain and the Origins of the First World War* (London: MacMillan, 1977), p.194. 'Army Council Decisions 1913 Number 734', pp.446–8, WO/163/18, Public Record Office, Kew (hereafter PRO).

26. Phillip Chetwode to Archibald Wavell, 20 June 1938, 6/VI/26, and George de S. Barrow to Archibald Wavell, not dated, 6/VI/10, Papers of Field Marshal Viscount Allenby, Liddell Hart Centre, King's College, London. Archibald Wavell, *Allenby, A Study in Greatness* (London: Harrap, 1940), pp.136–8.

27. Haig war diary entries, 7 and 9 Sept. 1914, Acc. 3155.98 Haig Papers. See also Charrington to Clark, 14 March 1935, I/7/1, Papers of H.C.S. Charrington, Liddell Hart Centre, King's College, London.

28. This is shown by Wilson's diary entries for August and September 1914 referring to French, in particular 22 September, 'of course he has no brains at all'. Papers of Field Marshal Sir Henry Wilson, Imperial War Museum, London (hereafter Wilson Papers). See also Holmes, op. cit., p.217.

29. Talbot-Rice to his parents, 4 Nov. 1914, 7511–80, Papers of Captain J. Arthur Talbot-Rice, 5th Lancers, National Army Museum, London.

30. Lumley, op. cit., p.258.

31. Haig war diary entry 18 April 1915, Acc. 3155.101, Haig Papers.

32. Minister for War Colonel-General Erich von Falkenhayn, quoted in the 'Editor's Notes' of *United Services Magazine*, Vol. LI, New Series (1914), p.226.

33. Rawlinson diary entry, 14 March 1915, Papers of Field Marshal Lord Rawlinson, Churchill Archive Centre, Churchill College, Cambridge (hereafter Rawlinson Papers). See also Wilson diary entry, 15 March 1915, Wilson Papers, and Rawlinson to Kitchener, 23 March and 1 April 1915, Papers of Field Marshal Lord Kitchener, PRO PRO 30/57 WB/17–18.

34. Prior and Wilson, op. cit., p.72.

35. Haig war diary entry, 9 July 1915, Acc. 3155.101, Haig Papers. Travers, *The Killing Ground*, p.127.

36. Julian Byng to Philip Chetwode, 30 May 1917, Folder Three, Papers of General Sir Philip Chetwode, Imperial War Museum, London (hereafter Chetwode Papers).

37. H. C. B. Rogers, *The Mounted Troops of the British Army 1066–1945* (London: Seely Service, 1959), p.233. Haig war diary entry, Haig to Robertson, 3 Feb. 1916, Acc. 3155.104, Haig Papers

38. See Haig war diary entry, 7 June 1916, on the King's visit, and also Robertson to Haig, 19 May 1916, Haig to Robertson 20 May 1916, and Haig to Robertson, 29 May 1916, all Acc. 3155.106, Haig Papers. See also 'Minutes of the War Committee Meeting, 9 November 1916, Statement of the Secretary of State for War', PRO CAB 22/65, pp.4–5.

39. Anon., *A Short History of the 1st King's Dragoon Guards* (Aldershot: Gale & Polden, 1929), p.38.

40. *Statistics of Military Effort*, pp.65–6, 207–8. See also Haig war diary entry, 1 Feb. 1917, and Note 79 on Army Commanders' Conference, 3 Feb. 1917, Acc. 3155.110, Haig Papers.

41. Haig war diary entry, paper 32(b), p.31, and entries 8 and 18 Jan. 1916, Acc. 3155.104, Haig Papers.

42. Haig war diary entry, secret memorandum to Rawlinson, 13 April 1916, p.78, Acc. 3155.105, Haig Papers. See also Prior and Wilson, op. cit., pp.147–50.

43. Haig war diary entry, 9 April 1916, Acc. 3155.105, Haig Papers.

44. Hubert Gough, *The Fifth Army* (London: Hodder & Stoughton, 1931), pp. 132–7. *Official History, France and Belgium 1916*, Vol. I, pp.193, 267. See also Travers, *The Killing Ground*, pp.86, 89–91, on the possible historical origins of the all-arms force in Haig's thinking.

45. 'Fifth Army General Staff War Diary April–December 1916', entries for 11–29 April and 13–28 June, PRO WO 95/518. 'Reserve Army AA&QMG War Diary April–December 1916', note from Fourth Army showing composition of Reserve Army, 19 June 1916, and note from Fourth Army cancelling the above note, 23 June 1916, PRO WO 95/523. '12th Division General Staff War Diary January–August 1916', entries April–June, PRO WO 95/1823. '25th Division General Staff War Diary, March–July 1916', entries May–July, particularly training exercise 13 June, PRO WO 95/2221. '3rd Cavalry Division General Staff War Diary October 1914–May 1919', entries March–July, PRO WO 95/1141. '1st Cavalry Division General Staff War Diary January 1915–September 1919', entries April–July, PRO WO 95/1097.

46. 'Fifth Army General Staff War Diary April–December 1916', entries for 23 and 28 June, and Fourth Army Order to Reserve Army, 22 June, PRO WO 95/518. *Official History, France and Belgium 1916*, Vol. I, Appendices, pp.89 and 150. See also Prior and Wilson, op. cit. pp.150–5.

47. Rawlinson diary entry, 1 July 1916, Rawlinson Papers. Gough, op. cit., p.137.

48. Quoted in Travers, *The Killing Ground*, p.153. See also Prior and Wilson, op. cit., pp.184–7.

49. Rawlinson diary entry, 14 July 1916, Rawlinson Papers. See also Haig war diary entry, 13 July 1916, Acc. 3155. 107, Haig Papers.

50. Brereton, op. cit., pp.326–7. E. Tennant, *The Royal Deccan Horse in the Great War* (Aldershot: Gale & Polden, 1939), pp.47–50. Terry Norman, *The Hell They Called High Wood* (London: William Kimber, 1984), pp.99–112.

51. Rawlinson diary entries, 11, 14 and 15 Sept. 1916, Rawlinson Papers. Haig war diary entry, 14 Sept. 1916, Acc. 3155.108, Haigh Papers.

52. Siegfried Sassoon, *Memoirs of an Infantry Officer* (London: Faber & Faber, 1930), p.163.

53. See for example Norman, op. cit., p.107, and Prior and Wilson, op. cit., p.10.

54. Haig war diary entry, 20 March 1917, note 337, Acc.3155.111, Haig Papers. See also 'Minutes of War Cabinet Meetings', p.5, 'Memorandum on Cavalry by Lord Curzon, 14

November 1916', PRO CAB 22/73, and Haig war diary entry, 23 Nov. 1916, 'Memoranda on Cavalry', Acc.3155.214h, Haig Papers.

55. *Official History, France and Belgium 1917*, Vol. I, Appendices, pp.100–4.

56. Julian Byng to Philip Chetwode, 30 May 1917, Folder Three, Chetwode Papers. L. B. Oats, *I Serve. The Regimental History of the 3rd Carabiniers* (Norwich: Jarrold & Son, 1966), pp.223–5.

57. *Official History France and Belgium 1917*, Vol. III, p.29. See also Woolcombe, op cit., Travers, *How the War Was Won*, pp.23–4, and William Moore, *A Wood Called Bourlon. The Cover-Up After Cambrai, 1917*, (London; Leo Cooper, 1988).

58. Haig war diary entry, Haig to Byng, 3 Nov. 1917, note 6, Acc. 3155.119, Haig Papers.

59. J. E. B. Seely, *Adventure* (London: Heinemann, 1930), p.273. See also *Official History France and Belgium 1917*, Vol. III, pp.307–9.

60. Haig war diary entry, Nov. 1917, Notes 111 and 115, Acc. 3155.119, Haig Papers. Woolcombe, op. cit., pp.136–7. Seely, pp. cit., pp.274–7. Brereton, op. cit, pp, 332–4. Travers, *How the War Was Won*, p.24.

61. Roger Evans, *The Story of the Fifth Royal Inniskilling Dragoon Guards* (Aldershot: Gale and Polden, 1951), p.149. Moore, op. cit. pp.156–7.

62. 'Minutes of War Cabinet Meetings', 7 Jan. 1918, CAB 23/13, p.187, evidence of Field Marshal Sir Douglas Haig. See also 'Minutes of War Cabinet Committee on Manpower Meetings', 4th meeting, Dec. 1917, CAB 23/14. Both in the Public Record Office, Kew.

63. Seely, op. cit. p.303. John Tolland, *No Man's Land. The Story of 1918* (London: Eyre Methuen, 1980), pp.108–9. This was by no means the only successful charge of the battle. See Michael Brander, *The 10th Royal Hussars (Prince of Wales's Own)* (London: Leo Cooper, 1969), p.98.

64. Haig war diary entry, 1 Aug. 1918, Acc, 3155.130, Haig Papers. Montgomery, op. cit. pp.23–4. *Official History France and Belgium 1918*, Vol. IV, p.55. '1st Cavalry Division General Staff War Diary January 1915–September 1919', paper 'Narrative of operations 1st Cavalry Division 8th to 11th August 1918', PRO. WO 95/1097. '2nd Cavalry Division General Staff War Diary Staff War Diary January 1916–April 1919', paper 6 Aug. 1918, PRO WO 95/118.

65. Rawlinson diary entry, 8 Aug. 1918, Rawlinson Papers. 'Fourth Army General Staff War Diary July–August 1918', paper 'Summary of operations 8 August', PRO WO 95/437. Brereton, op. cit., pp.338–9. Pomeroy, op. cit. pp.325–8.

66. Haig war diary entries, 19 and 21 Aug. 1918, Acc. 3155.130, Haig Papers.

67. Haig war diary entry, Douglas Haig to Henry Wilson (personal letter), 1 Sept. 1918, Acc. 3155.131. Haig Papers. See also Terraine, *Douglas Haig, The Educated Soldier*, pp.472–3.

CHAPTER EIGHT

The SHLM Project –
Assessing the Battle Performance of British Divisions

John Lee

There is no shortage of books in the English language to tell us of the technical brilliance and innovative genius of the German Army in the First World War. We have descriptions aplenty of the way the Germans learned the lessons forced on all combatants by the trench stalemate that set in towards the end of 1914. The taking of increasingly strong and sophisticated defences certainly required new methods of infantry attack, new training and weaponry, and new artillery equipments and tactics. One could study the historiography of fighting on the Western Front and be forgiven for thinking that it was only the German Army that had the wit to study the problem and devise 'modern' ways of overcoming the difficulties. This sort of admiration can be at the modest level of accepting that the Germans were a very professional military nation, with a widespread military culture based on universal conscription, and, of course, the unique and wonderful Great General Staff which constantly absorbed new ideas and spread them throughout the German Army. At the more extreme end of the spectrum we are asked to believe that the Germans created an entire army of storm troopers who were able to crush their opponents by the power of their attacks. It must be an abiding mystery to this school of history how Germany actually lost the war.[1]

This appreciation of the skill and mastery of the Germans is usually accompanied by a fairly dismissive treatment of their opponents. There might be some grudging respect for the French; there is usually a deafening silence about the British. If the latter are mentioned at all it is more than likely to be in fairly abusive terms: an army of amateurs, locked in by nineteenth-century colonial warfare doctrine. They were untrained and untrainable according to one (British) critic.[2]

Students of the British Army's conduct of war find it at best irritating, and at worst unacceptable, to read rapturous accounts of German training methods and tactical doctrine and practice, while the British, having been through similarly bitter experiences in the early years of the war, and also learning important and ultimately decisively successful lessons in war-fighting, get absolutely no credit for their achievement.

As a response to this imbalance in the literature, a number of like-minded historians have recently come together to organise some serious research into the battle performance of the divisions of the British Expeditionary Force on the Western Front during the First World War. This undertaking has been dubbed the 'SHLM Project', after the initials of its prime movers.[3] It had fairly unscientific beginnings, and it may be seen as a particularly British phenomenon, based on the long traditions of our army's regimental system, and our tendency to favour the achievements of a favourite unit with family or regional associations. Perhaps it is merely part of the human condition to prefer some 'tribal' connection against those of even close neighbours; are Bavarians better fighters than Saxons, Tennesseans better than 'damn Yankees', Gascons better than Parisians?

Most meetings of historians interested in the operational aspects of the war soon turn towards the relative merits of particular divisions of the British Army. A whole series of fascinating questions is raised, for which the answers are often frustratingly elusive. For example, why are some divisions so much more 'famous' than others, such as the 9th (Scottish) Division; Maxse's 18th (Eastern) Division; the Guards; the 'Incomparable' 29th? What became of the 21st and 24th Divisions after the débâcle at Loos, or the 31st Division after the tragedy at Serre on 1 July 1916? Is it significant that these divisions never produced a divisional history? Those well-versed in the historiography and literature of the war will be familiar with this type of discussion of the relative martial virtues of various nationalities and units.

As a general guide, we have Robert Graves' assertion that about one-third of the British divisions were worthy of élite status for their consistently good performance; about one-third were steady and reliable under most circumstances; the remaining third were deemed (by whom? by GHQ?) to be less than completely reliable.[4] This rough assessment is taken up by Tony Ashworth in his *Trench Warfare: The Live and Let Live System.*[5] We might have hoped that he would make some quantifiable observations about the incidence of 'live and let live' and the relative reliability of the divisions in question but he leaves it as a subject for further research. Many personal memoirs refer to the status of certain divisions. It is 'standard procedure' to rate one's own division as one of the best and link it with, say, the Guards, the New Zealanders, the Highland Division or the 29th. But it still comes as a surprise to see officers of the 35th Division, which did not perform too well as the Bantam division, write to the official historian, Edmonds, claiming that theirs was one of the five best divisions in the army in 1918.[6] Similarly, Peter Simkins' research into the 'Hundred Days' of offensive operations up to 11 November, 1918, produces among the high-achieving divisions some 'unfamous' divisions like the 19th and 34th composed of much-derided English county regiments.

We must mention two further instances of troops with very high opinions of themselves and with generally high reputations. Read any account by serving members of Harper's 51st (Highland) Division of the Territorial Force, as it was then known, and you will be told that the German Army had a list of the British divisions ranking them in the order in which they were to be feared by the Germans. Yes, sure enough, the 51st Division is top of that list; but this list is not published anywhere, and enquiries have failed to reveal it in any archive. What, by contrast, are we to make of Tommy Atkins' malicious humour when he insists that 'HD' stood for 'Harper's Duds'?

As for the Dominion troops – the Australians, New Zealanders, Canadians and South Africans – they are universally praised, and are often used to emphasise failings of British units by comparison. The Australians are particularly problematic in this regard, since certain commentators, not all of them Australian, seem to suggest that all the great victories achieved on the Western Front were won by these 'colonial supermen'. The New Zealanders have their own private frustration at being subsumed by the ANZAC acronym, while the Canadians, relatively speaking, seem a good deal less assertive in their claims.[7] The South Africans have their own pride, but share in the generally high reputation of their parent 9th (Scottish) Division.

Around 1991 all these ideas and questions were exercising the attention of Peter Simkins of the Imperial War Museum and his colleagues Chris McCarthy and Bryn Hammond. At a Western Front Association seminar in Birmingham in April 1991, he discovered the University of Birmingham's research project to create a database on all the divisional commanders of the British Army in the First World War. The work of John Bourne and Bob Bushaway in using a computer database to gather and interrogate the evidence showed the way forward. Leaning heavily on the computer skills of Bryn Hammond therefore, work began to create a useful proforma for gathering information on the battle performance of British divisions on the Western Front. Through meetings of the British Commission for Military History, Peter Simkins also drew John Lee into the work and so the SHLM Project was born.

The aim was to recruit research volunteers who would each 'adopt' a division and study all its battles on the Western Front under the guidance of the core team. Thus every division that served there from 1914 to 1918, and every major battle, would be covered. A set form was designed to facilitate the gathering of information in a standard format, which would be the basis of the input to the database. Exactly what questions should be asked in the first place and the ordering of information on the form itself evolved in a lengthy and complex process. The British victory on 20 September 1917 on the Menin Road Ridge was selected as a test-case for study (and John Lee undertook the analysis). Most importantly, the work of two early volunteers, Nick Perry (36th Division) and Tony Cowan (34th Division), proved vital in the evolution and final ordering of the form. They come respectively from the Northern Ireland Office and the Foreign Office: clearly this work appeals to the civil service mind. One early and probably obvious lesson was that separate forms were required to cover offensive and defensive fighting: one has to pose different questions for each.

How does one judge the performance of a division of troops in battle? First, the many factors must be tabulated, to ensure that every division in every battle is analysed in exactly the same way. After that, it is possible to ask interesting and important questions about the achievement of the British Army at different stages of the war. After much discussion and several editions of the SHLM form, including reference to the analytical work undertaken by Trevor Dupuy, the following factors were selected for analysis – weather, terrain, enemy defences and opposing forces, British infantry and artillery preparation, the execution and results of the attack, and the British and German losses in the battle.

We start by listing the basic identifying information. One form is completed for each division for each day it is engaged in a battle. The battles to be covered by the project are taken from the listing of the Official Nomenclature Committee set up after the war. The division and its commander are noted, together with the corps and army and their commanders. Patterns of success or failure as they develop will inform our appreciation of the work of all British generals.

The factors over which the British had no control are next grouped together. The state of the weather is enquired after in some detail. It is clearly a vital factor and will make a particularly interesting study once the first stage of the research is completed. The incidence of attacks in mist or fog, in rain or snow, in fine or wet weather has never been tabulated before. Similarly, the nature of the terrain over which the battle was conducted is noted in general terms – whether hilly, rolling or flat; wooded, bare or mixed; marshy or urbanised. After early research efforts, a section was added to describe the 'going' of the ground, as the infantry invariably passed some remark about it in their battle reports. This can range from 'firm' through 'slippery' to 'marshy'.

The nature of the enemy troops and defences is of the highest importance and receives scant attention in the literature. Questions posed cover all eventualities, from the formidable prepared positions of the Somme on the 1 July 1916, or the Hindenburg Line, to the fluid battlefields of the manoeuvre warfare of 1914 and 1918. A points system for evaluating the strength of a position has been worked out, based on its preparedness and the accretions of such elements as fortified woods, concrete pill boxes and wire belts.

A wholly unique aspect of the research is the attention given to the enemy troops engaged. The regiments and divisions are identified and, using allied intelligence summaries (notably the US Army's *Two Hundred and Fifty One Divisions of the Imperial German Army*), some attempt is made to rate their battle worthiness. At the present stage we are simply highlighting our regrettable lack of knowledge about the Germans and plans are in place to do a lot more work on German sources not generally available in English.

We next turn to the planning and preparation of the battle by the British. The state of the division in question is looked at. What was its strength? How long had it been in the line or in action? When had it last been used in battle? The task set for it in the battle under review is then studied. The frontage of attack and the depth of the objectives are clearly significant factors, and will repay comparative analysis at a later stage. The assault formation is noted – both by brigade and battalion – to see how the division chose to achieve its objective. As the data accumulates it will be interesting to see if any standard operational procedure emerges. The timing of the attack is carefully noted. It will be interesting to see how this influenced overall success or failure rates. We also note whether the troops were able to rehearse the attack. This was much more common in all stages of the war than many people realise. It certainly was not the sole prerogative of the Germans.

No battle of this war can be understood without a full appreciation of the role of the artillery, which is curiously lacking in many general accounts. For the first time there will be a full listing of all the artillery support available in battle, by number of guns (noting both the field artillery brigades and the heavy artillery groups allocated), by guns per yard of the front, by duration of bombardment (logged by days for the long bombardments of the middle period of the war and by hours or even minutes for the 'hurricane' bombardments favoured more in the later stages). The files of the Public Record Office are full of details and reports on this vital aspect of the war and they are being systematically unlocked by this project for the first time.

Other aspects of support in the attack are covered, such as the use of aircraft, gas, mines, machine gun or trench mortar barrages and, of course, the use of tanks. This new weapon is looked at in some detail with the intention of more carefully evaluating its true role in the war. Rather large claims are often made for it which really do require further analysis.

A lengthy section on the actual execution of the attack then follows, evaluating the relative success of the artillery support, the problems of the attacking infantry and, of course, the reaction of the enemy (such as, intensity of fire from front or flank, their counter-attacks). Finally, the relative success or failure of the attack, measured against the objectives set, is evaluated.

The number of casualties suffered are listed in the greatest possible detail and will be the subject of much serious analysis by the computer when complete. Similarly, and for the first time, we ask for as much detail as possible of the enemy losses, in men and materiel. The form closes with some general questions as to whether the troops were relieved on schedule, how the division was brought back up to strength and the like. It must be confessed that the section on the awarding of Victoria Crosses for the action is really there to provide a little extra interest for the patient researchers who have by now carried out the most painstaking and important work imaginable!

Having described the nature of the questions posed for assessing British attacks, it should be clear that only a slight change of emphasis is needed to convert them to British defences and German attack methods in the case of the British performance on the defensive.

Once completed, the database will be available to answer any combination of questions we care to set. We can compare different divisions in the same battles, or one division at different times in its history. We can ask what factors make for consistently successful attacks and what make for inevitable defeat. The possibilities are, more or less, limited only by the questioner's imagination.

It must be obvious to all that this sort of detailed and exhaustive analysis will greatly increase our understanding of military operations on the Western Front. It will combine the solid fact of the much-derided *Official History*; all unit histories; the huge and relatively untapped resources of the Public Records Office; and the often valuable archives of personal memoirs which can yield important extra details. The unit War Diaries in WO 95 at the Public Records Office are widely known. What is of particular interest are the files of the General Staffs of division, corps and army, with their details of planning, intelligence assessments and after-action analysis; of the Commanders, Royal Artillery and Heavy Artillery with their often decisive contribution; of the engineers, the machine gun officers, etcetera. Never before has all this been studied in a systematic way, and it will be a lasting monument to the men of the BEF for all time.

Once the task of assessing every day of major battle for every division is complete, a second stage of the project is under consideration. The whole thrust of the research is to show that the British Army was on a 'learning curve' throughout the war, improving its technique as it gained experience. The study will go deeper into the evolution of small unit tactics, of trench raids, of staff work. Given that morale itself is not quantifiable, it will look at factors which are, such as disciplinary offences, surrender incidents and examples of non-aggressive 'live and let live' arrangements. Once again the possibilities are endless and the end result will be of enduring benefit to all interested in the subject.

The SHLM Battle Assessment Study is already producing conference papers, lectures and booklets based on the early findings of its research. The task is a large one and is quite open-ended in the drive towards ever greater detail and more comprehensive sifting of source materials. Anyone interested in assisting in this work in any way should contact Peter Simkins, Chris McCarthy or Bryn Hammond at the Imperial War Museum, Lambeth Road, London SE1 6HZ.

NOTES

1. See Timothy T. Lupfer, *The Dynamics of Doctrine: The Changes in German Tactical Doctrine During the First World War* (Fort Leavenworth Paper No. 4, 1981); Bruce J. Gudmundsson, *Stormtroop Tactics: Innovation in the German Army 1914–1918* (New York: Praeger 1989); Martin Samuels, *Doctrine and Dogma: German and British Infantry Tactics in the First World War* (Westport, CT: Greenwood Press, 1992).
2. Samuels, op. cit., Ch. 8 and pp.177–79; cf Gudmundsson, op. cit., p.175. John Laffin, *British Butchers and Bunglers of World War One* (Gloucester: Alan Sutton, 1988) is one book of this type but is entirely in keeping with this particular author's output.
3. Peter Simkins, Bryn Hammond, John Lee and Chris McCarthy. The project has since been more carefully named 'The SHLM Battle Assessment Study 1914–1918'.
4. Robert Graves, *Goodbye to all That* (London: J. Cape, 1929; Penguin, 1960), p.152.
5. Tony Ashworth, *Trench Warfare 1914–1918: The Live and Let Live System* (London: Macmillan, 1980).
6. Colonel Sandilands to General Edmonds, 14 Aug. 1923, PRO, CAB 45/192.
7 See Bill Rawling, *Surviving Trench Warfare: Technology and the Canadian Corps 1914–1918* (University of Toronto Press, 1992); Reginald H. Roy (ed.), *The Journal of Private Fraser 1914–1918: Canadian Expeditionary Force* (British Columbia: Sono Nis Press, 1985).

Glossary of Terms and Abbreviations

AA and QMG – Assistant Adjutant and Quarter Master General

ADS – Advanced Dressing Station

APM – Assistant Provost Marshal

ATS – Anti-Tetanus Serum

BEF – British Expeditionary Force

C2 – Command and Control

CB – Counter Battery

CCS – Casualty Clearing Station

CIGS – Chief of the Imperial General Staff

CMP (or 'Redcaps') – Corps of Military Police

DCIGS – Deputy Chief of the Imperial General Staff

DF – Defensive Fire (a modern term similar to the 'SOS' fire of Great War terminology)

DPM – Deputy Provost Marshal

FOO – Forward Observation Officer

FPF – Final Protective Fire (similar to 'SOS' fire of Great War terminology)

GHQ – General Headquarters (i.e. the headquarters, in France, controlling the whole BEF)

GMP – Garrison Military Police

GS – General Staff

HE – High Explosive

HMSO – His Majesty's Stationery Office, London

IT – Inspectorate of Training

IWM – Imperial War Museum (Department of Documents, unless otherwise stated)

KOYLI – King's Own Yorkshire Light Infantry

LHCMA – Liddell Hart Centre for Military Archives, King's College, London

MDS – Main Dressing Station

MFP – Military Foot Police

MMP – Military Mounted Police

NAM – National Army Museum

POWs – Prisoner(s) of War

PRO – Public Record Office, Kew

'Q' Staff – Quartermaster General Staff

RA – Royal Artillery

RAMC – Royal Army Medical Corps
RAP – Regimental Aid Post
RE – Royal Engineers
RFA – Royal Field Artillery
RFC – Royal Flying Corps
RGA – Royal Garrison Artillery
RMPA – Royal Military Police Archives, Chichester
RNAS – Royal Naval Air Service
RP – Regimental Police
RWF – Royal Welch Fusiliers
rpg – rounds per gun
SMLE – Short Magazine Lee Enfield rifle
SS – Stationery Service (i.e., the BEF's publishing organisation)
WD – War Diary
WWDS – Walking Wounded Dressing Station

Selected Bibliography

OFFICIAL HISTORIES

Statistics of the Military Effort of the British Empire During the Great War (London: HMSO, 1922)

A. F. Becke, *Order of Battle of Divisions* (British official history, 6 vols; London: HMSO, 1937–45, reprinted by Sherwood and Westlake, 1986–89)

J. E. Edmonds (general editor), *History of the Great War, Based on Official Documents: Military Operations, France and Belgium* (i.e., British Official History, or OH; 14 vols. plus maps and appendices; London: Macmillan, 1922–49. Some volumes recently reprinted by IWM)

W. G. MacPherson *et al.*, *History of the Great War Medical Services* (12 vols. London: HMSO, 1921–31)

SELECTED BIOGRAPHICAL MATERIALS AND
EYEWITNESS ACCOUNTS

F. M. Cutlack (ed.), *War Letters of General Monash* (Sydney: Angus & Robertson, 1935)

Charles Douie, *The Weary Road: Recollections of a Subaltern of Infantry* (London: Murray, 1929)

J. C. Dunn, *The War the Infantry Knew* (first published 1938; new edn with introduction by K. R. Simpson, London: Jane's, 1987),

Robert Graves, *Goodbye to All That* (first published by Cape, 1929; London: Penguin edn, 1982)

'Mk VII' (Max Plowman), *A Subaltern on the Somme in 1916* (London: Dent, 1928)

Robin Prior and Trevor Wilson, *Command on the Western Front* (Oxford: Blackwell, 1992)

E. K. G. Sixsmith, *British Generalship in the Twentieth Century* (London: Arms & Armour, 1970)

John Terraine (ed.), *General Jack's Diary, 1914–18* (London: Eyre & Spottiswode, 1964)

John Terraine, *Douglas Haig: The Educated Soldier* (London: Hutchinson, 1963; Leo Cooper, 1990)

Aubrey Wade, *The War of the Guns, Western Front, 1917 and 1918* (London: Batsford, 1936)

Denis Winter, *Haig's Command, a Resassessment* (London: Viking, 1991)

David R. Woodward, *Lloyd George and the Generals* (East Brunswick, NJ: Associated University Presses, 1983)

TECHNICAL STUDIES AND OTHER WORKS

R. J. Q. Adams (ed.), *The Great War, 1914–18: Essays on the Military, Political and Social History of the First World War* (London: Macmillan, 1990)

Eric Andrews, *The Anzac Illusion: Anglo-Australian Relations during World War 1* (Cambridge University Press, 1993)

Tony Ashworth, *Trench Warfare 1914–1918: The Live and Let Live System* (London: Macmillan, 1980)

Jonathan Bailey, *Field Artillery and Firepower* (Oxford: Military Press, 1989)

Arthur Banks, *A Military Atlas of the First World War* (first published 1975; new edn, London: Leo Cooper, 1989)

Ian F. W. Beckett and Keith Simpson (eds), *A Nation in Arms: A Social Study of the British Army in the First World War* (Manchester University Press, 1985)

Shelford Bidwell and Dominick Graham, *Firepower, British Army Weapons and Theories of War, 1904–45* (London: Allen & Unwin, 1982)

Gregory Blaxland, *Amiens 1918* (London: Muller, 1968)

Brian Bond (ed.), *The First World War and British Military History* (Oxford: Clarendon Press, 1991)

Peter Chasseaud, *Topography of Armageddon* (London: Mapbooks, 1991)

Rose E. B. Coombs, *Before Endeavours Fade, a Guide to the Battlefields of the First World War* (first published 1976; new edn, London: After the Battle, 1986)

John Ellis, *Eye-deep in Hell, The Western Front 1914–18* (London: Croom Helm, 1976)

M. Farndale, *History of the Royal Regiment of Artillery: Western Front 1914–18* (Woolwich: RA Institution, 1986)

D. J. Fletcher, 'The Origins of Armour', in J. P. Harris and F. H. Toase (eds), *Armoured Warfare* (London: Batsford, 1990)

C. H. Foulkes, *Gas, the Story of the Special Brigade RE* (Edinburgh and London: Blackwood, 1934)

Paddy Griffith, *Battle Tactics on the Western Front, The British Army's Art of Attack, 1916–18* (Yale University Press, 1994)

Bruce I. Gudmundsson, *Stormtroop Tactics, Innovation in the German Army*

1914–18 (Westport, CT: Praeger, 1989)

Bruce I. Gudmundsson, *On Artillery* (Westport, CT: Praeger, 1993)

Guy Hartcup, *The War of Invention* (London: Brasseys, 1988)

Ian V. Hogg, *The Guns 1914–18* (London: Pan/Ballantine, 1973)

T. T. Lupfer, *The Dynamics of Doctrine: The Changes in German Tactical Doctrine During the First World War* (Fort Leavenworth, KS: US Army Command and General Staff College, 1981)

Martin Middlebrook, *The First Day on the Somme* (London: Allen Lane, 1971)

Martin Middlebrook, *The Kaiser's Battle* (London: Allen Lane, 1978)

F. Mitchell, *Tank Warfare, the Story of the Tanks in the Great War* (London: Nelson, n.d.; No. 15 in 'The Nelsonian Library', reprinted Donovan, 1987)

Jonathan Nicholls, *Cheerful Sacrifice, the Battle of Arras 1917* (London: Leo Cooper, 1990)

Terry Norman, *The Hell They Called High Wood* (London: Kimber, 1984)

Barrie Pitt, *1918: The Last Act* (first published 1962; London: Papermac edn, 1984)

R. E. Priestley, *The Signal Service in the European War of 1914 to 1918 (France)* (Official RE History; Chatham: Mackay, 1921)

Bill Rawling, *Surviving Trench Warfare* (University of Toronto Press, 1992)

M. Samuels, *Doctrine and Dogma, German and British Infantry Tactics in the First World War* (Westport, CT: Greenwood, 1992)

G. D. Sheffield, *The Redcaps: A History of the Royal Military Police and its Antecedents from the Middle Ages to the Gulf War* (London: Brassey's, 1994)

Peter Simkins, *Kitchener's Army: The Raising of the New Armies, 1914–16* (Manchester University Press, 1988)

John Terraine, *The First World War 1914–18* (first published 1965; London: Papermac edn, 1983)

John Terraine, *The Smoke and the Fire* (London: Sidgwick & Jackson, 1980)

John Terraine, *White Heat: The New Warfare 1914–18* (London: Sidgwick and Jackson, 1982)

Tim Travers, *The Killing Ground: The British Army, the Western Front and the Emergence of Modern Warfare 1900–1918* (London: Allen & Unwin, 1987)

Tim Travers, *How The War Was Won: Command and Technology in the British Army on the Western Front, 1917–18* (London: Routledge, 1992)

Index